BULLYING SOLUTIONS

Evidence-based approaches to bullying in Australian schools

Editors

Helen McGrath & Toni Noble

BULLYING SOLUTIONS

Evidence-based approaches to bullying in Australian schools

Pearson Education Australia
Unit 4, Level 3
14 Aquatic Drive
Frenchs Forest NSW 2086

www.pearsoned.com.au

Publisher: Diane Gee-Clough
Senior Project Editor: Rebecca Pomponio
Copy Editor and Proofreader: Kathryn Lamberton
Senior Permissions Coordinator: Liz DeRome
Cover and internal design by Ellie Exarchos
Cover illustration by Getty Images
Typeset by Midland Typesetters, Maryborough, Vic.

Printed in Malaysia (CTP – CLP)

1 2 3 4 5 09 08 07 06 05

Bullying solutions : evidence-based approaches to bullying in Australian schools.

Includes index.
ISBN 0 7339 7166 4.

1. Bullying in schools – Australia – Prevention.
I. McGrath, Helen. II. Noble, Toni.

371.78

PEARSON
Longman
An imprint of Pearson Education Australia (a division of Pearson Australia Group Pty Ltd)

CONTENTS

FOREWORDS

The Alannah and Madeline Foundation

What is the Alannah and Madeleine Foundation? Why is it mentioned in this book?

The Alannah and Madeline Foundation was established in 1997 to honour two little girls, Alannah and Madeline Mikac, who lost their lives during the Port Arthur tragedy. The Foundation has the simple and important mission of providing loving support and practical assistance to child victims of violence and sudden family loss. Recognising that bullying is a very serious issue that can lead to violence against self and others, one of the initiatives of the Foundation was the establishment of the National Coalition Against Bullying (NCAB). Chaired by the former Chief Justice of the Family Court of Australia, Alastair Nicholson AO, NCAB conducts national conferences working with, and seeking the support of, all education sectors and government departments. In their work in this area, members of NCAB identified a need in schools for practical advice on the delivery of anti-bullying programs and have come together to write *Bullying Solutions: Evidence-based approaches to bullying in Australian schools*.

In its exploration of the issue of bullying in Australian schools and discussion of recent anti-bullying initiatives, *Bullying Solutions* shares the Foundation's message that the cycle of violence against children must be broken and that bullying should not be tolerated. This book provides expert advice to educators and those working with children, as well as practical tools for action, all aimed at tackling the important issue of bullying in our schools.

For further information on the Foundation's other initiatives, including the *Children Ahead Program* and the *Better Buddies Program*, please visit <www.amf.org.au>

John Bertrand AM
Chairman
The Alannah and Madeline Foundation

The Alannah and Madeline Foundation.
TAKING CARE OF THE LITTLE THINGS.

The National Coalition Against Bullying

NCAB exists because of the dedicated and committed work of the Alannah and Madeline Foundation. The Foundation's own research, commissioned in 1998, indicates that in Australia over 700 acts of violent crime are committed against children every week. Consequently, the Foundation recognised that it needed to broaden the scope of its work beyond the school environment and initiated the National Coalition Against Bullying.

This book is significant because it is a genuine attempt to find solutions to the problem of bullying, and to ensure that there is much greater awareness of just how widespread the problem is. The chapters in this book provide evidence-based directions for the management and legal issues that face schools. They also provide clear, practical steps and strategies to prevent and deal with bullying. Our aim is to provide the latest information and strategies that will assist schools to become caring and safe places with values that can spill over into the surrounding communities.

In seeking solutions to the problem of bullying, the National Coalition Against Bullying has a tough but, I believe, ultimately achievable job to do.

Our objective is to raise awareness of the seriousness of bullying in Australia and to promote a tolerant, inclusive, balanced society in which bullying is on the public agenda as an issue that can and must be tackled.

No-one is suggesting that it is easy or simple to tackle the problem of bullying, because it is not. Short-term solutions will not provide long-term answers. Long-term solutions reside in the changing of a society that generally views bullying with indifference at best. We have to look at a gentler world where it is not okay to act like a thug, whether physically or verbally – a world where tormenting or harassing your schoolmates, your employees, your workmates or your family is not acceptable. This may take a long time but we can start now by encouraging a generation of school children to view respect, tolerance, reason, conciliation and talking, as opposed to violence and oppression, as a better way to lead their lives. The quality of information in this book is particularly high and most importantly is backed up by the experience and knowledge of specialists and researchers who are working with children and adults.

NCAB members act as if it is impossible to fail. It is a testament to their dedication that they have given their time to contribute to this book and are donating all author royalties to The Alannah and Madeline Foundation to enable it to continue its work.

For information about the NCAB please visit <www.ncab.org.au>

Alastair Nicholson AO
Chairman
The National Coalition Against Bullying

NATIONAL COALITION AGAINST BULLYING
An initiative of The Alannah and Madeline Foundation.
TAKING CARE OF THE LITTLE THINGS.

ABOUT THE CONTRIBUTORS

Margaret Armstrong

Margaret is a teacher, currently working as a senior program officer for Student Wellbeing and Drug Education at the Department of Education & Training in Victoria. For the past three years, she has been training and supporting schools implementing a restorative approach to behaviour management throughout the Southern Metropolitan Region. In 2004 she was granted a Churchill Fellowship to research restorative practices in schools internationally. Margaret can be contacted at <armstrong.marg.a@edumail.vic.gov.au>

Dr Dale Bagshaw

Dale is an Associate Professor and the director of the Conflict Management Research Group at the Hawke Research Institute, University of South Australia. Widely published, she directs postgraduate programs and conducts training programs internationally on mediation and conflict management, with a particular focus on families, schools and workplaces. Dale can be contacted at <dale.bagshaw@unisa.edu.au>

Tilly Barger

Tilly is the principal at Williamstown Primary School. She has extensive experience in primary education, including six years as a principal. She has also worked as a visiting teacher of the deaf and as a consultant in curriculum and special education. In 2003 she became involved with assisting the work of the Alannah and Madeline Foundation and the National Coalition Against Bullying (NCAB) through her involvement with the Teacher Release to Industry Program of the Department of Education and Training, Victoria. Tilly can be contacted at <Barger.Matilda.M@edumail.vic.gov.au>

Pam Carroll

Pam is a clinical psychologist and a member of the Australian Psychological Society who is currently completing her PhD at Flinders University, South Australia. The focus of her research is on the effectiveness of specific kinds of individual therapy for supporting young people with craniofacial conditions who have been bullied. She is also focusing on ways to develop more positive and caring community attitudes and behaviours towards young people with these conditions. Pam can be contacted at <Pam.Carroll@flinders.edu.au>

Evelyn Field

Evelyn is a former school counsellor and currently practises privately as a psychologist. She works with child, adolescent and adult victims of bullying. She presents extensively to parents and students and is the author of a self-help book on bullying for students and parents. Evelyn is a member of the National Coalition Against Bullying and a media spokesperson for the Australian Psychological Society. She can be contacted at <efield@netspace.net.au> or visit the website <www.bullying.com.au>

Andrew Fuller

Andrew is a clinical psychologist, family therapist and consultant in Melbourne, and a Fellow of the Departments of Psychiatry and Learning and Educational Development at the University of Melbourne. He is an ambassador for Mind Matters and a member of the National Coalition Against Bullying. His initiatives in bullying prevention are used in over 20 countries and he has received a national award for violence prevention. Andrew has published extensively and also works in communities and schools promoting the value of resilience in young people. Andrew can be contacted at <inyahead@satlink.com.au> or see his website <http://www.inyahead.com.au>

Dr Helen McGrath

Helen is a qualified teacher and currently part-time senior lecturer in the Faculty of Education at Deakin University in Melbourne. She is also a psychologist in private practice and a consultant to schools. Helen is a member of the National Coalition Against Bullying, the academic advisor (2004–2005) for the Commonwealth Government's National Safe Schools Framework's Best Practice Grants Program, and chief investigator for the Review of Good Practice for Reducing Bullying in Schools conducted by the Victorian Department of Education and Training (2005). She has published extensively in the area of school welfare and learning. In 2003 Helen and her co-author, Dr Toni Noble, received the Australian Psychological Society's Robin Winkler Award for Excellence in Applied Community Psychology Research. Helen can be contacted at <helenmc@deakin.edu.au> or access the website <www.bounceback.com.au>

The Hon. Alastair Nicholson, AO, RFD

Alastair was appointed Justice of the Supreme Court of Victoria in 1982 and Chief Justice of the Family Court of Australia in 1988. He retired from this position in 2004. Previously he had been appointed Judge Advocate General of the Australian Defence Force (1987–1992). He holds the rank of Air Vice-Marshal. Alastair was appointed as an Officer of the Order of Australia (AO) in 1992 and received the Reserve Force Decoration (RFD) in the same year. Alastair and his wife were for many years members of Kids in Care, a group providing emergency foster care to children. Since 1984 he has also been the Chairman of the ACSO Centre, a charitable organisation devoted to the provision of care, accommodation and counselling to ex-prisoners. He is a member of the Alannah and Madeline Foundation's Advisory Board, chair of the National Coalition Against Bullying and an honorary Professorial Fellow of the Department of Criminology at the University of Melbourne. Alastair can be contacted at <alasnich@bigpond.com>

Dr Toni Noble

Toni, a qualified teacher, is a consultant and part-time senior lecturer in the Faculty of Education at Australian Catholic University – National in Sydney. She is a member of the National Coalition Against Bullying and the academic advisor (2004–2005) for the Commonwealth Government's National Safe Schools Framework's projects being undertaken by schools linked to the New South Wales Association of Independent Schools. She has published extensively in the area of school welfare and learning. In 2003 Toni and her co-author, Dr Helen McGrath, received the Australian Psychological Society's Robin Winkler Award for Excellence in Applied Community Psychology Research. Toni can be contacted at <tnoble@mary.acu.edu.au> or visit the website <www.bounceback.com.au>

Dr Ken Rigby

Ken is a qualified teacher and guidance officer and currently an Adjunct Research Professor and educational consultant based at the University of South Australia (Underdale campus). Over the last 10 years he has become a leading international authority on bullying and has presented papers both nationally and internationally. He has published extensively, especially in the area of bullying. He has undertaken many consultancies for State and Commonwealth governments on bullying and has collaborated with international researchers on a range of projects. Ken can be contacted at <ken.rigby@unisa.edu.au> or visit the website <http://www.education.unisa.edu.au/bullying/>

Dr Phillip Slee

Phillip is Professor of Human Development at the School of Education at Flinders University, South Australia. He is a qualified teacher and registered psychologist. Phillip has published extensively in the field of bullying and school violence. Phillip has presented his work both nationally and internationally in workshops and lectures and is one of Australia's leading authorities on bullying. Over the years he has undertaken a number of consultancies for State and Commonwealth governments in relation to bullying and is currently conducting a number of international research projects on the topic of school violence in conjunction with researchers from China, Japan, Korea, Canada, England and the United States. Phillip can be contacted at <phillip.slee@flinders.edu.au> or visit the website <http://www.caper.com.au>

Maree Stanley

Maree is a qualified teacher and currently the director of the Alannah and Madeline Foundation's education projects. Maree was responsible for the establishment of the National Coalition Against Bullying. Buddy Bear, the friendly face of the Foundation's Better Buddies program, was also her brainchild. She is the project manager (2004–2005) for the Commonwealth Government's National Safe Schools Framework Best Practice Grants Program. Maree can be contacted at <maree.stanley@amf.org.au>

Margaret Thorsborne

Margaret has a background in teaching and counselling, and behaviour, conflict and trauma management. She is a restorative justice consultant who pioneered the use of restorative conferencing in schools. She is a published author in this field and has widened the use of restorative practice to workplaces for high level conflict and workplace bullying. She presents, trains, consults and works in schools across Australia, New Zealand, UK, Canada and USA. Margaret can be contacted at <marg@thorsborne.com.au>

INTRODUCTION

Helen McGrath and Toni Noble

Imagine a school where all members of the school community feel physically and psychologically safe and there are low levels of bullying. The school consistently and firmly communicates that bullying behaviour is unacceptable and has a well-developed anti-bullying policy which clearly outlines rights, responsibilities and procedures for reporting concerns about bullying. Rarely does a bullying situation become so entrenched that very serious reactions such as suspension are needed because all teachers are skilled in the use of management strategies which they immediately and effectively employ whenever a bullying situation arises. Different student strengths are valued, not just academic or sporting excellence, and students have many opportunities to build on their strengths and receive recognition. There is a culture of trust, cooperation and respect. All members of the school community share a strong sense of belonging to a good school. There are successful peer support systems operating and open discussion of the issue of bullying between students, teachers and parents. The school works hard to connect all members of the school community to each other and to the school, and social relationships and interactions are characterised by caring and respect for others and the school and acceptance of differences. Students are actively encouraged to be friendly and inclusive and to act responsibly in supporting others.

The chapters in this book outline what research tells us about how to develop this kind of school.

This book represents an exciting and unique opportunity to bring together the ideas and evidence-based knowledge of many leading experts working in the field of anti-bullying in Australia today. The chapters are bound by a common theme: what evidence-based practices can help schools reduce and manage the serious problem of school bullying. Encompassing a review of school and classroom practices that help both with the *prevention* of school bullying and with its *management*, the focus is on *informed practice* rather than *best practice*. Although both approaches emphasise the importance of using evidence to guide decision-making, the term 'best practice' implies that there is one effective way. On the other hand, the term 'informed practice' acknowledges that what works in one social context or school environment may not be appropriate in a different context. As Smith (2001) notes, it is vital to adapt approaches to suit the conditions of the particular school.

Bullying has been shown to exist in schools in at least 16 countries (Smith & Brain, 2000) and many experts in the field are now describing bullying as 'normative'. This *doesn't* mean that it is 'normal' and inevitable, but rather that power relationships are likely to occur in any human group where people can gain rewards for using antisocial power in antisocial ways against another. Power-oriented bullying behaviour is especially likely to occur in groups that are relatively enduring and where it is not easy for someone to leave, such as the school situation. A comparison can be made between schools and gardens. In any garden, no matter how well tended, there will be weeds. However, there will be fewer and more manageable weeds in gardens where 'weed prevention' (e.g. mulching) has been undertaken and where the gardener has been vigilant in watching for weeds and dealing swiftly with them. Similarly, in any school, no matter how well managed, some bullying is likely to occur. But there will be far less bullying and it will be more easily stopped in schools with a planned program of prevention and effective management practices.

There was relatively little interest in or research about bullying until the mid 1980s. This current third decade of bullying research is characterised by an awareness of the prevalence and seriousness of school bullying. This awareness enables schools to acknowledge their problems with bullying without fear of being judged a 'bad' school (Smith, 2004). We now know that bullying problems extend far beyond the individual students involved in bullying to include their peers, their parents, their teachers and the broader community.

This increased awareness of the extensive and negative effects of bullying has also influenced the general community's responses to bullying as reflected in more frequent media references to bullying and to the number of anti-bullying campaigns across the world. Probably the best known of these was the campaign in the UK in which the BBC and the Anti-Bullying Alliance urged the community to 'Make a Stand, Wear a Band'. The campaign was particularly directed towards young people and encouraged them to wear the wristband to show that they were determined to work together to 'beat bullying'.

A humanitarian and rights-based struggle to reduce the incidence of bullying and its harmful consequences for everyone involved has driven much of the research into bullying over the past 25 years (Smith, 2004). Ohsako (1999) has noted that the recent spate of research studies of bullying and the increasing public concern about its damaging effects are particularly characteristic of more 'settled' countries that do not have more immediate problems such as malnutrition and civil war. Concern about bullying reflects a growing awareness of the rights of all people to be safe from victimisation and abuse, including women, those with a different sexual orientation, people from different ethnic or religious groupings and people with disabilities.

When we look at the big picture of research into bullying interventions, we see a complex collection of limited successes and failures (Smith, 2004; Smith & Brain, 2000). We still have a lot to learn about what does work and what does not in anti-bullying interventions (Smith, 2001). Appropriately, all chapters in this book highlight the complexity of the task of reducing school bullying. They also highlight the crucial importance of this task to the psychological health and wellbeing of everyone involved, both in the short term at school and in the long term after leaving school.

The writers all optimistically believe that the evidence-based practices outlined in this book can make a difference. The practices identified as showing signs of success can not only help to reduce bullying but will also contribute to creating caring and supportive school communities where everyone feels safe and has a sense of belonging. This kind of positive school climate makes it more likely that effective learning will occur.

Anti-bullying initiatives have much in common with research into school effectiveness and the school reform agenda. Research into each has highlighted that any significant change in school or classroom practices requires time and a consistent and committed whole-school approach. The common directions are towards effective classroom management, effective engagement practices, connectedness, safety, belonging, and social and emotional learning. We now know that students' social and emotional learning facilitates their academic learning (Zins, Weissberg, Wang & Walberg, 2004) and that a student's level of social competence and their friendship networks are predictive of academic achievement (Caprara, Barbaranelli, Pastorelli, Bandura & Zimbardo, 2000; Wentzel, 2003; Wentzel & Caldwell, 1997; Wentzel & Watkins, 2002). The goals of anti-bullying initiatives also align with the teaching in schools of socio-moral values such as respect, support/care, cooperation, acceptance of differences and inclusion (McGrath & Noble, 2003). In summary, there are significant moral, social, emotional and educational advantages to addressing bullying problems in schools.

Purpose and structure of the book

Our purpose in putting this book together is to support the successful and ongoing work of the National Coalition Against Bullying (NCAB). The National Coalition Against Bullying has challenged all Australian schools to take a proactive stance on bullying. The NCAB brings together a group of individuals from key organisations across Australia to draw national attention to the issue of bullying. Author royalties will go to the Alannah and Madeline Foundation to support their work in caring for children who have been harmed, drawing national attention to the issue of bullying and helping to bring about social change in our schools and the community. We would like to thank the generosity of all chapter contributors in giving considerable time and their expertise to making this project possible.

We have organised the chapters into four sections. Section One establishes the context of bullying in terms of international research evidence and the legal perspectives on bullying in Australia. Section Two provides six chapters on strategies for the prevention of bullying and Section Three includes five chapters on management solutions for bullying. Section Four, entitled 'Putting it all together', provides resources that flow from the other sections of the book, including a safe school template, to support your school's work in the prevention and management of bullying.

Section One: An overview of bullying and possible solutions

In the first chapter, eminent Australian researcher and author on bullying Ken Rigby provides an overview of what the research tells us about bullying. He focuses on the key messages and conclusions from both national and international research, and stresses the importance of measuring the incidence of bullying behaviours based on an agreed clear definition of what bullying is (and is not). The effects of bullying and the factors that contribute to it are described in terms of individual differences, socio-cultural factors and school factors. He concludes that the success of anti-bullying programs reflects the level of commitment of the whole school to the reduction of bullying and the implementation of a *variety* of whole-school and class-based strategies, not just a single approach.

The second chapter has been written by Alastair Nicholson, former Chief Justice of the Family Court of Australia and current chair of the National Coalition Against Bullying. His deep understanding and experience with current law in Australia, especially pertaining to children, as well as his work with NCAB, provide him with a unique perspective on the legal ramifications of bullying and the importance of schools in meeting their duty of care in keeping students safe. He explains that in Australia bullying *per se* currently does not constitute a crime, but that many of the behaviours that are often associated with bullying *may* attract legal consequences. He reviews a number of national and international cases that provide some guidance on the possible legal consequences of school bullying. This review illustrates the legal muddy waters related to bullying and highlights the inappropriateness of most of the penalties involved when applied to children. He reminds us that legal processes related to bullying are often protracted and may be traumatic for all involved.

This ambiguity indicates that the current criminal law for controlling bullying has a number of serious limitations. Despite this, recent data shows an increase in actions for damages for negligence against schools and teachers arising out of bullying. Nicholson strongly emphasises that 'there can be no doubt that a school and its teachers owe a duty of care to their pupils to take reasonable care to protect them from injury'. Therefore, school authorities are well advised to set up sound anti-bullying policies and management systems for dealing with bullying, as the absence or inadequacies of such policies and systems may render them more liable to an action for damages. On a positive note, such infrastructure provides security and safety for the whole school community. Nicholson's chapter suggests that current legislation related to bullying is in urgent need of critical review and amendment.

Section Two: An overview of preventive solutions for bullying

In this section the research related to the prevention of bullying in schools is discussed. The section begins with Helen McGrath's overview of national and international multi-focus whole-school prevention programs in Chapter 3. These programs are based on the premise that broad whole-school prevention practices can help put a stop to bullying as well as antisocial behaviour, school violence, mental health problems, substance abuse, truancy and low achievement at school. Most of the programs have accessed large-scale sample sizes and research funding in the USA that are not available to such an extent in Australia. The benefits are that we can extrapolate the good practices in preventive programming that have been identified from these studies. The caveat is that we need to adopt and amend the practices in ways that appear to best suit our own school contexts and systems without altering their 'active ingredients'. Our next challenge is to identify and document the components that work best in the Australian context. Reference is made to the Friendly Schools Friendly Families Program from Western Australia, which has demonstrated very promising research outcomes.

In Chapter 4, Toni Noble provides a summary of the research on the key components of prevention. She concludes that successful prevention programs are school-wide and are available to all students, not just those who are 'at risk'. Her review of the research shows that programs involving partnerships with school, family and community work best, and that the earlier programs are introduced the better the outcomes. Longer programs are more effective than short ones. After discussing the importance of adopting a multi-factored approach, and describing the most effective components of such an approach, she focuses on specific strategies that teachers in classes can implement. Noble, along with most of the authors in this book, stresses that no program is likely to succeed without ongoing teacher commitment, even those that include the powerful components she identifies.

In Chapter 5, eminent Australian researcher and writer on bullying, Phillip Slee, focuses on the PEACE anti-bullying pack. He introduces the chapter by providing a rationale for preventing bullying that draws on current research evidence. He then outlines the major components of a framework for schools to assess the status of their anti-bullying policy, procedures and curriculum initiatives. PEACE is an acronym for Preparation, Education, Action, Coping and Evaluation, the key steps in initiating, conducting and evaluating an anti-bullying program. Given the possible risks of litigation, as outlined in Chapter 2, Slee's PEACE anti-bullying pack provides useful guidelines for implementing a program that helps schools ensure that they have fulfilled their duty of care in preventing bullying.

Research into the effectiveness of peer support is explored by Maree Stanley and Helen McGrath in Chapter 6, with particular focus on buddy systems. There is a reasonable level of research support for the effectiveness of a variety of peer support systems and structures in reducing school bullying and creating a caring and positive school culture. Such peer support has been shown to contribute to building positive peer relations, developing social and emotional learning, and creating peer and school connectedness.

In Chapter 7, school principal Tilly Barger provides an overview of one primary school's journey in implementing a values-based and social-skills-focused whole-school prevention program. Her chapter provides step-by-step details on how her school implemented many of the evidence-based components of effective prevention programs to 'turn the school around' from one that was dominated by poor student behaviour and bullying to a caring and supportive school underpinned by pro-social values in action. Their school-wide intervention was based on effective leadership, underpinned by a clearly articulated vision, the provision of teacher-friendly resources for each teacher, accessing parent support, and directly teaching children values and social skills. A testament to the success of the program is that the 'Willy Kids Are Friendly Kids' program has continued to evolve over 12 years and is still in operation.

In Chapter 8, Ken Rigby and Dale Bagshaw outline research into two promising prevention strategies for helping students to acquire understanding and personal skills that can contribute to reducing bullying. In general, school action against bullying has been more effective in primary schools than in secondary schools (Smith, 2001), so it is exciting to note that the research into each of these two strategies was conducted with secondary school students. The first strategy described used drama to teach students skills for responding constructively to conflict as opposed to using force (as students who bully do) or withdrawing (as students who are bullied tend to do). Conflict is not the same as bullying (see Chapter 14 for more details), but schools that work towards constructive management of conflict are clearly working towards a positive culture of harmony and acceptance of difference rather than a negative one of intimidation and prejudice. We also know that poorly resolved conflict situations between friends and classmates often lead to bullying situations. The documented outcomes for students were wide ranging and impressive, especially given the tight time frame of eight weeks. The group drama task also facilitated peer group connections and combined social and emotional learning with academic learning.

Research suggests that peers are involved in some capacity (from actively participating to passively onlooking) in 85 per cent of all bullying incidents (Atlas & Pepler, 1998) and that there is a trend towards increasing bystander apathy and increasing self-justification on the part of bullying students as students get older, especially in boys (Smith & Shu, 2000). The second research study documented in Chapter 8 focuses on training 'bystander students' to support peers who are being victimised. This is a strong evidence-supported trend in anti-bullying programs (e.g. Salmivalli, Kaukainen, Voetin & Sinisammal, 2004) and more detail is offered in Chapter 9. Rigby and Bagshaw found that few students in the research study were inclined to tell their teacher about observing bullying because they did not have confidence in the teachers knowing how to intervene effectively. This suggests that anti-bullying programs that advocate encouraging peers to report bullying to teachers are unlikely to succeed unless students can be convinced that the actions teachers will take will make a difference. Bystander support can produce positive outcomes for specific bullying incidents and hence make it less likely that a pattern of bullying will develop. The chapter also offers practical guidelines on what teachers can do to promote positive bystander behaviour.

Section Three: An overview of management solutions for bullying

The focus of this section is on management solutions for bullying.

In Chapter 9, Ken Rigby presents an overview of research into a range of approaches to managing bully/victim problems. As he notes, the distinction between dealing with (or managing) bullying and prevention is somewhat artificial in that the successful management of bullying should act as a deterrent to future bullying. A recurrent theme in this book, and mentioned in this chapter, is that a combination of actions have more chance of success than a single approach or action. Rigby highlights the importance of providing close school surveillance and safe places to play with activities at break times. He critiques punitive and non-punitive approaches, pointing out that non-punitive approaches acknowledge the positive power of the peer group to reduce bullying behaviour. Given that quite different punitive and non-punitive approaches can achieve similar results, Rigby reminds us that how consistently and accurately an approach is implemented is equally as important as its specific content. He concludes by noting the lack of focus on teaching systematic skills and understanding related to bullying in pre-service teacher training courses in Australian universities.

In Chapter 10, Andrew Fuller describes a resilience-based approach to helping children who have been bullied at school, which can be adapted for use by school counsellors or student welfare coordinators. His five-session plan is derived from solution-focused therapy, a practice that builds on existing strengths and resources to help individuals to find solutions. It is an optimistic model which is based on the premise that, with support and a focus on the 'here and now', rather than the past, a young person can use skills and strengths to create a more positive future for themselves, despite past traumatic events. Solution therapy is part of a social constructivist approach that emphasises the importance of language in shaping and moulding an individual's perception of events in their life (Berg, 2005).

The importance of 'restoring relationships' as a way of managing bullying underpins the work that Margaret Armstrong and Margaret Thorsborne describe in Chapter 11 on restorative responses to bullying. Restorative practices require a shift from traditional punitive management strategies to relational models that not only hold the wrongdoers accountable for their behaviour, but also provide support for the school community affected by the bullying. The focus of restorative practices is on restoring relationships, building empathy, making amends and negotiating solutions. The approach includes small group and individual conferences for less serious incidents, whole-class conferences for issues affecting all students and community conferences for serious cases of bullying. The authors draw on evaluations conducted in Victoria, Queensland and the ACT to confirm the positive outcomes of the restorative justice approach to bullying. They report that schools which are explicit about their core values and the practices aligning with those values are more likely to be successful in implementing restorative justice practices than those schools wedded to traditional discipline strategies.

A comparison of two non-punitive approaches to managing bullying is presented in Chapter 12 by Helen McGrath and Maree Stanley. The non-punitive approaches reviewed are the Method of Shared Concern (Pikas, 1989, 2002) and the No-Blame Approach (Maines & Robinson, 1992; Young, 1998). The chapter provides a teacher-friendly, step-by-step description of how each non-punitive approach is implemented. McGrath and Stanley also outline the research and theoretical support for and against the use of non-punitive measures to manage bullying and leave the reader to draw their own conclusions. They also identify factors that can increase the efficacy of non-punitive approaches. Many of these factors are similar to those that have been shown to improve school effectiveness.

In Chapter 13, Evelyn Field and Pam Carroll address strategies for working effectively with parents on the issue of bullying and, in particular, with parents of students who are bullied or who bully others. The authors provide general guidelines on communicating with parents about the problem of bullying at school, as well as specific suggestions for assisting parents to help their child develop 'social survival skills' and resilience, which in turn will make it less likely that they will be bullied. They also identify some of the issues that parents might have in relation to bullying situations.

Section Four: Putting it all together

Chapter 14 makes practical links between all of the previous chapters. The main component of the chapter is a safe school template for use in schools. This is supported by a number of related resources such as a safe schools checklist, definitions and examples of bullying, assessment tools for bullying, and the use of focus group discussions and a range of specific kinds of anti-bullying resources.

The chapters in this book represent both a contemporary and a comprehensive foundation for evidence-based prevention and management practices to reduce bullying in Australian schools. Implementing new anti-bullying practices is a slow journey and these practices can take from three to five years to become institutionalised. It is imperative to maintain a sense of optimism that schools using evidence-based practices can make a significant difference to the lives of young people who are bullied, and who bully, and to everyone else in the school community affected by the bullying.

Not so many years ago smoking in shared places was tolerated by the community. Despite the harm that it caused, both to smokers and non-smokers, smoking was prevalent in restaurants, workplaces and public venues, and on planes and other public transport. The community campaigns directed against smoking over the last 20 years have significantly changed attitudes, behaviours and legislation to the point where it is now difficult to imagine that such a situation was tolerated and endured. Hopefully, in 20 years from now we will recall bullying in much the same way.

REFERENCES

Atlas, R. S. & Pepler, D. J. (1998). Observations of bullying in the classroom. *The Journal of Educational Research*, 92(2), 86–97.

Berg, I. K. (2005). *Solution focused brief therapy*. Retrieved April 9, 2005, from <www.brief-therapy.org>

Caprara, G. V., Barbaranelli, C., Pastorelli, C., Bandura, A. & Zimbardo, P. G. (2000). Prosocial foundations of children's academic achievement. *Psychological Science, 11*(4), 302–306.

Maines, B. & Robinson, G. (1992). *The No-Blame Approach*. Bristol: Lucky Duck Publishing.

McGrath, H. & Noble, T. (2003). *BOUNCE BACK! A Classroom Resiliency Program. Teacher's Handbook. Level One: K–2; Level Two: Years 3–4; Level Three: Years 5–8*. Sydney: Pearson Education.

Ohsako, T. (1999). The developing world. In P. K. Smith, Y. Morita, J. Junger-Tas, D. Olweus, R. Catalano & P. Slee (Eds.). *The nature of school bullying: A cross-national perspective* (pp. 359–375). London and New York: Routledge.

Pikas, A. (1989). The Common Concern Method for the treatment of mobbing. In E. Roland & E. Munthe (Eds.), *Bullying: An international perspective* (pp. 91–104). London: David Fulton in association with the Professional Development Foundation.

Pikas, A. (2002). New developments in the Shared Concern Method, *School Psychology International*, 23(3), 307–326.

Salmivalli, C., Kaukainen, A., Voetin, M. & Sinisammal, M. (2004). Targeting the group as a whole: The Finish anti-bullying intervention. In P. K Smith, D. Pepler & K. Rigby (Eds.), *Bullying in schools: How successful can interventions be?* (pp. 251–275). Cambridge: Cambridge University Press.

Smith, P. (2004). Bullying: Recent developments. *Child and Adolescent Mental Health*, 9(3), 98–103.

Smith, P. K. (1999). England and Wales. In P. K. Smith, Y. Morita, J. Junger-Tas, D. Olweus, R. Catalano & P. Slee (Eds.), *The nature of school bullying: A cross-national perspective* (pp. 68–90). London: Routledge.

Smith, P. K. (2001). Should we blame the bullies? *The Psychologist, 14*(2). Retrieved May 14, 2005, from <www.luckyduck.co.uk>

Smith, P. K. & Brain, P. (2000). Bullying in schools: Lessons from two decades of research. *Aggressive Behavior*, 26, 1–9.

Smith, P. K. & Shu, S. (2000). What good schools can do about bullying: Findings from a survey in English schools after a decade of research and action. *Childhood*, 7, 193–212.

Wentzel, K. R. (2003). Sociometric status and adjustment in middle school: A longitudinal study. *Journal of Early Adolescence*, 23, 5–28.

Wentzel, K. R. & Caldwell, K. (1997). Friendships, peer acceptance, and group membership: Relations to academic achievement in middle school. *Child Development*, 68, 1198–1209.

Wentzel, K. R. & Watkins, D. E. (2002). Peer relationships and collaborative learning as contexts for academic enablers. *School Psychology Review, 31*(3), 336.

Young, S. (1998). The support group approach to bullying in schools. *Educational Psychology in Practice*, 14, 32–39.

Zins, J. E., Weissberg, R. P., Wang, M. C. & Walberg, H. J. (Eds.) (2004). *Building academic success on social and emotional learning: What does the research say?* New York: Teachers College Press.

SECTION ONE

AN OVERVIEW OF BULLYING AND POSSIBLE SOLUTIONS

CHAPTER 1

What international research tells us about bullying

Ken Rigby

Over the last 15 years or so a large base of research literature on bullying has been amassed, drawing from studies conducted in many countries (see Rigby, 2002a, 2002b; Smith et al., 1999). It has focused on a variety of areas, these being the most common:

1. Definition and measurement associated with bullying
2. Occurrence or prevalence of phenomena associated with bullying in schools
3. Consequences of bullying
4. Causes of bullying
5. Effectiveness of anti-bullying programs
6. Factors relating to the effective implementation of programs.

This chapter provides a brief survey of the contribution of international research to the study of bullying in schools and how it can be countered.

Defining bullying

Without an agreed definition of bullying, research into this area is unlikely to be of much value. In the early years of inquiry, some writers suggested definitions of bullying that were not acceptable to everyone. For example, Tattum and Tattum (1992) defined bullying as 'the wilful, conscious desire to hurt another and put him/her under stress' (p. 147). Behaviourally oriented researchers had problems with this formulation. For them, measuring 'behaviour' was more attractive (and practical) than attempting to measure a child's motives. It was pointed out that bullying needed to be distinguished from aggression in general. It is now generally agreed that bullying is a sub-set of aggression, that is, aggression that occurs in a situation in which there is an imbalance of power between perpetrator(s) and target(s) or 'victims'.

Probably the most influential formulation of what constitutes bullying has been proposed by Olweus (1993). According to him, bullying may be defined as a student being exposed, repeatedly and over time, to intentional injury or discomfort inflicted by one or more other students. This may include physical contact, verbal assault, making obscene gestures or facial expressions, and intentionally excluding the student. Bullying, he adds, implies an imbalance in power or strength in which one child is victimised by others. Bullying is thus conceived largely in behavioural terms, that is, it involves negative actions on the part of the perpetrator. However, it does not exclude the subjective element suggested by the Tattums; inference must still be made regarding the desire or, in Olweus's formulation, the intentionality, of the perpetrator.

Subsequently, it has been suggested that a distinction should be made between intentionally seeking to hurt someone, which may be termed 'malign bullying' and unintentional bullying, that is of a 'non-malign' nature (Rigby, 1996). It is clear from the reports of children that they are sometimes unaware that they are bullying someone. They are not trying to hurt their peers. But their peers *are* being hurt. They feel that they are being bullied. In practice, determining whether bullying has occurred is generally based on the reports of 'victims'.

There are two further issues that concern researchers in defining bullying. Olweus and many others insist that bullying involves 'repeated actions' of a negative kind. Yet it is not unreasonable to call an action 'bullying' even if it occurs on one occasion. Children have been known to be traumatised as a result of a single experience of intense bullying. Secondly, researchers commonly seek to avoid 'value judgments' in their definitions of phenomena. Yet clearly to call someone a 'bully' or some action 'bullying' is to make a value judgment. Such judgments may of course be accepted at some times but not others. In Elizabethan times wife-beating under the mildest provocation would not be called bullying; in 19th-century England senior private school boys were licensed to chastise their 'fags' for not cleaning their boots. Variations in norms over time and from place to place complicate the notion of what constitutes bullying. Such difficulties are recognised in some conceptualisations. Thus Farrington (1993), a British criminologist, saw 'oppression' as crucial to what bullying is. He defined bullying as 'repeated oppression, psychological or physical, of a less powerful person by a more powerful person'. To this, one may add that bullying, especially in schools, typically involves a plurality of perpetrators, rather than a single perpetrator. The view that bullying involves immoral or socially unacceptable behaviour is consistent with the most general – and the most parsimonious – definition of bullying as 'the systematic abuse of power' (Smith, Pepler & Rigby, 2004).

Although there has been progress towards consensus in conceptualising bullying in schools, some high-profile research continues to confuse bullying with other related concepts. For instance, an international project has recently reported research findings purportedly comparing countries according to the level of victimisation in their schools (Thomson & Fleming, 2002). Their index of bullying in a school was how unsafe children felt at schools, for example, about having property stolen from them. Whilst children who are bullied often feel unsafe, it does not follow that children who feel unsafe (for whatever reason) are being bullied by their peers. A clearer understanding of what constitutes bullying is still needed.

Measuring bullying

By far the most common way of measuring bullying is by means of self-reports in answer to questions contained in anonymous questionnaires. This approach was pioneered by Olweus (1993). His questionnaire was translated from Norwegian into English for use in schools in England (Smith, Sharp, Eslea & Thompson, 2004). Other translations have been made for use in a number of other countries, including Germany, Belgium and Italy. In Australia, the Peer Relations Questionnaire (PRQ) and the shorter Peer Relations Assessment Questionnaire (PRAQ), in part adaptations of the original Olweus model, have been widely employed in schools (Rigby, 1999). Non-verbal measures using illustrations of bullying have been developed for use with very young children. These measures have been shown to be reliable and valid, more so when answered by older students reporting on how often they had been bullied at school in the recent past. Alternative measures of the occurrence or frequency of bullying have employed peer nomination procedures (Perry, Kusel & Perry, 1988), teacher assessments (Alsaker & Valkanover, 2001) and direct behavioural observations (Pepler & Craig, 1995). Some researchers have also sought to assess the attitudes of children towards victims (Rigby, 1997b), the behaviour of bystanders in the presence of bullying (Salmivalli, Lagerspetz, Bjorkqvist, Osterman & Kaukiainen, 1996), and the attempted coping responses of children when they are bullied (Kristensen & Smith, 2003).

Occurrence or prevalence of phenomena associated with bullying in schools

Estimates of the occurrence of bullying in schools vary widely. There are a number of reasons for this. Definitions of bullying sometimes differ; for example, as we have seen, Thomson and Fleming (2002) see being bullied as the same thing as being unsafe; others don't. It is unfortunate that standardised procedures with at least face validity for assessing bullying have not been widely used. Questionnaires typically contain different preambles relating to what constitutes 'bullying'. Item content often varies and the precise wording of items and response categories used in questionnaires also often differ.

Comparisons between countries have been particularly difficult to make. In part, this is because the words used to describe bullying in different countries have different connotations. For example, in Italy, the word 'prepotenze' is typically used in questionnaires assessing bullying. This word implies a severe and physically aggressive action against a partner, and does not cover a great deal of negative behaviour of a less severe kind usually implied by the English word 'bullying' (Fonzi et al., 1999). Similar problems arise when comparisons are made with statistics reported in Japan, where the word used to describe bullying, namely, 'ijime', describes negative actions performed by groups of classmates rather than by individuals (Morita, Soeda, Soeda & Taki, 1999).

In estimating the occurrence of bullying, there are also problems associated with the sampling. The age of the children being sampled is one crucial factor. Reported bullying typically reduces with age. It has also been found to be higher in some studies (but not in all) in areas of low socio-economic status (Rigby, 2002a). The racial mix of students in a school may also constitute a further factor in areas in which racial prejudice is rife. Figures for boys and girls often differ, with boys reporting being bullied more often physically, and girls reporting experiencing more indirect forms of bullying, for example, social exclusion (Crick & Grotpeter, 1995).

Research into the occurrence of bullying may also be restricted by ethical requirements insisted upon in some countries but not in others. For instance, in Australia, ethics committees in universities and education departments commonly disallow research in schools that makes use of peer nomination procedures, that is, those in which students indicate who the children are who frequently engage in bullying others and/or are themselves bullied. This method is probably the most useful one for reliably identifying bullies and victims and is employed routinely in many countries such as the UK and the USA. An ethical requirement that only children who have parental permission to complete questionnaires about bullying, even if answered anonymously, further ensures that samples of students from which conclusions are drawn are unrepresentative and the nature of the bias is unknown.

As yet, there have been no reports from which reliable inferences can be made about the level of bullying experienced in Australian schools compared with those surveyed overseas. Nevertheless, in absolute terms, the level of reported victimisation appears to be high, with as many as 19 per cent of students between the ages of 7 and 17 reporting being bullied in some way on a weekly basis (see Figure 1.1). Comparable data from overseas countries is still needed to place bullying in Australia in an international context.

Consequences of bullying

For the most part, studies of the consequences of bullying in schools have concentrated upon health outcomes for children who are persistently bullied by their peers. Results from cross-sectional surveys suggest that being victimised by peers is related to comparatively low levels of psychological wellbeing and social adjustment and to high levels of psychological distress and adverse physical health symptoms (see, for example, the work

Figure 1.1 Reported victimisation in Australian schools, based on N = 37 997 students

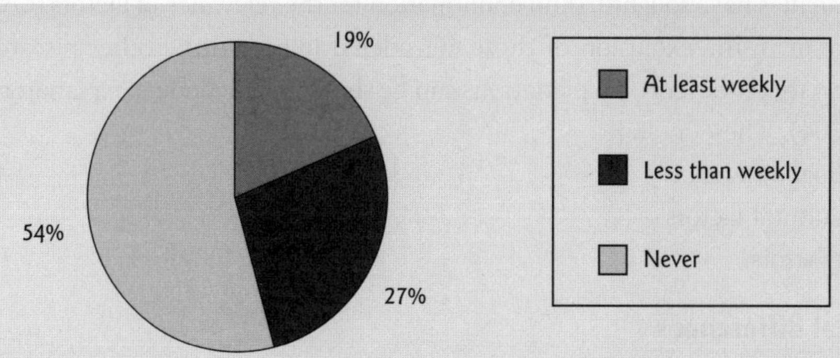

Source: Rigby (1997a)

of Crick and Grotpeter (1995) in the United States; Forero, McClellan, Russel and Bauman (1999) and Rigby and Slee (1999) in Australia; Kaltialo-Heino, Impala, Martine, Impala and Rateen (1999) in Finland; and Williams, Chambers, Logan and Robinson (1996) in England. Such research does not shed light on the direction of causation. It is theoretically possible that having low self-esteem and being psychologically depressed attracts bullying and that bullying is a cause rather than a consequence, or as some claim, both a cause of being bullied and a consequence (Egan & Perry, 1998).

To establish a clear causal relationship between bullying and health status has required researchers to collect data on the health status of children and how often they have been bullied at one point in time and then repeat the testing at a later stage, say one or two years later. Where such longitudinal studies have been done, the results strongly suggest that being repeatedly bullied actually impacts upon the child's mental and/or physical health. In Australia, such studies have been conducted with adolescent students by Rigby (1999) and by Bond, Carlin, Thomas, Ruin and Patton (2001). Overseas, similar findings with young children have been reported by Kochenderfer and Ladd (1996) and by Egan and Perry (1998). Some research has suggested that there can be persistent negative effects of being bullied on mental health into adult years (Olweus, 1992; Smith, Singer, Hoel & Cooper, 2003). The current position is that it is extremely likely that severe bullying is likely to induce deterioration in mental and possibly physical health. For a more comprehensive examination of international research in this area, see Hawker and Boulton (2000) and Rigby (2003a).

Causes of bullying

This is a somewhat controversial area of research into bullying. In part, this is because some researchers have sought to find confirmation for the relevance of factors *they* believe are important to the exclusion of those considered important by other researchers. It seems likely that a variety of explanations can be shown to have some explanatory power (Rigby, 2004). These include:

- individual differences
- socio-cultural factors
- school factors.

Individual differences

Bullying is sometimes seen as a consequence of individual differences which enable the more powerful to impose themselves upon the less powerful. This may be regarded as a necessary but not sufficient factor in accounting for bullying. Researchers have identified personality factors that make bullying more likely; for example, children who repeatedly bully others tend to be generally aggressive (Olweus, 1993) and Machiavellian (Sutton & Keogh, 2000) and show low levels of empathy (Slee & Rigby, 1993). Children who are repeatedly victimised by peers have been characterised as relatively introverted (Slee & Rigby, 1993); having low self-esteem (Egan & Perry, 1998) and lacking in assertiveness (Sharp & Cowie, 1998). Some evidence has been adduced suggesting that such differences between bullies and victims have a genetic basis (O'Connor, Foch, Todd & Plomin, 1980). However, it is generally conceded that explanations based upon personality differences provide only one part of the story.

Sociocultural factors

Emphasis is sometimes placed upon sociocultural explanations for bullying in schools. These relate to differences of a sociological kind and include such factors as gender, race or ethnicity, social class and religious affiliation. Children are thought to come to school with hostile attitudes learned from their families and the community towards members of other groups (Espelage, Bosworth & Simon, 2000). These may motivate them to act negatively towards some of their peers and, if possible, victimise them in some way. Sociocultural factors are sometimes held to explain why boys bully others more than girls do and why boys bully girls more than vice-versa. It is argued that boys typically aspire to become tough and dominant, thereby constructing a satisfying masculine identity (Connell, 1995; Gilbert & Gilbert, 1998). Accordingly, they seek out those they can dominate, often by bullying them. Typically their victims include girls, whom they see as being in some sense 'inferior', and boys who do not conform in their behaviour to that expected of the stereotypical male, that is, effeminate types and those suspected of being gay. Research clearly shows that boys are more likely to bully others than girls and that cross-gender bullying most commonly involves boys as the perpetrators (Rigby, 2002a). Further, the bullying of children who are thought to be gay is prevalent in many schools (Rivers, 2001).

Some international research has suggested that bullying may be motivated by racial or ethnic prejudice and by social prejudice relating to differences in socioeconomic status. However, the research has produced inconsistent outcomes. Studies in some countries have reported that there are ethnic or social groups that are bullied in schools more than others, for example, Aboriginal children in Australia (Rigby, 2002a). But in some countries no significant associations have been found (see Rigby, 2002a for a review of the research evidence). In conclusion, sociocultural explanations for bullying provide further reasons why some (but not all) children may be bullied in schools.

School factors

It is evident from international research that, while some bullying can be explained as due to the importation of prejudiced thinking, relayed by children from the wider community, the school ethos itself may contribute to the level of bullying experienced by the children who attend. It has been reported that bullying in one school may be four times higher than bullying in another school, even when the schools are located in similar socioeconomic areas with the same ethnic mix (Rigby, 1996). How a school manages the problem of bullying is a crucial factor. When schools have been able to achieve a very positive classroom climate wherein children work constructively and enjoy their studies, bullying has been found to be relatively low (Roland & Galloway, 2004).

Effectiveness of anti-bullying programs

Research has pointed toward a number of possible solutions, many of which have been incorporated into actual intervention programs. An outline of these measures is given in Chapter 9. Drawing upon an extensive range of anti-bullying programs worldwide, the degree to which measures have been successful in reducing bullying is described in detail in Rigby (2002b) and Smith, Pepler and Rigby (2004). Here is a brief summary of the outcomes from this research.

Outcomes from anti-bullying programs

1. The range of reported outcomes is very broad. For example, the first national Norwegian intervention to reduce bullying, conducted in the 1980s, resulted in approximately 50 per cent reduction in reported victimisation. By contrast, several similar programs led to little or no improvement, for example, anti-bullying programs undertaken in Germany, Belgium, and Southern Carolina.
2. On average, reductions in bullying have been around 15 per cent of children being victimised at school. They have generally been greater in primary than in secondary schools.
3. It seems unlikely that variations in outcomes from interventions are closely related to specific program content. Not only have similar programs, for example those based on the Olweus model, produced widely different results, but programs that are radically different in content have at times produced quite similar results. The Finish intervention reported by Salmivalli, Kaukainen, Voetin and Sinisammal (2004) utilising a problem-solving approach proposed by Swedish psychologist, Anatol Pikas

(2002), produced a similar reduction in bullying (around 40 per cent) to that reported in Oslo by Olweus using a more traditional punitive approach (Olweus, 2004).

4. Generally, reductions have been greater where the implementation of programs has been most thorough, in some case approaching a 70 per cent reduction (Salmivalli et al., 2004).

Factors in the effective implementation of programs

Recently, research into the effectiveness of anti-bullying programs has focused on the importance of rigorous implementation (Olweus, 2004; Roland & Galloway, 2004; Salmivalli et al., 2004; Smith, Pepler & Rigby, 2004). These factors have been reported as associated with relatively good reductions in bullying in schools:

1. Teachers see the issue as important.
2. Teachers regard the level of bullying as unacceptably high.
3. Teachers are personally and emotionally concerned when they encounter cases of bullying.
4. There is comprehensive staff involvement in the actual development of the school anti-bullying policy.
5. Teachers fully comprehend what is expected of them in the program.
6. Principals play a positive part in promoting anti-bullying procedures, for example, in placing bullying on the school agenda at staff meetings, organising meetings with parents, ensuring good surveillance of student behaviour at breaks.
7. The school's anti-bullying policy is communicated to members of the school community, including parents.
8. Regular classroom meetings are held with children about bullying.
9. Curriculum-based work is being done with children, for example, group discussions, role plays, assertiveness training, and especially the promotion of positive action on the part of student bystanders.
10. Appropriate action is being consistently taken by schools when cases of bullying are identified.
11. There is good teacher management of classes leading to a cooperative classroom environment that promotes positive relations between students.

Conclusions on research into bullying

The last 20 years has seen remarkable achievements in research into bullying in schools. A great deal is now known about the occurrence and consequences of bullying in schools in many countries. Plausible explanations, both psychological and sociological, have been proposed to account for some children being involved in bully/victim problems more that others and for the variation in the level of bullying between schools. Yet there remains considerable uncertainty and controversy over which explanations are most convincing. Probably each of the different explanations explains some cases of bullying and some variation between schools, but not all. Although much of what is now being done in schools to counter bullying is supported by research findings, very few studies achieve a target of 50 per cent reduction in bullying – and some have reported minimal or zero improvement. Currently it cannot be said that variations in the specific content of anti-bullying programs account for differences in outcomes. It seems likely on the available evidence that when a program is implemented with the full and cooperative support of the staff in a school the outcomes are substantially better.

REFERENCES

Alsaker, F. D. & Valkanover, S. (2001). Early diagnosis and prevention of victimization in kindergarten. In J. Juvonen & S. Graham (Eds.), *Peer harassment in school* (pp. 175–195). New York: Guilford.

Bond, L., Carlin, J. B., Thomas, L., Ruin, K. & Patton, G. (2001). Does bullying cause emotional problems? A prospective study of young teenagers. *British Medical Journal, 323*, 480–484.

Connell, R. (1995). *Masculinities*. Sydney: Allen and Unwin.

Crick, N. R. & Grotpeter, J. K. (1995). Relational aggression, gender and social psychological adjustment. *Child Development*, 66, 710–722.

Egan, S. K. & Perry, D. G. (1998). Does low self-regard invite victimization? *Developmental Psychology*, *34*, 299–309.

Espelage, D., Bosworth, K. & Simon, T. (2000). Examining the social context of bullying behaviours in early adolescence. *Journal of Counselling and Development*, *78*, 326–344.

Farrington, D. P. (1993). Understanding and preventing bullying. In M. Tonny & N. Morris (Eds). *Crime and justice* (p. 17), Chicago: University of Chicago Press.

Fonzi, A., Genta, M. L, Menesini, E., Bacchin, D., Bonino, S. & Costabile, A. (1999). Italy. In P. K. Smith, Y. Morita, J. Junger-Tas, D. Olweus, R. Catalano & P. T. Slee (Eds.), *The nature of school bullying: A cross-national perspective* (pp. 140–156). London: Routledge.

Forero, R., McClellan, L., Russel, C. & Bauman, A. (1999). Bullying behaviour and psychosocial health among school students in NSW, Australia. *British Medical Journal*, *319*, 344–348.

Gilbert, R. & Gilbert, P. (1998). *Masculinity goes to school*. St Leonards, NSW: Allen and Unwin.

Hawker, S. J. & Boulton, M. J. (2000). Twenty years' research on peer victimization and psychosocial adjustment: A meta-analytical review of cross-sectional studies. *Journal of Child Psychology and Psychiatry*, *42*, 441–455.

Kaltialo-Heino, R., Impala, M., Martine, M., Impala, A. & Rateen, P. (1999). Bullying, depression and suicidal ideation in Finnish adolescents: School survey. *British Medical Journal, 319*, 348–350.

Kochenderfer, B. J. & Ladd, G. W. (1996). Peer victimisation: Cause or consequence of school maladjustment. *Child Development, 67*, 1305–1317.

Kristensen, S. M. & Smith, P. K. (2003). The use of coping strategies by Danish children classed as bullies, victims, bully/victims, and not involved, in response to different (hypothetical) types of bullying. *Scandinavian Journal of Psychology, 44*, 479–485.

Morita, Y., Soeda, H., Soeda, K. & Taki, M. (1999). Japan. In P. K. Smith, Y. Morita, J. Junger-Tas, D. Olweus, R. Catalano & P. T. Slee. *The nature of school bullying: A cross-national perspective* (pp. 309–323). London: Routledge.

O'Connor, M., Foch, T., Todd, S. & Plomin, R. (1980). A twin study of specific behavioral problems of socialisation as viewed by parents. *Journal of Abnormal Child Psychology*, 8, 189–199.

Olweus, D. (1992). Victimisation by peers: Antecedents and long term outcomes. In K. H. Rubin & J. B. Asendorf (Eds.), *Social withdrawal, inhibition and shyness in children* (pp. 315–342). Hillsdale, NJ: Erlbaum.

Olweus, D. (1993). *Bullying at school: What we know & what we can do*. Oxford and Cambridge, MA: Blackwell.

Olweus, D. (2004). The Olweus bullying prevention programme; design and implementation issues and a new national initiative in Norway. In P. K. Smith, D. Pepler & K. Rigby (Eds.), *Bullying in schools: How successful can interventions be?* (pp. 13–36). Cambridge: Cambridge University Press.

Pepler, D. J. & Craig, W. M. (1995). A peek behind the fence: Naturalistic observations of aggressive children with remote audiovisual recording. *Developmental Psychology, 31*(4), 548–553.

Perry, D. G., Kusel, S. J. & Perry, L. C. (1988). Victims of peer aggression. *Developmental Psychology, 24*, 807–814.

Pikas, A. (2002). New developments: A Shared Concern Method. *School Psychology International, 23*(3), 307–326.

Rigby, K. (1996). *Bullying in schools – and what to do about it*. Melbourne: ACER.

Rigby, K. (1997a). *Manual for the Peer Relations Questionnaire* (PRQ). Point Lonsdale, Victoria, Australia: The Professional Reading Guide.

Rigby, K. (1997b). Attitudes and beliefs about bullying among Australian school children. *Irish Journal of Psychology, 18*(2), 202–220.

Rigby, K. (1999). Peer victimisation at school and the health of secondary students. *British Journal of Educational Psychology, 22*(2), 28–34.

Rigby, K. (2002a). *New perspectives on bullying*. London: Jessica Kingsley.

Rigby, K. (2002b). *A meta-evaluation of methods and approaches to reducing bullying in pre-schools and in early primary school in Australia*. Canberra: Commonwealth Attorney-General's Department. (Phone 1800 708 777 for free copies.)

Rigby, K. (2003a). Consequences of bullying in schools. *Canadian Journal of Psychiatry*, *48*, 583–591.

Rigby, K. (2003b). *Stop the bullying: A handbook for schools* (Rev. ed.). Melbourne: Australian Council for Educational Research (ACER).

Rigby, K. (2004). Addressing bullying in schools: Theoretical perspectives and their implications. *School Psychology International*, *25*, 287–300.

Rigby, K. & Slee, P. T. (1999). Suicidal ideation among adolescent school children, involvement in bully/victim problems and perceived low social support. *Suicide and Life-threatening Behavior*, *29*, 119–130.

Rivers, I. (2001). The bullying of sexual minorities at school: Its nature and long-term correlates. *Education and School Psychology*, *18*(1), 32–46.

Roland, E. & Galloway, D. (2004). Is the direct approach to reducing bullying always the best? In P. K. Smith, D. Pepler & K. Rigby (Eds.), *Bullying in schools: How successful can interventions be?* (pp. 37–80). Cambridge: Cambridge University Press.

Salmivalli, C., Kaukainen, A., Voetin, M. & Sinisammal, M. (2004). Targeting the group as a whole: The Finish anti-bullying intervention. In P. K. Smith, D. Pepler & K. Rigby (Eds.), *Bullying in Schools: How successful can interventions be?* (pp. 251–275). Cambridge: Cambridge University Press.

Salmivalli, C., Lagerspetz, K. M. J., Bjorkqvist, K., Osterman, K. & Kaukiainen, A. (1996). Bullying as a group process: Participant roles and their relations to social status within the group. *Aggressive Behavior*, *22*, 1–15.

Sharp, S. & Cowie, H. (1998). *Counselling and supporting children in distress*. London: Sage.

Slee, P. K. & Rigby, K. (1993). The relationship of Eysenck's personality factors and self-esteem to bully/victim behaviour in Australian school boys. *Personality and Individual Differences*, *14*, 371–373.

Smith, P. K., Morita, Y., Junger-Tas, J., Olweus, R., Catalono, R. & Slee, P. (Eds.) (1999). *The nature of school bullying: A cross-national perspective*. London: Routledge.

Smith, P. K., Pepler, D. & Rigby, K. (Eds) (2004). *Bullying in schools: How successful can interventions be?*. Cambridge: Cambridge University Press.

Smith, P. K., Sharp, S., Eslea, M. & Thompson, D. (2004). England: The Sheffield project. In P. K. Smith, D. Pepler & K. Rigby (Eds.), *Bullying in schools: How successful can interventions be?* (pp. 99–124). Cambridge: Cambridge University Press.

Smith, P. K, Singer, M., Hoel, H. & Cooper, C. L. (2003). Victimization in the school and the workplace: Are there any links?. *British Journal of Psychology*, *94*, 175–188.

Sutton, J. & Keogh, E. (2000). Social competition in school: Relationships with bullying, Machiavellianism and personality. *British Journal of Educational Psychology*, *70*(3), 443–456.

Tattum, D. P. & Tattum, E. (1992). *Social education and personal development*. London: Fulton.

Thomson, S. & Fleming, N. (2002). Summing it up: Mathematics achievement in Australian schools. In TIMSS 2002 (*TIMSS Australia Monograph No*. 6). Melbourne: ACER.

Williams, K., Chambers, M., Logan, S. & Robinson, D. (1996). Association of common health symptoms with bullying in primary school children. *British Medical Journal*, *313*, 17–19.

CHAPTER 2

Legal perspectives on bullying

Alastair Nicholson

Overview

The law has not been designed to cope with bullying, nor has there been any conscious design of laws that are specifically directed at bullying. This means that any attempt to invoke the law is really an attempt to fit the bullying conduct complained of into a legal framework that has really been designed for something else. The result is that legal remedies are rarely very satisfactory in coping with the problem of bullying.

In discussing this topic, reference will be made to a number of decided cases in the UK, Canada and Australia. Such cases provide guidance as to the proper interpretation of the law, but it is important to remember that decisions made in higher courts carry more weight than those made in lower courts. There is often room for legitimate disagreement about the correctness of a particular decision or whether it represents the law.

The objectives of the criminal law are basically to denounce and punish the individual and to deter both the individual and others who might engage in similar conduct. Another important objective is to reform behaviour. This has unfortunately slipped down the agenda somewhat in recent years, although it retains considerable importance in relation to crimes committed by children and young persons. However, the methods for achieving these objectives, such as imprisonment, detention and fines, are comparatively blunt instruments in relation to bullying situations and are normally only relevant when the bullying constitutes a serious crime. There are some alternative remedies, such as family group conferences, discussed later in this chapter, which do hold out some prospect of being useful and appropriate in a bullying context, but they are usually available only, if at all, when a crime as such has been committed.

Civil law also presents difficulties in relation to bullying. In relation to this discussion, it is designed to provide a remedy to individuals who suffer damage at the hands of others, arising either out of the commission of a tort or a breach of contract. A tort is a wrong committed by one person against another and includes personal injuries caused by negligence, assault, breach of statutory duty, nuisance, defamation and the like.

In the context of bullying the most relevant torts are assault, negligence and breach of statutory duty. It is beyond the scope of this chapter to discuss all of the ramifications of actions for damages involving schools, teachers and pupils. A very full discussion can be found in the recent book, *Schools, Courts and Law* (Stewart & Knott, 2002). This chapter will concentrate only on the law as it relates to bullying.

As is discussed below, assault is both a crime and a tort and persons may be sued for assault whether or not they have been charged or convicted of the crime of assault. Negligence is usually defined as a failure to take reasonable care for the safety of a person to whom a duty of care is owed. In the case of a school, a duty of care is clearly owed to the pupils when they are at the school or engaged in school activities. The duty of care is owed by the school authority, the head teacher, teachers and others, such as outside experts, e.g. psychologists and other specialists. A breach of the duty of care gives rise to damages if the injury was foreseeable by the body or person owing the duty and the injury was, on the balance of probabilities, caused by the breach. It is unnecessary for the extent of the injury to have been foreseeable. The issue of whether the duty of care extends outside the school grounds is not without difficulty and is discussed later as well.

In practical terms, individual teachers are unlikely to suffer financial loss as a result of damages claims for negligence. The normal practice in Australia is for the school authority, or its insurer (if any) to accept the financial responsibility for such claims and for the costs of defending them. A teacher's personal liability is only likely to arise if the school authority becomes insolvent and is uninsured. A school authority may possibly seek to recover from a teacher in circumstances where the teacher's serious misconduct has caused the harm by, for example, encouraging or taking part in the bullying behaviour, or extreme neglect. As well as the teacher concerned, the school authority may also be liable for a crime committed by a teacher against a pupil.[1]

In the case of breach of contract, the relevant remedy is an action for damages or an injunction against a school authority for failing in an express or implied duty to provide safe premises and a safe environment. Such a claim can also usually be framed in tort.

The problem for the present purposes is that the usual remedy in a civil action is damages. That may be useful in seeking compensation from a school authority for breach of contract or the negligence of the school, teachers or persons in authority, but it is a remedy that is only available after, and usually a considerable time after, the damage has been suffered.

The possibility of being subject to such an action is of course useful in encouraging school authorities to set up proper systems and policies for dealing with bullying because the absence or inadequacy of such policies is likely to render them liable in damages.

The problem is that the somewhat cumbersome mechanism of a civil action can do nothing to prevent the victim of bullying from suffering or continuing to suffer from it.

It is true that civil courts do have the power to grant injunctions preventing the repetition of the conduct complained of. However, firstly, the conduct must be established to the court's satisfaction and the injunction obtained, which takes time, and secondly, it is necessary to go back to the court in the event of a breach and prove the breach, and then the court has the power to punish the perpetrator for contempt. This is a very tortuous and often expensive process. The remedy of damages is obviously useless against a schoolyard bully.

There is a third category of proceeding that may have relevance to the control of bullying: the seeking of an apprehended violence or intervention order from a court. The availability of these orders arose out of legislation directed at the control of family violence and later extended to providing a remedy for stalking. They are readily available from the Magistrate's Court or, where appropriate, the Children's Court, with minimal formality. They are usually directed at restraining the perpetrator from coming to or within a specified distance of the victim and, not uncommonly, from harassing them either by telephone or electronic means. Failure to comply with such an order exposes the offender to criminal penalties and in that sense they resemble the civil injunction.

In Victoria, at least, these orders have begun to be widely used as a response to bullying. But this has given rise to some concerns, including the unsuitability of such orders in many school-related situations and the difficulties of meaningful enforcement, as well as the question of whether they really achieve anything in the control of bullying.

These concerns are undoubtedly justified, but it is suggested that if serious attention was to be given to the way in which they might be adapted to control bullying then there may be some merit in their use. At present, in Victoria, due to resource problems in the Children's Court, there are no reliable up-to-date statistics as to the use of these remedies and, more importantly, no evidence as to their effectiveness or otherwise.

If the use of such remedies was to be combined with the power to order something along the lines of a Family Group Conference, it is considered that some meaningful benefit might be obtained. Also, it is time that proper research was conducted as to the efficacy of the existing legal remedies for bullying and to ways in which effective remedies could be offered.

There are other legal proceedings that may be of relevance to bullying. Anti-discrimination laws have been successfully invoked in appropriate cases and, in some states and territories, criminal injuries compensation may be available to victims.

Starting with a definition

In considering bullying from a legal point of view, it is important to have an understanding of what bullying is. Any definition is, of necessity, imprecise because of the wide range of behaviour that can constitute bullying. Also, any concise definition must be expanded by further explanation in order to define what is not bullying as well as what is meant by the term.

Olweus (1993) has defined bullying as 'Repeated negative ill-intentioned behaviour against another who has difficulty defending him/herself'. The Canadian National Strategy on Community Safety and Crime Prevention (2004) also draws upon Olweus in defining bullying:

> Bullying is the assertion of power through aggression. Bullies acquire power over their victims physically, emotionally and socially. This can be done in many ways: by physical size and strength, by status within the peer group, by knowing the victim's weaknesses or by recruiting support from other children, as in group bullying. Emotional and social bullying may perhaps be the most frequent and harmful forms. Bullying can be physical or verbal. It can be direct (face-to-face) or indirect (gossip or exclusion) … With repeated bullying, the bully's dominance over the victim is established and the victim becomes increasingly distressed and fearful.

Rigby (2003) has given the following description of bullying:

> Bullying involves a desire to hurt + hurtful action + a power imbalance + (typically) repetition + an unjust use of power + evident enjoyment by the oppressor and a sense of being oppressed on the part of the victim.

A more detailed discussion of the definition can be found in other chapters, but the above definitions, particularly the description adopted by Rigby, will suffice here.

The relevant law

It is important to remember that bullying as such is not a concept known to the law and, in particular, that in Australia it does not constitute an offence. However, the Acts that constitute bullying may attract legal consequences. Accordingly, it follows that there are a number of branches and sub-branches of the law that are or may be relevant to the question of bullying.

1. Criminal law

As has been pointed out, bullying *per se* is not a crime. Bullying behaviour may offend the criminal law but it does not necessarily do so. There are no criminal remedies directed specifically at bullying in Australia. On the other hand, the increased number of statutes directed at stalking and harassment has widened the reach of the criminal law in this regard.

Criminal law may be relevant in controlling some types of bullying, but it has a number of serious limitations, including:

- Strict proof of criminal conduct is required, which involves proof beyond reasonable doubt of the guilt of the offender. This involves not only proof that the offender committed the act complained of, but that he/she did so intentionally, knowing that it was wrong to do so.
- Children may lack criminal responsibility and thus be incapable of committing a crime or, if between 10 and 14, have diminished responsibility and thus it may be impossible to prove the necessary intent to constitute a crime.
- A defence may be available to charges of assault on the basis that the children were engaged in 'rough and undisciplined play' even in the absence of the victim's consent to such 'play' provided that the perpetrators held a genuine belief that the victim was consenting, even if that belief was unreasonably held (Furniss, 2000).

- Legal processes are often protracted and may be traumatic for the victim as well as the perpetrator.
- The law is only concerned with actions that constitute an offence and many aspects of bullying, such as emotional abuse, do not usually constitute an offence against the criminal law.
- The penalties for the commission of criminal offences are often quite inappropriate when applied to children.
- Police and prosecuting authorities may be unwilling to act, except in the case of what they regard as serious offences.

In general, the use of the criminal law is practically confined to acts of violence or harassment, usually involving older children. It is important to note that it is the *acts* that are punished by the criminal law and not the fact that they may have taken place in a situation where bullying is present, although the latter fact may exacerbate the punishment imposed.

While there are many cases that come to the criminal courts that may have involved an element of bullying, there are only a limited number that are reported in law reports as having emanated from a school environment. There is room for more research in this area. The fact that reported examples of such cases are relatively uncommon does not mean that they do not occur, but rather that they do not often reach the superior courts. Often press reports are the best source of such cases but they have limitations as to content. There are, however, some interesting recent examples.

In Canada, on 26 March 2002, a 16-year-old girl was found guilty of uttering threats and criminal harassment following the suicide of one of her classmates two years previously. The judge's comments indicated that the victim had been bullied repeatedly giving her reason to fear for her life ('B.C. girl convicted in school bullying tragedy', 2002). The perpetrator was subsequently sentenced to 18 months probation, following a 'sentencing circle' involving the victim's mother and the convicted girl and her family (Joyce, 2002). This case was later described by an Ontario judge as the first case in Canada targeting bullying and harassment (Zuker, 2002). Again, however, it is clear that the charges were of specific offences rather than bullying. Furniss (2000) records similar cases in England in 1997 and 1998.

In New Zealand, in 2003, six youths were sentenced to varying terms of imprisonment for anally assaulting a classmate with a broomstick at a party in 2001 and another was sentenced to imprisonment for the same offence in 2002 ('Broomstick bullies sentenced', 2003). The victim was aged 17 at the time of the offence, as were those convicted. Again it should be noted that the offence concerned was not bullying but the commission of a serious assault. The incident attracted considerable publicity and is commonly referred to as the Taradale Broomstick Case (Hay-Mackenzie, 2002). It occurred outside the school environment and was attempted to be justified as some sort of rugby 'initiation'.

All of these cases involved what would normally be described as 'serious' criminal activity. Furniss (2000) raises the question as to what is or is not serious in such a context. This is a difficult question and the answer must be, I believe, that it depends upon the particular circumstances, and that a degree of common sense must be observed. The above cases were obviously serious. It seems to me that if the conduct in question either has led to or is likely to lead to serious consequences then appropriate action should be taken by teachers and the school authorities to inform police.

The following section outlines particular aspects of the criminal law that may be relevant in these more serious cases of bullying.

Assault

The crime of assault in all its forms covers a multiplicity of conduct ranging from the very serious and life threatening to the trivial. It can also give rise to claims for injunctions preventing a repetition of the conduct complained of and actions for damages in civil proceedings. However, some sense of proportion can and should be observed.

For example, quite minor actions such as a kiss can constitute an assault, as can many minor physical contacts, but it would be obviously impracticable to invoke the criminal or civil law in most such cases. There are, however, others where the invocation of the criminal law would be expected as a matter of course, such as cases of assault involving brutal beating or wounding with a weapon. Even in a case of wounding, however, the wound may be minor and inflicted in circumstances where the matter may best be dealt with in the school environment. For example, the weapon might well be a small pen knife, the wound little more than a scratch and the circumstances in which someone was injured with it may be less than clear. It is difficult to see what assistance it would be to involve police and the law in such circumstances unless what occurred was an obvious intentional and serious assault. As is suggested above, perhaps the best approach involves the application of common sense, having regard to the magnitude of the conduct.

It should be noted that threats to kill or inflict serious injury also constitute criminal offences (see Appendix 2A for relevant details of the Victorian Crimes Act). This may be of relevance in cases of serious bullying and all states and territories have provisions proscribing this type of conduct.

Stalking

Similarly, in most states and territories, stalking is created as a criminal offence, which may be very relevant in a bullying context, particularly in those states and territories where it extends to electronic communications (see Appendix 2B for details of the relevant Crimes Act).

Protection and Apprehended Violence Orders

These orders are aimed at preventing criminal conduct, but are not strictly a part of the criminal law. However, breach of these orders can lead to criminal sanctions. This is important for, in Victoria at least, as we shall see, it is open for a child to seek an order against another child, which if breached exposes the child to the sanctions of the criminal law.

The effect of such orders may be to prohibit the person complained of from having any contact with the victim and to prevent them from engaging in certain forms of conduct towards the victim.

The purpose of these orders has traditionally been to protect family members from the actions or threatened actions of other family members. However, the definition has gradually been extended to protect persons against the behaviour of other persons, whether or not they are family members.

In particular, stalking is now a crime in virtually all jurisdictions and it is usually possible to obtain orders of this nature in order to protect people against this behaviour whether perpetrated by a family member or someone else.

In Victoria, for example, legislation operates to extend the provisions of the *Crimes (Family Violence) Act 1987* to stalking (see Appendix 2C). That Act was previously confined to proceedings where a family member sought protection against the actions of another family member. The extended legislation enables proceedings in respect of stalking to be brought against anyone, including a child, regardless of whether they are a family member or not. In the case of children, any proceedings under that Act must be brought in the Children's Court.

Intervention orders are available in Victoria in a number of circumstances appropriate to bullying situations (see Appendix 2C for details of the relevant Crimes Act).

The practical effect of the combination of these legislative provisions is that in Victoria an application may be made on behalf of a child in the Children's Court against another child or children who are not family members seeking intervention orders against them. It is unlikely that the legislation ever contemplated this outcome.

However, there have been many instances of the use of these provisions in Victoria by children who claim to be suffering from bullying. In an address to the ANZELA

Conference 2001, Judge Jennifer Coate (2001), who is in charge of the Children's Court in Victoria, indicated that in the years 2000/2001 there were 291 applications for intervention orders involving bullying issues relating to children and that these applications had doubled from the previous year. Judge Coate, who is also a former school teacher, has expressed the view that these provisions are singularly impractical in a school situation:

> We do all know that homes, schools and communities are the places in which we nurture, guide and teach our young people how to grow, develop and be responsible citizens. Part of that is about conflict resolution. We haven't yet had the debate about whether this is the way that we should be teaching young people to be resolving their conflicts. My view is that it is not. What has happened is that they are resorting to the courts when we don't quite know how they have got there, why they've got there, and what they hope to achieve.
>
> What I am suggesting is that the time has come for proper, informed and sensible debate – to create a system and develop appropriate information. (p. 11)

She went on to comment that most applications came from schools and neighbourhoods in metropolitan areas with very few from the country. She expressed great concern that there was no evidence of the value of this process, or whether it produced positive outcomes for victims, or in assisting perpetrators understand the consequences of their behaviour. She also said that it was unclear whether referrals were coming from schools or why they were coming.

The thrust of her paper was directed to the need for much better planning, liaison and communication between schools, education authorities, police and juvenile courts.

Although this paper was given some years ago, recent inquiries of the Children's Court in Victoria do not suggest that this situation has changed or improved. In my view there is considerable substance in Her Honour's concerns. If the courts are to have a place in the prevention of bullying it is vital that any interventions are properly directed and useful. While one can understand the very real concerns of parents and children with nowhere else to go, the present *ad hoc* system seems to be not only unsatisfactory but may well be counterproductive. If we are going to provide remedies in our juvenile courts for bullying they need to be done under properly thought-out legislation backed by appropriate research, and courts must be properly funded and staffed to deal with these problems. These cases are usually best dealt with outside the courtroom, and if the courts were properly equipped, this could often be achieved, even after the cases have been referred to them, except in extreme cases where no other option is available.

Electronic harassment

As has been pointed out, in a number of states the use of SMS, e-mail and the like as a means of harassing persons is a crime punishable by imprisonment. Again, however, this is a very blunt instrument, the use of which carries with it all of the difficulties to which Judge Coate (2001) refers. It also carries with it the difficulties of proof of intent and the effect of diminished criminal responsibility of children.

Possible solutions to deficiencies in the use of intervention orders

This problem is a very real one and one that must be addressed. The question really is: what is the appropriate way of doing so? One approach might be the further development of what is known as Family Group Conferencing to adapt it to cover situations of bullying. This is a New Zealand concept that has been widely adopted in juvenile justice systems throughout the world. There are various models, but the one that is about to be implemented by legislation in Victoria is that, upon the offender admitting his/her guilt, there is an option of a Family Group Conference as an alternative to a traditional sentencing process. This involves the offender and his/her legal representative and parents, or other close relatives, the magistrate or judge, and the victim and his/her family or close relatives meeting together in order to work out the best solution to the problem. It has proved to be highly effective in relation to what are often quite serious offences by juveniles and would be obviously well suited to situations where the crime has been committed in the context of a school bullying situation. It is of interest to note that the sentencing process in the Canadian case previously discussed involved the use of a 'sentencing circle', which is a type of Family Group Conference. (Chapter 11 on restorative justice outlines how a version of this concept can be used with bullying within a school.)

While such conferences are (or will be) available in some states and territories in relation to the commission of offences, they are not presently available in circumstances where an intervention order is sought to prevent bullying. It is obvious, however, that they would be likely to have considerable value in this situation. Such a process would be far more likely to produce a satisfactory outcome than either criminal or civil proceedings or the current system of applying for intervention orders.

At present, juvenile courts are not equipped to offer such services. In order to do so effectively, it would clearly be necessary not only to have the resources and skills to conduct such conferences but also the greater availability of psychologists/counsellors to juvenile courts. There is some provision for this in most Children's Courts in Australia but the facilities are overtaxed and clearly could not cope with the increased workload that would be likely to occur if such a program were to be implemented.

Crimes compensation

In most states and territories there is provision for crimes compensation where people suffer injury as the result of the commission of a crime. It is unnecessary to prove fault other than the fact of the commission of the crime. In circumstances where the bullying conduct amounts to the commission of a crime and the victim has suffered injury (including psychological damage), some compensation may be payable. The amount is usually modest and of course the availability of compensation of this nature does nothing to control the commission of the offence in question.

2. Civil law

Civil damages are also available for behaviour that constitutes an offence under the criminal law and the courts may also order that the conduct complained of not be repeated (an injunction). Proof is not as strict and it is only necessary to prove both the commission of the act complained of and (where intent is an element) the intention of the person concerned, on the balance of probabilities. This means that the issue in question is treated as proved if the court is satisfied that it is more probable than not that the conduct occurred or that the necessary intent was present. Intent is not always an ingredient of civil claims. In cases of negligence or breach of statutory duty, it is unnecessary to prove that the offender intended to do harm or even intended to do the act complained of. What must be proved is that the alleged offender failed to take reasonable care in circumstances where he/she/it owed a duty of care to the injured person, either by acting in such a way as to negligently cause the harm or by negligently failing to act to prevent the harm from occurring. There may also be avenues for claims under anti-discrimination law in appropriate cases.

Claims in negligence

For our purposes, negligence may be broadly defined as a failure to take *reasonable* care for the safety of a person to whom a duty of care is owed. Whether the care taken has been reasonable is a question of fact in each case.

There can be no doubt that a school and its teachers owe a duty of care to their pupils to take reasonable care to protect them from injury. If a child is injured as a result of bullying, this can fall within the category of negligence if a failure to take reasonable care can be established and the fact that the child might be injured was reasonably foreseeable.

In a decision of the House of Lords in England in the case of *Phelps v. Hillingdon London Borough Council*[2], Lord Slynn defined the issues in cases involving actions against schools and teachers as follows:

> As to the first question, it is long and well-established, now elementary, that persons exercising a particular skill or profession may owe a duty of care in the performance to people who it can be foreseen will be injured if due skill and care are not exercised, and if injury or damage can be shown to have been caused by the lack of care. Such duty does not depend on the existence of any contractual relationship between the person causing and the person suffering the damage. A doctor, an accountant and an engineer are plainly such a person. So in my view is an educational psychologist or psychiatrist, a teacher including a teacher in a specialised area, such as a teacher concerned with children having special educational needs. So maybe an education officer performing the functions of a local education authority in regard to children with special educational needs. There is no more justification for blanket immunity in their cases than there was in *Capital & Counties Plc. v. Hampshire County Council* [1997] Q.B. 1004.
>
> I fully agree with what was said by Lord Browne-Wilkinson in *X Minors* (supra) at page 766B-E that a head teacher owes 'a duty of care to exercise the reasonable skills of a headmaster in relation to such [sc. a child's] educational needs' and a special advisory teacher brought in to advise on the educational needs of a specific pupil, particularly if he knows that his advice will be communicated to the pupil's parents, 'owes a duty to the child to exercise the skill and care of a reasonable advisory teacher'. A similar duty on specific facts may arise for others engaged in the educational process, e.g. an educational psychologist being part of the local authority's team to provide the necessary services.

In the case of a school authority the question would usually be posed as to whether the school authority had acted in all the circumstances in the way that a reasonable school authority would act. For example, it could be established that a reasonable school authority would now have adopted a policy on bullying and that such a policy would at least conform to that in common use in similar schools. Likewise it would be expected that the existence of such a policy would be widely known to teachers and pupils at the school and that it would be applied. If it could be established that the particular school either did not have such a policy, or that it was not widely known or was not applied, then this would be evidence of negligence which would leave the school open to an action for damages. Similar considerations apply to government departments such as the education departments of the various states and territories, for whose actions their respective governments would be liable.

While there is still some debate in England as to whether a school authority can be separately liable for negligence, as distinct from the negligence of its staff, in Australia the High Court made it clear in the case of *Commonwealth of Australia v. Introvigne*[3] that a school authority can be independently liable.

In the case of a principal or teacher the test is the same, that is, has the teacher acted as a reasonable teacher would in all of the circumstances? Some English and Australian cases in the past have sought to equate the duty of care of a teacher with that of a parent. However, recent cases have suggested that the standard is that of 'exercising the ordinary skill of an ordinary competent man [*sic*] exercising that particular art'. In the High Court of Australia case of *Geyer v. Downs*[4], Murphy and Aickin JJ made it clear that they thought the attempt to equate the duty of a careful father to his children to that of a schoolmaster with up to 400 children in his care was unreasonable. They preferred the formulation stated in *State of Victoria v. Bryar*[5] where the High Court agreed with the formulation of Winneke CJ set out in *Richards v. State of Victoria*[6] as being that 'the duty of care owed by' (the teacher) 'required only that he should take such measures as in all the circumstances were reasonable to prevent physical injury to' (the pupil). The reference to physical injury was in the context of that case, but psychological and emotional damage is also compensable. The issue in Geyer's case was whether a duty of care to a pupil arose in circumstances where she was injured by being struck with a softball bat in the school grounds some 10 minutes before school commenced. The evidence was that the children were unsupervised and the argument for the defendant was that as the school day had not commenced no duty of care arose. The majority of the court made it clear that there was no rule that there could be no duty of supervision outside 'ordinary school hours' or 'before school started'. The court took the view that the headmaster, by permitting entry prior to 9 am and knowing the risk of injury from children playing ball games in a small, crowded playground without supervision, had created a factual situation in which he was under a duty to ensure that there was adequate supervision.

The standard of care required is reasonable care. Perfection is not expected and the circumstances are taken into account so that what might be expected of a teacher in one set of circumstances (for example, in the control of pupils in the classroom) might be more stringent than in another, such as when in charge of a large number of pupils on a school excursion.

Richards v. The State of Victoria was a 1960s case where two boys aged 16 became involved in a fight in the classroom and one suffered serious injury. The teacher did not attempt to prevent or end the argument that preceded the fight and took no steps to stop it. A jury found the teacher and thus the State of Victoria to be negligent and awarded substantial damages. The decision was set aside on appeal because of what the court found to be misdirections by the trial judge to the jury.

The court rejected the argument that because of the relatively mature age of the students the teacher owed the plaintiff no duty of care. It was also argued that the injury to the plaintiff was not foreseeable in that the teacher had no reason to suppose that a fight would develop out of the argument that took place in the classroom. The evidence was that the teacher took no action but in fact continued writing on the blackboard as the argument was taking place. However, the court took the view that it would have been open to the jury in the circumstances to conclude that the teacher should have reasonably foreseen that a fight might develop and injury result.

However, they also considered that such a finding would not have necessarily justified a finding that the teacher failed in his duty of care to the plaintiff. In a curious passage they in effect thought that a reasonable teacher might have thought that to permit a fight to occur would be of value in moulding a boy's approach to settling differences with his fellows on future occasions. This latter view is one that a modern court would be unlikely to take. It seems to reflect the values of the 1960s or even earlier. However, they were nevertheless correct in their view that it did not necessarily follow that the teacher had failed in his duty of care to the plaintiff. It would still be necessary to ask the question as to whether the teacher's intervention would have had any effect. The answer might well depend upon the stage at which he became aware of the problem.

In considering a submission that there was no evidence that the teacher's failure to act had caused the injury, the court thought that a jury could have concluded that the injury would probably have been prevented if the teacher had intervened at an earlier stage. However, once the fight had started, they doubted whether he was obliged to physically intervene, the evidence being that the two boys were much larger than he was. The court said that before the jury could find him liable upon this basis, it would have had to have been satisfied that any such physical intervention would have been likely to prevent the injury.

Apart from clearly stating the existence of a duty of care and the need to provide proper supervision in the classroom, this case is important in raising issues of just what is expected of a teacher in a classroom situation and the sort of event that is regarded as reasonably foreseeable. The case also suggests that there does come a point where a teacher is not necessarily required to physically intervene when actual violence commences. This must be qualified by the particular circumstances, however, and there would be many situations where some physical intervention would be required, particularly in the case of smaller children.

Richards' case was not strictly a case of bullying, but it makes it clear that argumentative and aggressive conduct by pupils requires some action by a teacher in a classroom situation in order to curb it. I consider that this duty would be a heavier one if the teacher was, or should have been, aware of a past history of bullying by one or more of those involved. *Haines v. Warren* was a NSW Court of Appeal decision relating to an assault in a playground by a known bully. It supports the view that a history of bullying is relevant in determining the extent of a teacher's duty of care.[7] The case has some unsatisfactory features in that the two judges forming the majority both agreed that the appeal by the defendant should be dismissed but one did so because he thought that the school was in breach of its duty to supervise the children in the playground and the other because there had been a failure to curb the behaviour of the bully.

In order to recover damages in cases where bullying is alleged, it must also be established that the child has suffered actual harm, whether physical or psychological, and that the harm suffered was reasonably foreseeable. As to the latter, it can be said that if a child suffers harm as a result of bullying at school, then that harm would normally be regarded as reasonably foreseeable by teachers and school authorities. This would not necessarily be the case, however, if the harassment/aggression was a 'one off' incident. Even then, if the incident occurred when the children were not properly supervised, or if there was a prior history of bullying behaviour by the perpetrator, as occurred in the Haines case, the school and teachers would be liable.

When the bullying takes place outside the school, the legal situation is not as clear as if it occurs within the school grounds. In *Bradford-Smart v. West Sussex County Council*[8], the English Court of Appeal upheld the decision of a trial judge dismissing the plaintiff's case for damages. She was a nine-year-old girl who had been the victim of bullying at her previous school and her mother had expressed concern to her teacher when she commenced at her new school in 1990.

The trial judge rejected evidence that she had been bullied at her new school, but accepted that she had been bullied on the bus going to and from school, which included threats as to what would happen when she got to school. He also accepted, however, that the bullying was not allowed by the school, and did not spill over to what happened at school. In the Court of Appeal Hale LJ (as she then was) said:

> 32. The school does not have the charge of its pupils all the time and so cannot directly protect them from harm all the time. At a day school that charge will usually end at the school gates, although the school will have a duty to take reasonable steps to ensure that young children who are not old enough to look after themselves do not leave the school premises unattended: see *Lewis v Carmarthenshire County Council* [1953] 1 WLR 1439, CA, at 1443 (the speeches in the House of Lords proceeded on the same assumption: see *Carmarthenshire County Council v Lewis* [1955] AC 549). One can think of circumstances where it might go beyond that, for example if it were reasonable for a teacher to intervene when he saw one pupil attacking another immediately outside the school gates. It will clearly extend further afield if the pupils are on a school trip, educational, recreational or sporting. But the school cannot owe a general duty to its pupils, or anyone else, to police their activities once they have left its charge. That is principally the duty of parents and, where criminal offences are involved, the police. There was evidence from Mr Watling, an educational consultant, that some schools do patrol 'areas of concern' outside school to prevent incidents after children have left. But we agree with the judge that this is a matter of discretion rather than duty.

She also expressed the view that while a school could conceivably be liable for failing to prevent bullying that occurred outside the school, the occasions when it would be liable would be few and far between. She said that it was also necessary to consider whether the steps that it is suggested should have been taken, and were not, would have prevented the bullying. She also pointed out that it was necessary to establish that the bullying had caused the injury.

This case may be regarded as of doubtful authority in Australia. The majority of the NSW Court of Appeal in the case of *The Trustees of the Roman Catholic Church for the Diocese of Bathurst v. Koffman*[9] took the view that a school was liable in negligence where the pupils of another school threw objects at the plaintiff that caused him an eye injury outside the school grounds. The incident occurred at a bus stop where the plaintiff, then aged 12, was on his way home from the primary school that he attended. The bus stop was situated outside the Bathurst High School some 300 to 400 metres from his school. It appears that the plaintiff and a friend somewhat provoked the situation by climbing trees at the bus stop and calling out to other pupils. Some high school students then started throwing sticks and rocks at the plaintiff and his friend, leading to the injury to his eye. Sheller JA, with whom Priestley JA agreed, took the view that the nature and duty of care of the teacher to the pupil is dictated by the particular circumstances. He said:

> If a pupil is injured while the school is supervising or should have been supervising that pupil's activities, the duty of care the school authority owes the pupil depends on the relationship of proximity which itself derives from the fact that the injured person is a pupil. Other necessary ingredients are a risk of injury foreseeable to a reasonable person in the position of the school authority and the failure to do what a reasonable person in that position would do by way of response to the risk; *Wyong Shire Council v Shirt* (1980) 146 CLR 40 at 47. The relationship of employer and employee imposes duties of care upon the employer to the employee. The relationship exists from the day the employee is 'employed' to the day the employee is dismissed or terminates the employment. Ordinarily the employer will owe a duty to the employee in the workplace and not for accidents occurring in the employee's home. This is not because the relationship ceases when the employee leaves work for the day but because the duty does not extend to ensuring, for example, that the floor in the employee's bathroom at home is not slippery. Similarly I do not think the relationship of teacher and pupil begins each day when the pupil enters the school ground and terminates when the pupil leaves the school ground. Undoubtedly however a particular duty of care arises because of the pre-existing relationship.

He further commented:

> I do not think its extent (the duty) is necessarily measured or limited by the circumstance that the final bell for the day has rung and the pupil has walked out the school gate.

In the circumstances of this case, he thought that the school was under a duty to supervise the students waiting for the bus.

The dissenting judge, Mahoney P, adopted the more conventional view expressed by Hale LJ in Bradford-Smart's case, with some modification. He was prepared to accept that the school might be under a duty of care to shepherd younger pupils across a busy and dangerous road outside the school. He was also prepared to accept that if a pupil was habitually molested at a point some distance from the school, the school might have an obligation to draw this to the attention of police and the child's parents. He was of the view that the school was not however obliged to provide a member of staff or otherwise to provide supervision of children waiting for a bus three or four hundred metres from the school.

Leave to appeal against this decision was subsequently refused by the High Court of Australia.

A useful discussion of these cases is to be found in Yeo (1997) where the author distinguishes between the view as expressed by Mahoney P in Koffmann's case and Hale LJ in Bradford-Smart's case, which attaches some sort of geographical boundary to the duty of care of the school, and that of the majority in Koffman's case, where the emphasis is placed on the nature of the relationship between the pupil and the school and its teachers. The learned author comments:

> A school owes a duty of care to its pupils when they are journeying to and from school or school-related activities. The preceding discussion has argued that the majority of the Court of Appeal of New South Wales in *Koffman* was correct in viewing this duty as existing throughout the entire journey. This approach is consistent with the firmly entrenched notion that the school's duty of care is premised on the relationship which it has with its pupils. That relationship is based on the authority and control which the school exercises over its pupils. Since schools have the right to take disciplinary or preventative action against unruly or risk-producing conduct of its pupils performed when travelling to and from school, it follows that the school-pupil relationship exists and, consequently, the school owes its pupils a duty of care during those times.
>
> But a finding that the school has a duty of care to its pupils is insufficient to establish liability in negligence. Additionally, the plaintiff must persuade the court that the school breached its duty of care by failing to meet the requisite standard of care. In determining the appropriate standard of care, it has been suggested that the standard should correspond in degree with the level of control that the school has over the pupil. Thus, the greater the control exercised by the school, the higher the standard of care that can be expected of it; the lower the control, the lesser its standard of care. This conceivably provides the underlying explanation as to why schools are generally not liable for accidents that have occurred to their pupils a considerable distance away

> from the school, but are more likely to be held liable for accidents occurring immediately outside the school grounds or at pedestrian crossings or bus stops which were supervised by the school.

I agree with the views of the majority of the NSW Court of Appeal.[10] It seems to me to be incorrect that the school's duty of care ends at the school gates and that, rather, the pupil-teacher and pupil-school relationship extends well beyond that. I can understand the application of what might be called the geographical test applied by Hale LJ and Mahoney P in relation to the more normal incidents of negligence. A school or teacher could not normally be expected to be in breach of a duty of care if a child is assaulted by a stranger outside his or her home or is hit by a negligent motorist. However, if the school and its teachers are made aware that bullying is taking place on the way to and from school, then the question might be posed as to who would be in a better position to protect the child than they would. The police can only act if a crime has been committed and it is asking much of parents to adopt an effective method of prevention. In my view it is strongly arguable that once the school or its teachers become aware that a child is being or is likely to be bullied on the way to or from the school, then it/they are under a duty of care to take steps to prevent this from occurring. This would be particularly so where the perpetrators were students at the same school but, as we have seen, this is not necessarily a requirement.

It may also be that the school and/or teachers could be liable, even if the bullying took place at home. In this regard I particularly have in mind electronic bullying by means of SMS, e-mail or telephone by other pupils at the school. This need not necessarily occur while the victim is at school and is perhaps more likely to occur out of school hours. Applying the above principles, it might be said that the relationship between the pupils and the school is such that the school is in a position to attempt to control or prevent the continuation of such bullying and has a duty of care to do so. This could even extend to physical or direct verbal bullying by fellow pupils in some circumstances. Schools and teachers do have disciplinary or other remedies available to them to control such behaviour and I think it arguable that a failure to act to control such behaviour could render them liable in such circumstances. The law in this regard is far from clear, but I think that schools and teachers would be well advised to err on the side of caution and not ignore such behaviour when it comes to their attention.

Actions for damages for negligence against schools and teachers arising out of bullying are by no means uncommon in Australia (*Nine News*, 2004). It would appear that a similar situation applies in the United Kingdom where a recent news report was to the effect that a 15-year-old girl in Scotland had received legal aid for an action for damages and her lawyer is quoted as saying that he had 30 other clients considering bringing similar actions (*BBC News*, UK edition, 2004). Similarly, in New York, the *Daily News* carried a report on 28 April 2004 of a jury awarding US$195 000 to a boy who was bullied and physically injured when aged eleven (Shifrel, 2004).

However, very few cases go to court for final determination as most are settled previously, usually by the school authority paying an agreed sum by way of damages. Anecdotally, they are increasing in number, and this is not surprising given the increased awareness in the wider community of the possibility of recovering damages by way of litigation. This tendency towards litigation is often the subject of criticism, but the other side of the coin is that bullying is most insidious, widespread and damaging and the question can reasonably be posed as to why schools and teachers should be protected from the consequences of negligently failing to prevent it. Indeed, the very threat or fear of litigation may well assist in producing action from those best in a position to prevent school bullying.

Breach of statutory duty

There are various statutes and regulations governing the conduct of schools. These vary in different jurisdictions and it is beyond the scope of this work to examine them. They may involve occupational health and safety, or the provision of safe places of assembly and the like. Independent of negligence, the law provides a separate course of action in damages for breach of such duties if the nature of the duty imposed by the statute is such that it can be concluded that the legislature intended that a breach would be compensable. The obligation to provide a safe environment could lead to a successful claim under this head in the case of injury by bullying. In relation to breaches of statutory duty by education authorities, Lord Slynn was of the view in the Hillingdon case above that the general nature of the duties imposed on education authorities as part of a national scheme of education in the UK meant that Parliament did not intend to create a statutory remedy by way of damages. Similar arguments would no doubt be advanced in actions against state and territory education departments.

Usually, however, the breach of such duties is also evidence of negligence and forms part of the case in negligence. But proof of a breach of statutory duty is often powerful evidence of negligence and it is important to ascertain whether such a breach has occurred.

Claims based upon contract

Such claims would usually be available only in respect of children attending independent schools because there would be no contract as such with government education authorities. The claim would normally be a claim by the parents and not the child alleging a breach of the terms of their contract with the school. The success or otherwise of such a claim would depend upon the nature of the contract.

It would usually be an implied, if not express, term of such a contract that the school would provide a reasonably safe environment for the child. If a child was subject to bullying in circumstances where the school authorities should have prevented it, then that would amount to a breach of contract resulting in damages. Damages would be confined to the financial loss sustained by the parents.

Usually, a claim in negligence would be available in circumstances where a breach of contract could be established, but a claim in contract would give the parents an additional avenue to recover financial loss that they had sustained. They would still be liable to pay the fees for the period that the child attended the school but such a claim could be set off against the school's claim for fees that might be owed to it.

A recent example of a case where the contract with the educational institution was in issue was that of *GE v. Taylors Institute of Advanced Studies Limited.*[11] This judgment was delivered at an interlocutory stage of the proceedings between a 20-year-old pupil and the educational institution, known as Taylor's College. The plaintiff had been suspended by the college after being charged by police with a number of serious criminal charges involving other students. The matter arose out of a dispute over an allegedly stolen mobile phone, which also involved allegations of bullying by the plaintiff. The plaintiff sought an interlocutory injunction restraining the college from suspending him, alleging a breach of contract by the college of implied terms in the contract that it would not suspend him without grounds being established and without giving him an opportunity to show cause why he should not be suspended.

It emerged in evidence that the college had a bullying policy which, amongst other things, provided that bullying behaviour was not acceptable. It also provided rules for the conduct of students and contained a provision that a breach of the rules or unacceptable behaviour entitled the enrolment of the student to be cancelled.

Because of the nature of the proceedings, the judge did not finally determine them. However, he considered the contract and formed the view that the injunction should not be granted as he had considerable doubt that any legal right of the plaintiff had been infringed. The final outcome of the proceedings is unknown, but it does suggest that a school is on reasonably firm ground in suspending a pupil in such circumstances.

Assault and trespass against a person

As has been mentioned, assault and trespass against a person may be a crime, as well as giving rise to a civil action for damages. School authorities would not normally be liable for an assault unless the assault was committed by a teacher. They may, however, be liable in negligence in circumstances such as occurred in Richards' case discussed previously. Intent is a necessary ingredient of actions for assault and the same problem of proving this in the case of children arises as it does in connection with the criminal law. The action lies only against the bully and not his/her parents. Since the main remedy is damages, this remedy is a very limited one.

Anti-discrimination proceedings

There have been a number of proceedings under anti-discrimination legislation for bullying, particularly in NSW. These are important remedies in appropriate cases. For example, in *FP and FQ on behalf of FR v. Department of Education and Training*[12], a complaint on behalf of a child of Korean birth of race discrimination at school was held to be substantiated and the department was ordered to pay $10 000 by way of damages. The evidence disclosed that the school's anti-bullying measures did not address the issue of race, and the child who had been subjected to racial bullying was thus able to recover.

In another case where disability discrimination was alleged, namely *S on behalf of M & C v. Director General, Department of Education & Training*[13], the tribunal rejected a claim on behalf of two sisters. One child was born with a cleft palate and also had impaired hearing and the other suffered from Attention Deficit Hyperactive Disorder (ADHD). The children had suffered from bullying but the Tribunal was of the view that the respective schools had not been guilty of any discrimination on the grounds of disability. It did, however, criticise one of the relevant schools for an inflexible application of its disciplinary code.

These cases I believe highlight the fact that in anti-discrimination cases it is discrimination that must be established and not simply bullying. A similar view was taken in the Canadian case of *Jubran and Deputy Chief Commissioner, British Columbia and Human Rights Commission.*[14] In that case Stewart J set aside a finding of discrimination by the British Columbia Human Rights Tribunal. The Tribunal had found that the child had attended secondary school from 1993 to 1998 where he had been treated as a pariah who was attacked and derided upon the basis that he was a homosexual. In fact he was not homosexual and the other students knew it but chose to attack him in this way. In short, the judge found that although he had been bullied he was not discriminated against because of his sexual orientation. The distinction was a very fine one in that had the child in fact been homosexual or had his tormentors believed that he was homosexual the claim by him would have been successful.

It follows, therefore, that care must be taken before resorting to claims based upon discrimination laws and that they are far from providing a legal remedy for bullying except in specific cases.

Conclusion

The law offers some remedies for bullying, but very few of them are entirely satisfactory. On the other hand, it is important that the law is adapted to assist in the control of this problem. Clearly, resort to the law should be regarded as the very last option but there are cases where no other remedy is possible. I have discussed ways in which the law might be better adapted to deal with such cases. There is certainly an opportunity for Australian legislatures to address this problem. It is important that when they do so, however, they act upon the basis of proper consideration and research. Our children deserve this, rather than the application of *ad hoc* or ill thought out provisions that are likely to do more harm than good. I think that what does emerge is that in the absence of legislative intervention the present unsatisfactory situation in relation to bullying will continue, to the detriment of all of our children. It is also clear that much greater cooperation is needed between schools and education authorities, juvenile courts, police and lawmakers in order not only to arrive at a satisfactory solution to the problem, but to ensure that it works thereafter.

REFERENCES

BBC News, UK edition. (2004, January 20). [Transcript]. Retrieved December 29, 2004, from <http://news.bbc.co.uk/1/hi/scotland/3414483.stm>

B.C. girl convicted in school bullying tragedy. (2002, March 25). *CBC News*. [Transcript]. Retrieved January 5, 2005, from <http://www.cbc.ca/story/canada/national/2002/03/25/wesley020325.html>

Broomstick bullies sentenced. (2003, May 16). *New Zealand Herald*. Retrieved January 5, 2005, from <http://www.nzherald.co.nz/index.cfm?ObjectID=3502438>

Coate, J. (2001). *Contemporary developments in the law relating to children and the Children's Court: Keynote address to the Australian & New Zealand Education & the Law Association (ANZELA) Conference, 5 October 2001.*

Furniss, C. (2000), Bullying in schools: It's not a crime – is it? *Education and the Law, 12*(1), 9–19.

Hay-Mackenzie, F. (2002). Tackling the bullies: In the classroom and the staffroom. *Australia and New Zealand Journal of Law and Education, 7*(2), 87–140.

Joyce, Greg (2002, May 14). Girl convicted of bullying attends sentence circle. Canada: CNEWS, *Law and Order*. [Transcript]. Retrieved January 5, 2005, from <http://www.canoe.ca/CNEWSLaw0205/14_bully-cp.html>

National Strategy on Community Safety and Crime Prevention (2004, January 28). Bullying in Canada. Canada: National Crime Prevention Centre. Retrieved December 29, 2004, from <http://www.prevention.gc.ca/en/library/publications/fact_sheets/bullying/>

Olweus, D. (1993). *Bullying at school: What we know and what we can do*. Oxford and Cambridge, MA: Blackwell.

Parents to sue over school bullying (2004). *Nine News*. [Transcript]. Retrieved January 3, 2005, from <http://news.nineemsn.com.au/other.aspx?id=2433>

Rigby, K. (2003). *Stop the bullying* (Rev. ed.). Melbourne: ACER.

Shifrel, Scott (2004, April 28). Jury strikes 195G blow for bullied Queens boy. New York: *Daily News*. Retrieved December 29, 2004, from <http://nydailynews.com/front/story/188228p-162856c.html>

Stewart, D. J. & Knott, A. E. (2002). *Schools, courts and the law*. Frenchs Forest, NSW: Prentice Hall.

Yeo, S. (1997). A school's liability to pupils journeying to and from school. *Torts Law Journal*, 5(3), 276–286.

Zuker, Hon. Marvin A. (2002). Bullying, school violence and youth crime. *The Law Journal UK*. Retrieved January 5, 2005, from <http://www.thelawjournal.co.uk/Bullying.htm>

ENDNOTES

1 *Lepore v. State of New South Wales* (2001) 52 NSWLR 420; *S v. The Corporation of the Synod of the Diocese of Brisbane* (2001) QSC 473.
2 [2000] 3 WLR 776.
3 [1982] 41 ALR per Mason J at 586. See also the discussion of this case in Hay McKenzie (2002).
4 (1977) 138 CLR 91 at 102.
5 [1970] ALR 809.
6 (1969) VR 136 at 138, 140–1.
7 *Haines v. Warren* (1987) Aust Torts Rep ¶80–115.
8 [2002] EWCA Civ 7.
9 (1996) Aust Torts Reps ¶81–399.
10 See also the reference to Koffman's case by Gleeson CJ in *Modbury Triangle Shopping Centre Pty Ltd v. Anzil* (2000) 75 ALJR 164 at 168.
11 Kellam J, Supreme Court of Victoria (unreported judgment delivered 16 September 2003), http://www.austlii.edu.au/cases/vic/VSC/2003/354.html

12 [2003] NSWADT 68.
13 [2001] NSWADT 43.
14 Stewart J (2003) BCSC 6 (CanLIl).

APPENDIX 2A: CRIMES ACT 1958 (VICTORIA), SECTIONS 20 AND 21

20. Threats to kill

A person who, without lawful excuse, makes to another person a threat to kill that other person or any other person –

(a) intending that that other person would fear the threat would be carried out; or

(b) being reckless as to whether or not that other person would fear the threat would be carried out –

is guilty of an indictable offence.

Penalty: Level 5 imprisonment (10 years maximum).

21. Threats to inflict serious injury

A person who, without lawful excuse, makes to another person a threat to inflict serious injury on that other person or any other person –

(a) intending that that other person would fear the threat would be carried out; or

(b) being reckless as to whether or not that other person would fear the threat would be carried out –

is guilty of an indictable offence.

Penalty: Level 6 imprisonment (5 years maximum).

APPENDIX 2B: CRIMES ACT 1958 (VICTORIA), SECTION 21A

Note: Similar sections have been included in the *Crimes (Threats and Stalking) Amendment Act 1994 No. 83* (NSW) and *The Statutes Amendment (Stalking) Act 2001* (South Australia).

Section 21A of the Victorian Crimes Act reads in part as follows:

(1) A person must not stalk another person.

Penalty: Level 5 imprisonment (10 years maximum)

(2) A person (the offender) stalks another person (the victim) if the offender engages in a course of conduct which includes any of the following –

- (a) following the victim or any other person;
- (b) contacting the victim or any other person by post, telephone, fax, text message, e-mail or other electronic communication or by any other means whatsoever;
- (ba) publishing on the Internet or by an e-mail or other electronic communication to any person a statement or other material –
  - (i) relating to the victim or any other person; or
  - (ii) purporting to relate to, or to originate from, the victim or any other person;
- (bb) causing an unauthorised computer function (within the meaning of Subdivision (6) of Division 3) in a computer owned or used by the victim or any other person;
- (bc) tracing the victim's or any other person's use of the Internet or of e-mail or other electronic communications;
- (c) entering or loitering outside or near the victim's or any other person's place of residence or of business or any other place frequented by the victim or the other person;
- (d) interfering with property in the victim's or any other person's possession (whether or not the offender has an interest in the property);
- (e) giving offensive material to the victim or any other person or leaving it where it will be found by, given to or brought to the attention of, the victim or the other person;
- (f) keeping the victim or any other person under surveillance;
- (g) acting in any other way that could reasonably be expected to arouse apprehension or fear in the victim for his or her own safety or that of any other person –

with the intention of causing physical or mental harm to the victim or of arousing apprehension or fear in the victim for his or her own safety or that of any other person.

(3) For the purposes of this section an offender also has the intention to cause physical or mental harm to the victim or to arouse apprehension or fear in the victim for his or her own safety or that of any other person if –

(a) the offender knows that engaging in a course of conduct of that kind would be likely to cause such harm or arouse such apprehension or fear; or

(b) the offender in all the particular circumstances ought to have understood that engaging in a course of conduct of that kind would be likely to cause such harm or arouse such apprehension or fear and it actually did have that result.

APPENDIX 2C: CRIMES (FAMILY VIOLENCE) ACT 1987 (VICTORIA), SECTION 4, INTERVENTION ORDERS

(1) The Court may make an intervention order in respect of a person if satisfied on the balance of probabilities that –

  (a) the person has assaulted a family member or caused damage to property of a family member and is likely to again assault the family member or cause damage to property of the family member; or

  (b) the person has threatened to assault a family member or cause damage to property of a family member and is likely to assault the family member or cause damage to property of the family member; or

  (c) the person has harassed or molested a family member or has behaved in an offensive manner towards a family member and is likely to do so again.

(2) The order may impose any restrictions or prohibitions on the person that appear necessary or desirable in the circumstances to the court.

SECTION TWO

AN OVERVIEW OF PREVENTIVE SOLUTIONS FOR BULLYING

CHAPTER 3

What research tells us about whole-school programs for preventing bullying

Helen McGrath

Introduction

When researchers Wang, Haertel and Walberg (1997) examined research on the relative influence of 30 different categories of educational and social and psychological variables on academic performance, their conclusion was that social and emotional variables exerted the most powerful influence. Many writers and researchers have argued that more attention needs to be paid to the socioemotional needs of students not only in terms of increasing academic outcomes, but also in terms of student safety and wellbeing (e.g. Anderman & Maehr, 1994; Hargreaves, Earl & Ryan, 1996; Maehr & Midgley, 1996). In the past 10 years, there has been an increasing focus on developing prevention programs that address those three objectives i.e. achievement, safety and wellbeing (Catalano et al., 2003). The main focus of most of these programs has been on the development of school community and positive peer relations and the teaching of social and emotional competencies. The assumption behind these school-based programs is that early prevention will help prevent and reduce the likelihood of low achievement, dropping out of school, substance abuse, violence, antisocial behaviour, bullying, mental health problems, truancy and suicide.

This chapter describes some of the more successful and well-known whole-school preventive programs and summarises the themes that emerge from the research into their effectiveness.

Earlier prevention programs

Earlier preventive school programs tended to be 'selected' programs which were delivered only to those students identified as already 'at-risk' for negative social, emotional and/or learning outcomes (Catalano et al., 2003). They also tended to employ a 'rifle' approach which used a small and specific set of program components rather than a multi-component approach (termed a 'shotgun' approach). Many writers and researchers have been highly critical of this narrow and less effective approach (e.g. Catalano, Berglund, Ryan, Lonczak & Hawkins, 2002). As a result of these criticisms, there has been a marked shift in the last decade to 'universal' prevention programs which focus on social and emotional learning opportunities for all students rather than only addressing the specific social and emotional needs of some students.

Contemporary research

Recent research evaluations of newer programs have provided many insights into 'good practice' in the development and implementation of preventive programs. Many have also been long term. In some cases, the researchers were able to follow up students even after they had left school to ascertain the long-term effects of the program they had participated in. As Greenberg et al. (2003) have concluded:

> There is a solid and growing empirical base indicating that well-designed well-implemented school-based prevention and youth development programming can positively influence a diverse array of social, health, and academic outcomes. (p. 470)

Common components of prevention programs

The components of any individual prevention program are many and varied but there is also a great deal of overlap of components across program categories. Irrespective of whether a program is labelled 'anti-violence', 'youth development', 'anti-bullying' or 'pro-social', most of them include aspects such as teaching values, building community, creating connectedness, teaching social skills, bibliotherapy (the use of appropriate texts), cooperative learning, buddy systems, classroom meetings, teaching empathy and emotional literacy, parental involvement and the teaching of conflict management.

Limitations in program evaluations

The recent international push for evidence-based prevention programs and directions has been welcomed by most Australian educational systems. However, it can be difficult to determine the value of specific program evaluations for the following reasons.

Lack of methodological rigour

Many researchers and reviewers have noted a relative lack of methodological rigour in some studies (e.g. Scheckner, Rollin, Kaiser-Ulrey & Wagner, 2002; Zbar, Brown, Bereznicki & Hooper, 2003). As well, significant variations have been found between classrooms, indicating that there may be strong teacher effects that have not yet been isolated (Greenberg, Domitrovich & Bumbarger, 2001). Research into values education programs, for example, suggests that programs are effective only if teachers are perceived to put the values into practice themselves (Deakin, Crick & Prosser, 1997; Ling, Burman & Cooper, 1998; Williams, 1993).

Consistency and thoroughness of implementation

Some teachers and schools clearly implement more of a program than do others and this can affect the results if not taken into account. Fullan (1998) has argued that successful implementation of a new intervention program is likely to be effective only if it is perceived to meet a clear need. This view was confirmed in Kallestad and Olweus's (2003) study of 89 teachers who implemented the Olweus Bullying Prevention Program. They found that the degree of implementation varied considerably among teachers and schools. In particular, they found that more demanding activities such as role-play, class rules, and class meetings were used less frequently by some teachers. They found that the main differences in how often and how effectively the program was implemented were attributable to teacher factors such as:

- How much bullying they believed was happening in their own classroom.
- How much they saw themselves and their school as important agents of change for counteracting bully/victim problems among their students.
- How much they had actually read and understood the available program information.

- How much they empathised with the students who were being bullied.
- How aware they were about what was actually happening among the students during recess periods.

Different methodologies

Many reviewers have also noted that there is often a marked contrast between the methodologies used to evaluate different programs. This makes it more difficult to form general conclusions about what constitutes good practice (De Roche & Williams 1998; Greenberg et al., 2001). Some of the more informal research studies have collected mostly anecdotal evidence, surveyed teachers or collected teacher observations. In many of these studies, teacher awareness has been a potential source of bias. More formal research evaluations have attempted to control for such potential bias (e.g. by having independent observers and control groups) and have used experimental or quasi-experimental pre- and post-intervention designs. So far, most researchers have focused on evaluations of single programs, but Catalano et al. (2003) have suggested that a research study which compared the relative effectiveness of different preventive models in different schools could help to identify the strengths and weaknesses of each program for different contexts.

Generalisability

Many studies that showed great promise have not been able to be replicated by independent investigators. One such example is the Olweus Bullying Prevention Program, which was shown to reduce bullying by 50 per cent in the original study (Olweus, 1993). However, other researchers (e.g. Roland, 1989) have not been able to produce the same results when implementing a very similar program. It has been suggested that in some cases there is so much external support for the implementation of a program that the program is not generalisable to more 'realistic' school contexts where such external support is less available.

Absence of long-term follow-up

In some studies, there has been an absence of long-term follow-up to evaluate the maintenance of program effects (Catalano et al., 2003; Conduct Problems Prevention Research Group, 1999; Greenberg et al., 2001; Weissberg & Greenberg, 1998). Since many programs appear to have a 'sleeper effect' (i.e. they show stronger impacts at long term follow-up than they did at the conclusion of the program), Greenberg et al. (2001) have argued that it is likely that the effects of many prevention programs have been underestimated.

Moderating factors

Another significant limitation is that there has not been enough focus on factors which might moderate the effects of a program, such as a student's gender or background or differences between school sites (Greenberg et al., 2001).

Despite the fact that there is still room for improvement in the implementation of school-wide school-based programs and their evaluations, it needs to be kept in mind that long-term naturalistic research is fraught with inevitable limitations. It is very difficult to ensure program fidelity in real-life educational conditions when many different teachers, classrooms and schools are involved. Inevitably there will be different levels of teacher enthusiasm, commitment and skill in the implementation of a specific program despite, in some cases, similar levels of professional development.

Specific prevention programs

The following overview looks at a number of preventive welfare programs. These are:

- The Friendly Schools Friendly Families Program
- The Child Development Project
- The Seattle Social Development Project
- The Raising Healthy Children Program
- The Peace Builders Program
- The Roots of Empathy Program
- The W.I.T.S. Program
- The Second Step Program.

The Friendly Schools Friendly Families Program

This 'universal' Australian program was evaluated in 20 primary schools in Western Australia and involved more than 4000 students and 450 teachers (Cross, Hall, Roberts & Young 2003; Cross et al., 2003). A randomised control design was used and students were followed up for four years. The basic assumption behind the program was that effectiveness in reducing bullying and increasing pro-social behaviour would be the result of many small moves, not just one approach. Some of the key components of the program were:

- open communication about bullying
- a consistent and positive response from all teachers towards bullying behaviour
- the teaching of peer support skills to enable all students in a bystander role to discourage bullying

- resilience skills that would be needed if students were bullied
- modified playground environments that would be more stimulating to students
- the teaching of social skills and pro-social values
- high visibility of playground supervisors during lunch and recess breaks
- school pride campaigns
- teacher professional development.

In schools that implemented the program, students were less likely to be bullied, less likely to bully others and were more likely to tell a teacher if they were being bullied or they knew of bullying that was occurring (Cross, 2004).

The Child Development Project

The Child Development Project (CDP) <http://www.devstu.org/cdp/> began in 1982 and is ongoing. It is a program that is designed to create school communities that are caring and supportive and that address students' needs for a sense of belonging. It is delivered as a whole-school program and some of its key features are:

- class meetings, which are used for setting goals and norms, planning activities, confirming class values and identifying and solving problems
- a buddy program, which pairs older and younger students for academic and recreational activities and helps to create powerful cross-age relationships, teach important social skills and create a caring ethos in the school
- school-wide community-building activities, which link students, parents and teachers, e.g. family film nights, creating a family heritage museum.

The CDP has been extensively and rigorously evaluated in several studies over the last seven years in quasi-experimental studies (e.g. Battistich, Schaps, Watson, Solomon & Lewis, 2001; Solomon, Battistich, Watson, Schaps & Lewis, 2000). Results suggest that the program has led to an increase in student behaviour that is consistent with pro-social values (especially respect for the rights and needs of others and cooperation), an increase in students' use of effective social skills (especially conflict management skills), and an increase in student engagement, motivation, aspirations and liking for school. The program also produced a decrease in bullying, violence, delinquency and substance abuse.

The largest and most recent study of the CDP (Battistich et al., 2001) focused on an ethnically and socio-economically diverse sample of over 14 000 students from 12 program schools and 12 comparison schools in six districts across the USA. After three years of the program, students in five of the 12 program schools demonstrated:

- a greater sense of the school as a caring community (33 per cent higher than would be expected if they had not experienced the program)

- more liking for school (12 per cent higher than would be expected if they had not experienced the program)
- stronger academic motivation (24 per cent higher than would be expected if they had not experienced the program)
- more frequent reading of books outside of school (8 per cent higher than would be expected if they had not experienced the program)
- a higher sense of self-efficacy (6 per cent higher than would be expected if they had not experienced the program)
- better conflict resolution skills (17 per cent higher than would be expected if they had not experienced the program)
- more concern for others (10 per cent higher than would be expected if they had not experienced the program)
- more frequent altruistic behaviour (8 per cent higher than would be expected if they had not experienced the program)
- less use of alcohol (13 per cent lower than would be expected if they had not experienced the program) and marijuana (19 per cent lower than would be expected if they had not experienced the program).

A follow-up study was carried out with former students from three of the primary schools with high levels of implementation of the CDP. When these students were in Years 6 to 8, they continued to show positive effects from the program compared to comparison students. Specifically, they had higher academic results, a greater sense of community, higher educational aspirations, more liking for school, greater trust in and respect for teachers, greater involvement in positive activities such as sports, clubs and youth groups, and less bullying and other forms of misbehaviour at school. In addition to these positive outcomes, students also reported that they had significantly fewer friends who were involved in school misbehaviour or delinquency, and significantly more friends who were positively engaged with school than did comparison students.

The United States Center for Substance Abuse Prevention has selected the CDP as a model drug prevention program, and the United States Department of Education has recognised it as a promising violence prevention program.

The Seattle Social Development Project

The Seattle Social Development Project (SSDP) was a comprehensive school-wide prevention program from school entry to Year 6, although not all students received the program. It had a strong emphasis on creating and maintaining strong school and family bonds. Some of its features were:

- parent training
- proactive classroom management
- interactive teaching, and cooperative learning
- social skills training (especially conflict management and anger management)
- academic support.

The program evaluation (Hawkins et al., 1992) involved 598 students and compared those who had received the program for the whole six years, those who had only received the program in Years 5 and 6, and control students in other matched schools who did not receive the program at all. The results indicated that, compared to students in the control schools, the students who received the program showed lower levels of aggression, engaged in less violent, bullying and delinquent behaviour, used alcohol less, were more attached and committed to their schools, and were less involved with antisocial peers. The students who had received the full program were followed up six years after the program when they were 18 years old. The findings indicated that they reported significantly stronger attachment to school, increased achievement (especially for boys), and less involvement in bullying or violent behaviour and school misbehaviour than did the control students (Hawkins, Catalano, Kosterman, Abbott & Hill, 1999; Hawkins, Guo, Hill, Battin-Pearson & Abbott, 2001).

Significantly fewer subjects in the program group than in the control group had committed violent acts, reported heavy alcohol use in the past year or engaged in sexual activity. There were no long-term differences between the students who had only received the program for two years and the control students, providing a strong argument for exposing students to long-term prevention programs rather than short-term ones.

The Raising Healthy Children Program

The Raising Healthy Children Program (RHC) was designed to both replicate and extend the Seattle Social Development Project. Like the SSDP, it was based on the social development model (Catalano & Hawkins, 1996) and was a universal preventive program. However, the RCH program additionally attempted to ensure that effective program practices were implemented school-wide rather than just implemented by a group of trained teachers of selected year level groups. The program was multifaceted, included teachers, parents, and students, and was designed to influence developmentally appropriate risk and protective factors in the family, school, peer, and individual domains (Catalano et al., 2003). The features of the program were similar to those in the SSDP, but, in addition, both teachers and parents taught social competencies.

The 497 students who participated in the RCH program were Year 1 and 2 students across 10 primary schools in the North Pacific region of the US. Ten paired control schools were also part of the evaluation. Data were collected four times during the 18-month period. The first set of data was collected prior to the program and was used as baseline data. The second, third and fourth sets of data were collected during the following 18 months. The evaluation was multifaceted and included parent, teacher, and student outcome measures. Results showed that, compared to their peers in the control schools, students who had received the RHC program:

- had significantly higher teacher-reported academic performance
- had a stronger commitment to school
- demonstrated a significant decrease in bullying and other antisocial behaviours
- demonstrated a significant increase in social competency.

The Peace Builders Program

The Peace Builders Program (Krug, Brener, Dahlberg, Ryan & Powell, 1997) is a school-based primary-school prevention program from Arizona, which teaches pro-social values and social competencies, using activities to improve daily interactions among students, teachers, other school staff, and parents. Social competencies such as being positive and avoiding put-downs are also taught and students are encouraged to follow the rule of '*seek good role models, correct hurts, and right wrongs*'. Teachers and parents provide positive rewards and feedback for pro-social behaviours.

Comparisons were made between 2393 students (K–5) in program schools and 1506 students in control schools. After one year of the program, overall visits to the nurse with physical injuries or to escape bullying decreased by 13 per cent in the intervention schools compared to an *increase* of 3 per cent in the control schools. As well, students in Years 1 and 2 who received the program were rated much more socially competent by their teachers, and students in Years 3–5 were rated moderately more socially competent but much less aggressive (Flannery et al., 2003). Follow-up data suggested that these effects were maintained a year later.

The Roots of Empathy Program

The Roots of Empathy is a Canadian classroom-based preventive program that aims to reduce aggression through the fostering of empathy and emotional literacy. The program is directed towards children aged 3 to 14 years. The core of the program is a series of monthly classroom visits by a local parent and their infant. Children are taught to observe the baby's development and non-verbal behaviour, celebrate its milestones, interact with the baby, and learn about an infant's needs and individual temperament. An outside instructor also works with the class the week before and the week after each family visit using a developmentally appropriate emotional literacy curriculum and relevant texts. The empathy and emotional literacy skills and the social skills (e.g. understanding and respecting others' opinions) taught in the program help to create caring classrooms. The assumption underlying the program is that, if children understand how others feel, they are less likely to hurt each other through bullying, exclusion and violence. Variations of this program have used puppies rather than infants.

Using a quasi-experimental control group pre-test and post-test design, Schonert-Reichl and her colleagues (Schonert-Reichl, Smith & Zaidman-Zait, 2002) focused on 132 children from Years 1–3 drawn from 5 classrooms who had received the Roots of Empathy Program and 5 comparison classrooms. Children were individually interviewed before and after the program and assessed on their emotional/social understanding using a series of instruments. Teachers rated participating children on dimensions of aggressive and pro-social behaviours both before and after the program. In the first evaluation (2000–2001), program children, relative to comparison children, demonstrated significant improvements in emotional knowledge, social understanding and pro-social behaviours with peers. They also displayed less aggression and bullying towards peers. In contrast, children in the comparison classrooms who had not received the program showed significant increases in bullying and other forms of proactive aggression across the school year. Similar outcomes were obtained in a second evaluation (Schonert-Reichl, Smith, Zaidman-Zait, & Hertzman, 2003) which used similar methodology and focused on 670 children in Years 4–7 from 38 classrooms across Canada.

The W.I.T.S. Program

The W.I.T.S. Rock Solid Primary Program for the Prevention of Peer Violence (http://www.youth.society.uvic.ca/resources/wits/manualpdf/10evaluation) was a three-year longitudinal program conducted in Canada. It aimed to increase children's interpersonal negotiation skills for handling peer aggression and threats of bullying and to reduce peer aggression in schools, classrooms and unstructured environments (playgrounds, halls, etc.). It was based around the acronym WITS (**W**alk away, **I**gnore, **T**alk, **S**eek a Supervisor). A stuffed walrus called WITSUP was a core part of the program and there were activity books, bookmarks, pens and pencils to reinforce the WITS messages and to help take these messages to the family.

Baseline data were collected in August 2000 and follow-up data were collected in April 2001, using the same measures (Centre for Youth and Society, 2001). A pre/post-intervention control group design was used with 432 children in Year 1 across 11 program schools and 6 control schools. The evaluation found the following effects, based on children's self-reports:

- Average Year 1 classroom levels of pro-social acts increased in both the high and the low poverty program schools. In the equivalent control schools pro-social acts actually decreased.
- Relational bullying decreased, but only in low poverty program schools.
- Physical bullying decreased in all low poverty schools but increased in all high poverty schools. However, increases in bullying in the high poverty *control* schools were much greater than increases in the high poverty *program* schools.

The Second Step Program

Second Step is a curriculum-based universal prevention program aimed at reducing social, emotional and behavioural problems and enhancing positive social interactions between students (Frey & Rivara, 1997). Grossman et al. (1997) conducted a study which assessed the effectiveness of this program with students in Years 2 and 3 only. The study used a control group design with 12 program schools and 12 non-participating control schools. Teachers from the program schools received 2 days of program training and students received a total of 30 lessons. Outcomes were assessed using teacher and parent ratings. In addition, students from each participating classroom were randomly selected for direct behavioural observations in the classroom, playground and cafeteria. Results suggested that students who participated in the program had significantly lower levels of negative physical playground behaviour and significant increases in pro-social behaviour in the playground/cafeteria. On the other hand, control students showed an increase in physically aggressive behaviours and bullying behaviours and no improvement in pro-social behaviour during the same time period (Grossman et al., 1997). These changes were maintained at the follow-up six months later (Conduct Problems Prevention Research Group, 1999; Frey, Hirschstein & Guzzo, 2000; Grossman et al., 1997).

Conclusions about good practice in preventive programs

Basic principles of good practice in the development and implementation of prevention programs have emerged from evaluation studies as well as from large-scale reviews and meta-analyses of a wide range of studies. These are summarised below.

Universal programs are better

School-based prevention programs that are universal (i.e. delivered to all students) are more effective than remediation programs or programs delivered only to selected 'at risk' students. Reviews of research suggest that it is more effective to develop strengths and protective factors than to target 'at risk' factors. However, there needs to be some attention paid to risk factors as well (e.g. Greenberg et al., 2001; Hawkins et al., 1992; Hawkins et al., 1999; Hawkins, Catalona & Miller, 1992).

School-wide programs are more effective

School-wide programs are more effective than those delivered only to selected classes within the school, and programs should be embedded in the curriculum and general life of the classroom and school. Briggs & Hawkins (1999) reviewed the research outcomes on the effectiveness of a variety of different preventive programs designed to teach protective behaviours in young children. Their conclusions were almost identical to those of the National Health and Medical Research Council's evaluation of effective health and welfare programs (National Health and Medical Research Council, 1996). Both found that the most effective prevention programs were those that were integrated with the curriculum as much as possible.

Focusing on multiple domains is more effective

Interventions which involve school, family and community work best (Dryfoos, 1990; Greenberg et al., 2003). By utilising these kinds of partnerships, communities can develop common conceptual models and common language and procedures (Greenberg et al., 2001).

A 'shotgun' approach is more effective than a 'rifle' approach

A multi-strategic approach using a collection of coordinated 'active ingredients' works better than a single approach and is an essential feature of any successful prevention program (Blum, 1998; Greenberg et al., 2001; Hawkins et al., 1992; Kellerman, Fuqua-Whitley, Rivara & Mervy, 1998; Resnick et al., 1997). Wilson, Gottfredson and Najaka (2001) have argued that the most important question at this stage is 'which combinations and sequences of strategies work best?' rather than 'which single program works best?' In their review of research, Catalano et al. (2003) concluded that effective programs usually contained at least five different aspects of social and emotional learning. Other reviews of effective programs suggest that the most effective approaches not only include multiple components but also focus on both promoting positive behaviour and reducing antisocial behaviour (Catalano, Haggerty, Gainey, Hoppe & Brewer, 1998).

Identifying the most active ingredients in a school-wide program package is important

Identifying the active ingredients and the processes involved in successful prevention programs enables schools to adapt the program to different school contexts and situations, and thus increases the likelihood of success (Hughes, 2000). The three 'active ingredients' which produce the greatest positive wellbeing and academic outcomes for the greatest number of students have been clearly identified (Catalano et al., 2002; Conduct Problems Prevention Research Group, 1999; Durlak & Wells, 1997; Frey et al., 2000; Greenberg & Kusche, 1998; Hawkins et al., 1999; Mytton et al., 2002; Resnick et al., 1997; Schaps, Battistich & Solomon, 1997; Seattle Social Development Research Project; Solomon et al., 2000; Wilson et al., 2001). These are:

- development of a caring community of learners which creates connectedness and a sense of belonging
- extensive classroom use of cooperative learning
- development of pro-social attitudes/values and the teaching of social skills.

Prevention programs are more effective when they are delivered to children early in their schooling

Most reviews of preventive research stress that programs which start when students are very young are more likely to be effective (e.g. Dryfoos,1990; Durlak & Wells, 1997; Greenberg et al., 2001; Greenberg et al., 2003; Grossman et al., 1997; Krug et al., 1997; O'Shaughnessy, Lane, Gresham & Beebe-Frankenberger, 2002; Severson & Walker, 2002; Walker, Severson, Feil, Stiller & Golly, 1998).

Long-term prevention programs are more effective than short-term ones

Short-term preventive interventions produce time-limited benefits. Multi-year programs are more likely to foster enduring benefits (Conduct Problems Prevention Research Group, 1999; Greenberg et al., 1999; Greenberg et al., 2001; Greenberg et al., 2003; Weissberg & Greenberg, 1998). Catalano et al. (2002) concluded that programs lasting nine months or more produced better outcomes.

Prevention programs are more effective when teachers' behaviour is consistent with what they are teaching

Students respond most positively to program components when they perceive that their teachers behave in ways that are in accord with what is being taught (e.g. Deakin, Crick & Prosser, 1997; Ling et al., 1998; Williams, 1993). Adolescents who perceive their learning environments as including respectful, caring teachers and peers participate more in class and complete more homework (Murdock, 1999; Trent, 2001).

Conclusion

The use of evidence-based 'good practice' which has been derived from research into school-wide prevention programs that meet the social and emotional needs of students can provide schools with powerful strategies for preventing and reducing bullying and antisocial behaviour and enhancing student wellbeing, positive and pro-social behaviour, and learning outcomes. In the long term these practices can develop the school community, enhance student safety and wellbeing, and become a significant aspect of overall school improvement.

REFERENCES

Anderman, E. M. & Maehr, M. L. (1994). Motivation and schooling in the middle grades. *Review of Educational Research*, 64(2), 287–309.

Battistich, V., Schaps, E., Watson, M., Solomon, D., & Lewis, C. (2001). Effects of the Child Development Project on students' drug use and other problem behaviors. *Journal of Primary Prevention, 21*, 75–99.

Blum, R. W. (1998). Healthy youth development as a model for youth health promotion: A review. *Journal of Adolescent Health, 22*, 368–375.

Briggs, F. & Hawkins, R. (1999). Keeping ourselves safe. *SET Special.* New Zealand: NZCER.

Catalano, R. F. & Hawkins, J. D. (1996). The social development model: A theory of antisocial behavior. In J. D. Hawkins (Ed.), *Delinquency and crime: Some current theories.* New York: Cambridge University Press.

Catalano, R. F., Berglund, M. L., Ryan, J. A. M., Lonczak, H. C. & Hawkins, J. D. (2002). *Positive youth development in the United States: Research findings on evaluations of positive youth development programs.* Washington, DC: US Department of Health and Human Services.

Catalano, R. F., Haggerty, K. P., Gainey, R. R., Hoppe, M. J. & Brewer, D. D. (1998). Effectiveness of prevention interventions with youth at high-risk of drug abuse. In W. J. Bukoski & R. I. Evans (Eds.), *Cost-benefit/cost-effectiveness research of drug abuse prevention: Implications for programming and policy.* (NIDA Research Monograph No. 176, pp. 83–110). Rockville, MD: National Institute on Drug Abuse.

Catalano, R. F., Mazzab, J. J., Harachia, T. W., Abbott, R. D., Haggerty, K. P. & Fleminga, C. B. (2003). Raising healthy children through enhancing social development in elementary school: Results after 1.5 years. *Journal of School Psychology, 41*(2), 143–164.

Centre for Youth and Society (2001). *Evaluation of the W.I.T.S. Solid Primary Program.* Canada: University of Victoria. Retrieved February 24, 2005, from <http://www.youth.society.uvic.ca/resources/wits/>

Conduct Problems Prevention Research Group (CPPRG) (1999). Initial impact of the Fast Track Prevention Trial for Conduct Problems: II. Classroom effects. *Journal of Consulting and Clinical Psychology*, 67, 648–657.

Cross, D. (2004, November). *Helping to make schools even safer: Where policy meets the playground.* Paper presented at the National Coalition Against Bullying Seminar, Melbourne.

Cross, D., Hall, M., Roberts, C. & Young, D. (2003). *Bullying prevention skills for primary school children: An intervention trial.* Western Australian Centre for Health Promotion Research. Perth: Curtin University.

Cross, D., Pintabona, Y., Hall, M., Hamilton, G., Erceg, E. & Roberts, C. (2003). The Friendly Schools Project: An empirically grounded school-based bullying prevention program. *Australian Journal of Guidance and Counselling, 13*(1), 36–46.

Deakin, R., Crick, R. & Prosser, G. (1997). An exploration of the spiritual, moral, social and cultural development of children in school: The whole child and school ethos – a qualitative study. Retrieved March 3, 2005, from <http://www.becal.net/toolkit/acorneres/acorneres.html>

De Roche, E. & Williams, M. (1998). *Educating hearts and minds: A comprehensive character education framework.* California: Corwin Press Inc.

Dryfoos, J. (1990). Adolescents at risk: A summary of work in the field – programs and policies. In D. E. Rogers & E. Ginzberg (Eds.), *Adolescents at risk: Medical and social perspectives* (pp. 128–140). San Francisco: Westview Press.

Durlak, J. A. & Wells, A. M. (1997). Primary prevention mental health programs for children and adolescents: A meta-analytic review. *American Journal of Community Psychology*, *25*(2), 115–152.

Flannery, D., Vazsonyi, A. T., Liau, A. K., Guo, S., Powell, K. E., Atha, H., Vesterdal, W. & Embry, E. (2003). Initial behavior outcomes for the Peace Builders universal school-based violence prevention program. *Developmental Psychology*, *39*(2), 292–308.

Frey, K. & Rivara, F. P. (1997). Effectiveness of a violence prevention curriculum among children in elementary school. *Violence Prevention Among Children*, *20*, 1605–1611.

Frey, K. S., Hirschstein, M. K. & Guzzo, B. A. (2000). Second Step: preventing aggression by promoting social competence. *Journal of Emotional and Behavioral Disorders*, 8, 102–112.

Fullan, M. (1998). The meaning of educational change: A quarter of a century of learning. In A. Hargreaves, A. Lieberman, M. Fullan & D. Hopkins (Eds.), *International handbook of educational change* (pp. 214–231). London: Kluwer Academic.

Greenberg, M., Lengua, L. J., Coie, J., Pinder Hughes, E. E. & The Conduct Problems Prevention Research Group (1999). Predicting developmental outcomes at school entry using a multiple-risk model: Four American communities. *Developmental Psychology*, *35*, 403–417.

Greenberg, M., Weissberg, R., O'Brien, M., Zins, J., Fredericks, L., Resnik, H. & Elias, M. (2003). Enhancing school-based prevention and youth development through coordinated social, emotional, and academic learning. *American Psychologist*, *58*, 466–474.

Greenberg, M. T. & Kusche, C. A. (1998). *Improving children's emotion regulation and social competence: The effects of the PATHS curriculum*. Paper presented at meeting of Society for Research in Child Development, Washington, DC.

Greenberg, M. T., Domitrovich, C. & Bumbarger, B. (2001). The prevention of mental disorders in school-aged children: Current state of the field. *Prevention and Treatment*, *4*, Article 1. Retrieved May 8, 2005, from <http://journals.apa.org/prevention/volume4/pre0040001a.html>

Grossman, D. C., Neckerman, H. J., Koepsell, T. D., Liu, P., Asher, K. N., Beland, K., Frey, K. & Rivera, F. P. (1997). Effectiveness of a violence prevention curriculum among children in elementary school. *Journal of the American Medical Association*, *277*, 1605–1611.

Hargreaves, A., Earl, L. & Ryan, J. (1996). *Schooling for change: Reinventing education for early adolescents*. New York: Falmer Press.

Hawkins, J. D. & Weiss, J. G. (1983). The social development model: An integrated approach to delinquency prevention. In R. J. Rubel (Ed.), *Juvenile delinquency prevention: Emerging perspectives of the 1980s*. San Marcos, TS: Institute of Criminal Justice Studies, South West Texas State University.

Hawkins, J. D., Catalano, R. & Miller, J. (1992). Risk and protective factors for alcohol and other drug problems in adolescence and early childhood: Implications for substance abuse prevention. *Psychological Bulletin*, *112*(1), 64–105.

Hawkins, J. D., Catalano, R. F., Kosterman, R., Abbott, R. & Hill, K. G. (1999). Preventing adolescent health-risk behaviors by strengthening protection during childhood. *Archives of Pediatrics and Adolescent Medicine*, *153*, 226–234.

Hawkins, J. D., Catalano, R. F., Morrison, D., O'Donnell, J., Abbott, R. & Day, L. (1992). The Seattle Social Development Project: Effects of the first four years on protective factors and problem behaviors. In J. McCord & R. Tremblay (Eds.), *The prevention of antisocial behavior in children* (pp. 139–161). New York: Guilford Press.

Hawkins, J. D., Guo, J., Hill, K. G., Battin-Pearson, S. & Abbott, R. D. (2001). Long-term effects of the Seattle Social Development Project on school bonding trajectories. *Applied Developmental Sciences*, *5*, 225–236.

Hughes, J. N. (2000). The essential role of theory in the science of treating children: Beyond empirically supported treatments. *Journal of School Psychology*, *38*, 301–330.

Johnson, D. & Johnson, R. (2000). *Cooperative learning methods: A meta-analysis*. Retrieved February 18, 2005, from <http://www.co-operation.org/pages/cl-methods.html>

Kallestad, J. K. & Olweus, D. (2003). Predicting teachers' and schools' implementation of the Olweus Bullying Prevention Program: A multilevel study. *Prevention & Treatment*, 6(21). Retrieved on May 13, 2005, from <http://journals.apa.org/prevention/volume6/pre0060021a.html>

Kellerman, A. L., Fuqua-Whitley, D. S., Rivara, F. P., Mervy, J. (1998). Preventing youth violence: What works? *Annual Review of Public Health*, *19*, 271–292.

Krug, E. G., Brener, N. D., Dahlberg, L. L., Ryan, G. W. & Powell, K. E. (1997). The impact of an elementary school-based violence prevention program on visits to the school nurse. *American Journal of Preventive Medicine*, *13*(6), 459–463.

Ling, L., Burman, E. & Cooper, M. (1998). The Australian study. In Stephenson, J., Ling, L., Burman, E. & Cooper, M. (Eds.), *Values in education* (pp. 35–60). London: Routledge.

Maehr, M. & Midgley, C. (1996). *Transforming school cultures*. Boulder, CO: Westview Press.

Murdock, T. B. (1999). The social context of risk: Status and motivational predictors of alienation in middle school. *Journal of Educational Psychology*, *91*, 62–75.

Mytton J. A., Di Guiseppi, C., Gough, D., Taylor, R., Roberts, I. & Logan, S. (2002). School based violence prevention programme: Systematic review of secondary prevention trials. *Archives of Pediatrics and Adolescent Medicine*, *156*, 752–762.

National Health and Medical Research Council (1996). *Effective school health promotion: Towards health promoting schools*. National Health and Medical Research Council's Health Advancement Committee. Canberra: Australian Government Publishing Service.

Olweus, D. (1993). *Bullying at school: What we know & what we can do*. Oxford and Cambridge, MA: Blackwell.

Olweus, D. & Alsaker, F. D. (1991). Assessing change in a cohort longitudinal study with hierarchical data. In D. Magnusson, L. R. Bergman, G. Rudinger & B. Törestad (Eds.), *Problems and methods in longitudinal research* (pp. 107–132). New York: Cambridge University Press.

O'Shaughnessy, T. E., Lane, K. L., Gresham, F. & Beebe-Frankenberger, M. E. (2002). Students with or at risk for emotional-behavioral difficulties. In K. L. Lane, F. M. Gresham & T. E. O'Shaughnessy (Eds.), *Interventions for children with or at risk for emotional and behavioral disorders* (pp. 3–18). Boston: Allyn & Bacon.

Patterson, G. R., Reid, J. B. & Dishion, T. J. (1992). *Antisocial boys*. Eugene, Oregon: Castalia.

Resnick, M., Bearman, P. S., Blum, R. W., Bauman, K. E., Harris, K. M., Hones, J., Tabor, J., Beuhring, T., Sieving, R. E., Shew, M., Ireland, M., Bearinger, L. H. & Udry, J. R. (1997). Protecting adolescents from harm. *Journal of the American Medical Association*, *278*, 823–832.

Roland, E. (1989). Bullying: The Scandinavian tradition. In D. P. Tattum & D. A. Lane (Eds.), *Bullying in schools* (pp. 21–32). Stoke-on-Trent: Trentham Books.

Schaps, E., Battistich, V. & Solomon, D. (1997). School as a caring community: A key to character education. In A. Molnar (Ed.), *The construction of children's character, Part II: 96th Yearbook of the National Society for the Study of Education*. Chicago: University of Chicago Press.

Scheckner, S., Rollin, S. A., Kaiser-Ulrey, C. & Wagner, R. (2002). School violence in children and adolescents: A meta-analysis of the effectiveness of current interventions, *Journal of School Violence*, *1*(2), 5–32.

Schonert-Reichl, K., Smith, V. & Zaidman-Zait, A. (2002). Effects of the Roots of Empathy Program on childrens' emotional and social competence. Unpublished manuscript. University of British Columbia. Retrieved March 3, 2005, from <http://www.rootsofempathy.org>

Schonert-Reichl, K. A., Smith, V., Zaidman-Zait, A. & Hertzman, C. (2003, April). *Impact of the 'Roots of Empathy' on social competence of elementary school children: Developmental and contextual considerations*. Paper presented as part of a symposium, Evaluating School Based Prevention Programs for Emotional and Social Competence: Considering Context, Process, Cumulative Effect, 70th Annual Meeting of the Society for Research in Child Development, Tampa, FL.

Severson, H. H. & Walker, H. M. (2002). Proactive approaches for identifying children at risk for sociobehavioral problems. In K. L. Lane, F. M. Gresham & T. E. O'Shaughnessy (Eds.), *Interventions for children with or at risk for emotional and behavioral disorders* (pp. 33–53). Boston: Allyn & Bacon.

Shechtman, Z. (1999). Bibliotherapy: An indirect approach to treatment of childhood aggression. *Child Psychiatry and Human Development*, *30*(1), 39–53.

Solomon, D., Battistich, V., Watson, M., Schaps, R. & Lewis, C. (2000). A six-district study of educational change: Direct and mediated effects of the Child Development Project. *Social Psychology of Education*, *4*, 3–51.

Trent, F. (2001, August). *Aliens in the classroom or: The classroom as an alien place?* Paper presented at the Association of Independent Schools NSW Sex, Drugs & Rock 'n' Roll Conference, Sydney.

Walker, H. M., Severson, H. H., Feil, E. G., Stiller, B. & Golly, A. (1998). First step to success: Intervening at the point of school entry to prevent antisocial behavior patterns. *Psychology in the Schools*, *35*(3), 259–269.

Wang, M. C., Haertel, G. D. & Walberg, H. J. (1997). Learning influences. In H. J. Walberg & G. D. Haertel (Eds.), *Psychology and Educational Practice* (pp. 199–211). Berkeley, CA: McCutchan.

Weissberg, R. P. & Greenberg, M. T. (1998). School and community competence-enhancement and prevention programs. In W. Damon (Ed.), *Handbook of child psychology* (Vol. 4) (5th ed.) (pp. 877–954). New York: Wiley.

Williams, M. (1993). Actions speak louder than words: What students think. *Educational Leadership*, *51*(3), 22–24.

Wilson, D. B., Gottfredson, D. C. & Najaka, S. S. (2001). School-based prevention of problem behaviors: A meta-analysis. *Journal of Quantitative Criminology*, *17*, 247–272.

Zbar, V., Brown, D., Bereznicki, B. & Hooper, C. (2003). *Values education study final report*. DEST. Retrieved February 24, 2005, from <http://www.dest.gov.au/schools/publications/2003/index.htm>

CHAPTER 4
Core components of a school-wide safe schools curriculum

Toni Noble

Introduction

The story of Columbine is a powerful reminder of a tragic outcome of school bullying. At Columbine High School in the United States two students consumed by rage and armed with an arsenal of guns and explosives went on a rampage, killing a teacher and 12 fellow students. The two students then turned their guns on themselves. There have been 11 other incidents in the United States where students have killed their classmates. What 'triggered' the students' attacks on their fellow students or Martin Bryant's massacre of innocent bystanders at Port Arthur in Tasmania? In all cases the young men who killed innocent others had experienced extreme stress as a result of being excluded, bullied, mocked and taunted.

These case studies clearly represent extreme reactions to being bullied and there is no doubt the responses of these young men were pathological and inexcusable. However, considerable research data supports the negative effects of being bullied and excluded. A meta-analytic review of 20 years of research has linked being bullied with depression, loneliness, anxiety, low self-esteem and poor social self-concept (Hawker & Boulton, 2000) and an Australian study has linked bullying with suicidal ideation and attempts at self-harm (Rigby & Slee, 1999). No study of social behaviour in any school anywhere in the world has shown an absence of bullying (Rigby, 2001). A large-scale Australian study of 38 000 students found that 19 per cent of students reported being bullied at least weekly and a further 27 per cent less than weekly (Rigby, 2004). Hence there is a compelling need to address the issue of bullying in our schools.

Bullying is a serious problem for everyone, for those who bully, for those who are bullied and for the communities in which bullying takes place.

A review of a number of meta-analyses of different prevention programs designed to prevent bullying and school violence provides useful guidelines on the most effective principles and practices in school prevention programs. These research findings illustrate that no single prevention or intervention strategy can guarantee the reduction of school bullying. Any program that is likely to succeed and to have long-term benefits for everyone involved needs to take a multi-factored approach to prevention.

This chapter outlines the research-based principles and practices of effective school-based prevention programs and then reviews the practices to prevent school bullying incorporated in the BOUNCE BACK! Classroom Resiliency Program (McGrath & Noble, 2003).

Guiding principles for good practice

Research shows that the six main contributors to effective school-based prevention programs are:

- Take a whole-school approach.
- Embed anti-bullying principles and processes in the curriculum.
- Start early.
- Plan for program maintenance, because long-term programs work best.
- Involve parents and the community.
- Use multiple strategies.

The following sections individually address each point.

Take a whole-school approach

Prevention programs which take a whole-school approach and work on building caring school communities that foster connectedness facilitate the establishment of safe schools. The human right to feel safe and supported at school underpins the National Safe Schools

Framework (2005). The framework's guiding principles highlight the responsibility of educators to provide protective pro-social school environments where everyone feels safe psychologically and physically. Feeling connected to school – operationalised as feeling 'close to people at school', 'happy to be at school', 'like I am part of this school' and that 'I feel safe at my school' (Resnick et al., 1997) – was identified as the most powerful protective factor of any school attribute studied for all health-risk behaviours including school violence and bullying.

The resilience research demonstrates that relationships are the key to both preventing school violence and bullying and successfully engaging students' intrinsic motivation to learn (Resnick et al., 1997). A new term 'Academic Care' has been coined to demonstrate this reciprocal interdependence of creating positive school environments and improving academic progress (Nadge, 2005). Researchers involved in CASEL (the Collaborative for Academic, Social and Emotional Learning) argue that:

> Social and emotional development and the recognition of the relational nature of learning and change are the fundamentals of human learning, work and accomplishment. Until this is given proper emphasis, we cannot expect to see progress in making schools safer, drug-free, with fewer students who don't care and want to drop-out, or with better tolerance of people who are different. (Elias & Weissberg, 2000, p. 264)

Embed anti-bullying principles and processes in the curriculum

Prevention programs that are embedded in the curriculum and the general life of the classroom and school are more effective than 'add-on' programs (Briggs & Hawkins, 1999; National Health and Medical Research Council, 1996; Scheckner, Rollin, Kaiser-Ulrey & Wagner, 2002). One of the major barriers to the sustainment of any new school initiative is the time it takes in an already crowded curriculum. The core business of teachers is to help their students achieve curriculum outcomes. If teachers see that anti-bullying initiatives can also achieve their curriculum outcomes, then these new initiatives are more likely to be maintained over time and hence be more cost-effective. A further benefit is that once teachers are trained they can employ the newly acquired principles and skills with subsequent classes.

Start early

Prevention programs are more effective when they are delivered to children early in their schooling. Most reviews of preventive research stress that programs which start when students are very young are more likely to be effective (e.g. Dryfoos, 1990; Durlak & Wells, 1997; Greenberg et al., 2003; O'Shaughnessy, Lane, Gresham & Beebe-Frankenberger, 2002; Scheckner et al., 2002; Severson & Walker, 2002; Walker, Severson, Feil, Stiller & Golly, 1998). The longer children are exposed to risk factors, the more likely they will acquire aggressive behaviours (Patterson, Reid & Dishion, 1992).

Plan for program maintenance

Not surprisingly, short-term preventive interventions produce time-limited benefits whereas multi-year programs are more likely to foster enduring benefits (Conduct Problems Prevention Research Group, 1999; Greenberg, Domitrovich & Bumbarger, 2001; Greenberg et al., 2003; Scheckner et al., 2002; Weissberg & Greenberg, 1998). Long-term programs provide more opportunities for students to revisit key concepts in developmentally appropriate ways. Such programs create more opportunities for students to understand, and practise, the key concepts and skills in different situations and contexts and for the underlying principles to be embedded in the school and class culture.

Involve parents and the community

Prevention programs and processes that are directed to multiple domains, i.e. school, family and community, work best (Dryfoos, 1990; Greenberg et al., 2003; Scheckner et al., 2002). For example, communicating the same messages through an anti-bullying policy and reinforcing the same pro-social values, skills and behaviours at the whole-school level and the class level, and including parents and the local community, is more productive than those programs simply targeting one domain, such as one or two classes (Cross, 2004; Greenberg et al., 2001).

Use multiple strategies

What strategies can schools put in place to provide caring communities, build positive relationships with teachers and peers and prevent school bullying? A clear message from the research is that no single approach will work and that programs with multiple strategies have more chance of success (Greenberg et al., 2001; Scheckner et al., 2002).

The following section outlines a range of evidence-based strategies for promoting a safe schools curriculum.

Core components of a safe schools framework

The following discussion reviews the 10 core components of an effective safe schools curriculum:

1. Development of positive student-teacher relationships
2. Facilitation of peer support
3. A values-based curriculum
4. Classroom structures that focus on peer support and processes of group participation
5. Teaching of social competencies
6. Programs based on cognitive-behavioural principles
7. Discipline procedures that help keep students feeling connected
8. A differentiated curriculum with a strengths-based approach
9. Literature-based programs for social and emotional learning
10. Ongoing professional development.

1. Development of positive student-teacher relationships

Outside families, teachers are among the most frequently encountered positive role models in the lives of children. Many different research studies are remarkably consistent in students' identification of the qualities of their best teachers. These qualities include teachers who listen, who notice when they're absent and who seem interested in them – in other words the students focus on the interpersonal quality of their relationship with their teachers (Dornbusch, Laird & Crosnoe, 1999; Ruddick, Day & Wallace, 1997; Trent, 2001; Werner, 2000). These 'best' teachers are also the ones who are most likely to connect them to school and enhance their commitment to learning.

2. Facilitation of peer support

It is currently estimated that peer bystanders observe bullying in 85 per cent of bullying incidents, which indicates the potential for reducing bullying behaviour by harnessing peer support (O'Connell, Pepler & Craig, 1999). When bystanders do discourage bullying, the bullying stops some 50 per cent of the time (Hawkins, Pepler & Craig, 2001). Relationship problems such as bullying require relationship solutions and children who bully or are bullied require support. A growing body of evidence is finding positive peer relationships as one of the most influential factors in improving school culture and student learning outcomes (Battistich, 2001; Battistich, Solomon, Kim, Watson & Schaps, 1995; Benard, 2004). For many young people one of their major reasons for coming to school is to socially and emotionally connect with their peers (Fuller, McGraw &

Goodyear, 1998). Students' sense of interconnectedness is critical to their acceptance of responsibility for the wellbeing of others. Helping students to become more active and responsible in offering peer support to students who are being bullied is now achieving greater prominence in anti-bullying initiatives (Rigby & Bagshaw, 2005; Stanley & McGrath, 2005).

3. A values-based curriculum

Safe schools are underpinned by core values in teacher and peer relationships – values such as caring, respect for others, cooperation and valuing diversity (National Safe Schools Framework, 2005; National Framework for Values Education in Australian Schools, 2005). The more students are connected to family, peers, school and teachers the better equipped they are to make values-based decisions. Explicitly teaching students values helps them to develop habits of thinking, feeling and acting that positively influence how they behave towards others.

4. Classroom structures focusing on peer support and processes of group participation

Small and large group strategies such as cooperative learning, peer tutoring, buddy systems and peer support programs (for example, peer mediation, circle of friends for students at risk of bullying or exclusion, circle time, student focus groups, classroom meetings, and class and school committees) allow students opportunities to practise the pro-social values and social skills of a caring community. All these strategies foster positive student-student interactions that help them to build empathy and to experience both being cared for and caring for others. These processes have been found to be critical components in effective school violence prevention programs (Johnson & Johnson, 1996).

Cooperative learning is an especially valuable group process because it can be used at any year level with any curriculum content. Over a thousand studies document the research benefits of cooperative learning (Benard, 2004). In studies with matched control groups, researchers have found the following benefits in cooperative learning: increases in academic scores and engagement in learning, social skills, empathy, motivation, acceptance of diversity (ethnic, racial, physical), conflict resolution, self-esteem, self-control, positive attitudes to school, and critical thinking (Johnson & Johnson, 1989, 2001; Slavin, 1995, 1990).

The key principles that characterise cooperative learning groups and make them different from unstructured group work are:

- *Positive interdependence* – group members have a shared goal and a shared belief that no-one succeeds unless everyone succeeds. All group members share their work and resources.
- *Individual accountability and responsibility* to the group. Everyone pulls their weight.
- *Social skills* are taught and practised within the group.

5. Teaching social skills

Social competence includes the skills, values and attitudes essential to forming positive relationships with others. Prevention programs that focus on teaching social skills and social perspective taking have shown considerable promise in promoting student well-being and reducing antisocial and bullying behaviours (Dryfoos, 1990; Tolan & Guerra, 1998). Research studies (Gresham, 1997; McGrath, 1998; Scheckner et al., 2002) have demonstrated that the best practices in the development of student social competencies involve the use of the following cognitive-behavioural steps:

- Class discussion of the reasons for learning this skill
- Identification and verbal rehearsal of the steps of the skill
- Dramatic role-plays where students practise the skill and receive constructive feedback from teacher and peers
- Realistic school or class-based games, tasks and activities that allow regular and naturalistic practice of the skill
- Briefing and debriefing of each practice opportunity to facilitate students' reflection on their use of the skill
- Targeted positive reinforcement for the effective use of the skill for those students who need more practice, feedback and support.

6. Programs based on cognitive-behavioural principles

The importance of strategies that incorporate cognitive-behavioural principles in effective anti-school violence and bullying programs was highlighted in the meta-analysis performed by Scheckner et al. (2002) and other well-controlled studies designed to improve classroom behaviour, self-esteem and pro-social competence in aggressive children (Greenberg et al., 2003; Gresham, 1997; Hansen, Nagle & Meyer, 1998; Lochman, 1992; Lochman, Lampron, Gemmer, Harris & Wyckoff, 1989; McGrath, 1998; Wilson, Gottfredson & Najaka, 2001). A key principle of cognitive-behavioural therapy (CBT) is that if we change the way we think, then we can change the way we feel and act. CBT is a highly successful form of behavioural change treatment for anger management, depression and anxiety. It also underpins training in optimistic thinking in young people (Gilham, Reivich, Jaycox & Seligman, 1995; Jaycox, Reivich, Gillham & Seligman, 1994; Seligman, 1995) – a critical variable in developing student wellbeing and their positive relationships with others. Optimistic thinking is a key component in maintaining a student's capacity to persevere in social, emotional or academic problem-solving, in facilitating their sense of hope that difficult situations will get better and in establishing positive relationships with others.

7. Discipline procedures that help keep students feeling connected

Instead of out-of-school suspensions for bullying and other discipline strategies designed to disconnect students, more positive approaches such as restorative justice (Armstrong & Thorsborne 2005) and shared concern, and for minor incidents classroom meetings or conferences (McGrath & Noble, 2003) attempt to keep students connected to their school and their classmates and build their sense of responsibility. Clear in all the resilience research is the value of 'letting go and moving on' after pain and mistreatment (Benard, 2004).

8. A differentiated curriculum with a strengths-based approach

A strengths-based approach to prevention and intervention now underpins the positive psychology movement (Peterson & Seligman, 2004; Seligman, 2002), the resilience research in education (Benard, 2004; Fuller, Bellhouse & Johnston, 2001; McGrath & Noble, 2003) and family intervention in social welfare (Geggie, De Frain, Hitchcock & Silberberg, 2000). A converging message from these different disciplines is the social, emotional and academic benefits of focusing on student strengths rather than risk factors and promoting these strengths in the natural context of the classroom and school rather than in remedial deficit focused withdrawal programs. Benard talks about 'turnaround teachers' who have high expectations for students, provide the necessary academic and behavioural support, and both recognise and help students and classmates to value each others' diverse strengths. A differentiated curriculum based on Gardner's multiple intelligences model has the capacity to build positive school and class communities where students value and celebrate student differences and, for students who struggle with learning, achieve more academic success (Kornhaber, Fierros & Veenema, 2004; McGrath & Noble, 2005; Noble, 2004). Given that students with learning difficulties are frequently targeted for bullying, there are clear advantages in establishing class learning communities where classmates respect each others' differences.

9. Literature-based programs for social and emotional learning

Shechtman (1999) conducted a school-based violence prevention program using relevant literature and videos as the primary prevention with Year 4 boys referred for aggression. Results indicated that five groups of program students compared to five control groups increased their pro-social behaviour and demonstrated reduced aggression, indicating that the use of relevant texts and videos can be an effective component of school-based prevention programs. The benefit of a literature-based approach to prevention is that it aligns with teachers' work and allows them to achieve their English curriculum outcomes concurrently with teaching an anti-bullying curriculum.

10. Ongoing professional development

In a review of the Olweus Bullying Prevention Program the most significant factors that influenced teachers' implementation of the program related to their perceptions of how much bullying was occurring in their classroom, their empathy with students who had been bullied, and how much they perceived they and their school were agents of change in counteracting bullying (Kallestad & Olweus, 2003). Whole-school surveys of bullying that provide school data on the incidence of bullying, in conjunction with teacher professional development, therefore represent important components to gaining teachers' commitment to any anti-bullying initiatives. Teacher involvement in the development of an anti-bullying school policy is also a crucial component in their actual implementation of programs (Rigby, 2004). The most effective prevention programs incorporated effective professional development and provided teachers with a wide range of good resources (Briggs & Hawkins, 1999; National Health and Medical Research Council, 1996). Nadge (2005) reports that once teachers understand the link between the teaching and the learning experiences they provide and their students' psychosocial development, they are able to adjust their practice accordingly.

The BOUNCE BACK! Classroom Resiliency Program

The second part of this chapter briefly describes the BOUNCE BACK! Classroom Resiliency Program as one example of how these program components can be included in a whole-school multi-strategic safe schools framework. In 2003 this program won the Robin Winkler Award for Excellence in Applied Community Research. This award is given for programs that address the prevention of bullying and other antisocial behaviours and the promotion of wellbeing in a community context such as schools. The program has 3 levels of classroom materials organised in 10 curriculum units that provide developmentally appropriate curriculum resources and activities from school entry through to the end of junior secondary.

The BOUNCE BACK program outlines strategies for developing positive relationships within the school community. It details a variety of evidence-based strategies for teaching students pro-social values (such as compassion, respect, acceptance of difference and friendliness) and social competencies (such as negotiation, conflict management and getting along with others). It also includes activities for teaching empathy as well as coping skills that help to develop students' capacity to 'bounce back' when they experience pain, difficulties, mistreatment or failure. There is a particular emphasis on optimistic thinking. Group-focused processes such as cooperative learning, cooperative games and circle time underpin the activities, and most are based on cognitive-behavioural principles. Many of the cooperative learning strategies promote higher order thinking and reasoning that can be applied to social or academic problem-solving.

A strong literature base embeds the program in the curriculum and is reflected in the 420 picture books and novels in the program that are used to introduce both the social and emotional skills that are taught and the anti-bullying and pro-social messages that are promoted. Curriculum differentiation is provided through the diverse range of learning activities, including music, hands-on experiential activities, games, and drama and role-play.

This program also includes a fully developed anti-bullying curriculum unit at each of the three levels, which is activity-based, literature-based and integrated with most key learning areas. The content focuses on teaching students a variety of skills for responding to bullying if targeted and dealing with peer pressure, as well as peer support skills that bystanders can use, and stresses the importance of seeking social support and teacher support. It also relates bullying to how animals and plants protect themselves (for younger children) and to legal issues and sporting issues (e.g. racial vilification), providing examples of historical and global mistreatment and oppression (for older students).

An abbreviated version of the BOUNCE BACK! program, focusing just on teaching coping skills (Turning the Tide), was trialled in a joint research project between the Drug Education section of the Department of Education in Victoria and the Faculty of Education at Deakin University (McGrath & Anders, 2000; McGrath & Noble, 2003). Eight teachers from eight different primary schools were involved in implementing the program in their Year 5 or 6 classrooms over 14 weeks. These teachers taught in diverse school communities that included working-class and middle-class schools, secular and private schools, and rural schools, inner-city and suburban schools.

All the teachers in the study found the program to be user friendly and easy to implement. At the end of 14 weeks of teaching the program, 7 of the 8 teachers reported greater confidence in teaching the coping skills that underpin the program. They also reported marked improvements and greater confidence in their ability to talk with and counsel their students when they were distressed. They believed that this occurred because they shared with their students an understanding of the coping skills covered in the program. This understanding enabled them to facilitate student management of personal issues as well as school-work issues. All teachers also reported that teaching the program improved their own personal and professional resilience and their capacity to cope with difficult times. The importance of teacher resilience in enhancing the social and emotional wellbeing of students and positive relationships is reflected in the following quotation by Hargreaves and Fullan (1998, p. 87):

> Too many of our teachers are starting to lose hope. We are in serious danger of undermining a fundamental truth of educational effectiveness – that the learning and emotional lives of students are profoundly dependent on the learning and emotional lives of teachers.

BOUNCE BACK is an acronym that stands for 10 coping statements which help students deal with difficult situations. The research study also demonstrated that the students in the 8 classes were able to learn, understand and recall the acronym with an 80 per cent success rate after 14 weeks teaching of the program. At the end of the program, students showed an increase in resilient thinking, especially optimistic and helpful thinking, as assessed by their capacity to solve problems in hypothetical difficult situations. In focus group interviews many students also reported using the coping skills in their own lives, including difficult family situations and peer group conflict. Some students mentioned that they had taught some of the coping skills to members of their family. During the 14 weeks of the program teachers also observed many students spontaneously using the coping skills and statements in real-life stressful situations and in supporting their classmates and friends.

These findings offer some sense of optimism that individual teachers can make a difference in facilitating both their own and student resilience.

The study does not explicitly evaluate the anti-bullying curriculum component. However, a strength of the BOUNCE BACK! program is its multi-factored approach to prevention. It would therefore be challenging to undertake a research study to isolate the most significant 'active ingredients' in reducing school bullying.

Conclusion

The research on school bullying prevention indicates the benefits of a whole-school approach to the development of schools that are psychologically and physically safe for all. The critical importance of positive teacher and peer relationships in helping students feel connected to school and facilitating their development of pro-social values and behaviours is highlighted. Programs that employ multiple strategies are more effective than those that focus on only one set of strategies. Structured positive classroom strategies that empower students and connect them with others are more effective in both the short term and the long term in reducing school bullying. Those programs that are embedded in the curriculum, start early in children's schooling, and revisit key concepts and skills over years are more likely to be successful. Teacher belief in the importance of their role in the reduction of bullying is a significant factor in gaining their commitment to any anti-bullying curriculum.

The BOUNCE BACK! Classroom Resiliency Program is a comprehensive program that includes many of these core components. It is a multi-year, multi-level program that employs multiple strategies to teach social and emotional competencies that are now seen as an integral part of academic learning. It also incorporates a comprehensive anti-bullying curriculum.

One clear message from the prevention research is that we still need to work hard at reducing the incidence of bullying in our schools. Another key message is that a number of pro-social positive prevention strategies are now emerging, providing hope and a sense of optimism that schools can make a significant difference in reducing the incidence of bullying for the benefits of all: the students who are bullied, the students who bully and the whole school community.

REFERENCES

Armstrong, M. & Thorsborne, M. (2005). Restorative responses to bullying. In H. McGrath & T. Noble (Eds.). *Bullying solutions: Evidence-based approaches to bullying in Australian schools.* Frenchs Forest: Pearson Education.

Battistich, V. (2001). Effects of an elementary school intervention on students' connectedness to school and social adjustment during middle school. In J. Brown (Chair), *Resilience education: Theoretical, interactive and empirical applications* (pp. 1–15). Seattle: AERA.

Battistich, V., Solomon, D., Kim, D., Watson, M. & Schaps, E. (1995). Schools as communities, poverty levels of student populations, and students' attitudes, motives, and performance: A multilevel analysis. *American Educational Research Journal, 32*, 627–658.

Benard, B. (2004). *Resiliency: What we have learned.* San Francisco: WestEd.

Briggs, F. & Hawkins, R. (1999). Keeping ourselves safe. *SET Special*. New Zealand: NZCER.

CASEL (Collaborative for Academic, Social and Emotional Learning) (2004). *SEL and academic performance: How evidence-based SEL programs work to produce greater student success in school and life*. Retrieved January 1, 2005, from <http://www.casel.org/downloads/Safe%20and%20Sound/2B_Performance.pdf>

Conduct Problems Prevention Research Group (1999). Initial impact of the fast track prevention trial for conduct problems: II. Classroom effects. *Journal of Consulting and Clinical Psychology*, 67, 648–657.

Cross, D. (2004, November). *Helping to make schools even safer: Where policy meets the playground*. Paper presented at the National Coalition Against Bullying Seminar, Melbourne.

Dornbusch, S. M., Laird, J. & Crosnoe, B. (1999). Parental and school resources that assist adolescents in coping with negative peer influences. In E. Frydenberg, *Learning to cope: Developing as a person in complex societies*. Oxford: Oxford University Press.

Dryfoos, J. (1990). Adolescents at risk: A summary of work in the field – programs and policies. In D. E. Rogers & E. Ginzberg (Eds.), Adolescents at risk: Medical and social perspectives (pp. 128–140). San Francisco: Westview Press.

Durlak, J. A. & Wells, A. M. (1997). Primary prevention mental health programs for children and adolescents: A meta-analytic review. *American Journal of Community Psychology*, 25(2), 115–152.

Elias, M. & Weissberg, R. (2000). Wellness in schools. In D. Cicchetti, J. Rappaport, I. Sandler & R. Weissberg (Eds.), *The promotion of wellness in children and adolescents* (pp. 243–269). Washington, DC: Child Welfare League Association Press.

Fuller, A., Bellhouse, B. & Johnston, G. (2001). *The heart masters: A program for the promotion of emotional intelligence and resilience in the middle to senior years of primary school*. Queenscliff, Vic.: Inyahead Press.

Fuller, A., McGraw, K. & Goodyear, M. (1998). *The mind of youth. Resilience: A Connect Project*. Department of Education, Victoria.

Geggie, J., De Frain, J., Hitchcock, S. & Silberberg, S. (2000). *The family strengths research report*. Family Action Centre, University of Newcastle.

Gilham, J. E., Reivich, K. J., Jaycox, I. H. & Seligman, M. E. P. (1995). Preventing depressive symptoms in schoolchildren: Two year follow-up. *Psychological Science*, 6(6), 343–351.

Greenberg, M. T, Domitrovich, C. & Bumbarger, B. (2001). *Preventing mental disorders in school-age children: A review of the effectiveness of prevention programs*. Report commissioned by the Center for Mental Health Services (CMHS), Substance Abuse Mental Health Services Administration, US Department of Health and Human Services.

Greenberg, M., Weissberg, R., O'Brien, M., Zins, J., Fredericks, L., Resnik, H. & Elias, M. (2003). Enhancing school-based prevention and youth development through coordinated social, emotional, and academic learning. *American Psychologist*, 58, 466–474.

Gresham, F. M. (1997). Social competence and students with behavior disorders: Where we've been, where we are, and where we should go. *Education and Treatment of Children*, *20*, 233–249.

Gresham, F. M. (2002). Social skills assessment and instruction for students with emotional and behavioral disorders. In K. L. Lane, F. M. Gresham & T. E. O'Shaughnessy (Eds.), *Interventions for children with or at risk for emotional and behavioral disorders* (pp. 242–258). Boston: Allyn & Bacon.

Hansen, D. J., Nagle, D. W. & Meyer, K. A. (1998). Enhancing the effectiveness of social skills interventions with adolescents. *Education and Treatment of Children*, *21*, 489–513.

Hargreaves, A. & Fullan, M. (1998). *What's worth fighting for out there*. New York: Teachers College Press.

Hawker, S. J. & Boulton, M. (2000). Twenty years research on peer victimisation and psychosocial malajustment: A meta-analytic review of cross-sectional studies. *Journal of Child Psychology & Psychiatry*, *41*(4), 441–445.

Hawkins, D., Pepler, D. & Craig, W. M. (2001). Naturalistic observations of peer interventions in bullying. *Social Development*, *10*, 512–527.

Jaycox, L. H., Reivich, K. J., Gillham, J. & Seligman, M. (1994). Prevention of depressive symptoms in school children. *Behaviour Research & Therapy*, *32*, 801–816.

Johnson, D. & Johnson, R. (1989). *Cooperation and competition: Theory and research*. Edina, MN: Interaction Book Company.

Johnson, D. & Johnson, R. (1996). Conflict resolution and peer mediation programs in elementary and secondary schools: A review of the research. *Review of Educational Research*, 66(4), 459–506.

Johnson, D. & Johnson, R. (2001). *Cooperative learning methods: A meta-analysis*. Retrieved February 9, 2005, from <http://www.co-operation.org/pages/cl-methods.html>

Kallestad, J. K. & Olweus, D. (2003). Predicting teachers' and schools' implementation of the Olweus Bullying Prevention Program: A multilevel study. *Prevention & Treatment*, 6(21). Retrieved February 9, 2005, from <http://journals.apa.org/prevention/volume6/pre0060021a.html>

Kornhaber, M., Fierros, E. D. & Veenema, S. A. (2004). *Multiple intelligences: Best ideas from research and practice*. Boston: Pearson Education Inc.

Lochman, J. E. (1992). Cognitive-behavioral intervention with aggressive boys: Three-year follow-up and preventive effects. *Journal of Consulting and Clinical Psychology*, 60(3), 426–432.

Lochman, J. E., Lampron, L.B., Gemmer, T. C., Harris, S. R. & Wyckoff, G. M. (1989). Teacher consultation and cognitive-behavioral intervention with aggressive boys. *Psychology in the Schools*, *26*, 179–188.

McGrath, H. & Anders, E. (2000). *The BOUNCE BACK Program: A pilot study*. Turning the Tide in Schools Drug Education Project. Department of Education, Victoria.

McGrath, H. & Noble, T. (2003). *BOUNCE BACK! A Classroom Resiliency Program. Teacher's*

Handbook. Level One: K–2; Level Two: Years 3–4; Level Three: Years 5–8. Frenchs Forest: Pearson Education.

McGrath, H. & Noble, T. (2005). *Eight ways at once. Multiple Intelligences + Revised Bloom's Taxonomy = 200 + Differentiated classroom strategies* (Books One & Two). Frenchs Forest: Pearson Education.

McGrath, H. L. (1998). An overview of prevention and treatment programs for developing positive peer relations. In K. Rigby & P. Slee (Eds.), *Children's peer relationships*. London: Routledge.

Nadge, A. (2005). Building resilience, building futures. *Journal of Pastoral Care in Education*, *23*(1), 28–32.

National Coalition Against Bullying: Alannah & Madeline Foundation. Retrieved February 9, 2005, from <http://www.ncab.org.au/>

National Framework for Values Education in Australian Schools (2005). Retrieved February 9, 2005, from <http://www.curriculum.edu.au/values/pdf/nat_framework.pdf>

National Health and Medical Research Council (1996). *Effective school health promotion: Towards health promoting schools*. National Health and Medical Research Council's Health Advancement Committee. Canberra: Australian Government Publishing Service.

National Safe Schools Framework (2005). Student Learning and Support Services Taskforce. Retrieved February 9, 2005, from <http://www.mceetya.edu.au/pdf/natsafeschools.pdf>

Noble, T. (2004). Integrating the Revised Bloom's Taxonomy with Multiple Intelligences: A planning tool for curriculum differentiation. *Teachers College Record*, *106*(1), 193–211.

O'Connell, P., Pepler, D. & Craig, W. (1999). Peer involvement in bullying: Insights and challenges for intervention. *Journal of Adolescence*, *22*, 437–452.

O'Shaughnessy, T. E., Lane, K. L., Gresham, F. & Beebe-Frankenberger, M. E. (2002). Students with or at risk for emotional-behavioral difficulties. In K. L. Lane, F. M. Gresham & T. E. O'Shaughnessy (Eds.). *Interventions for children with or at risk for emotional and behavioral disorders* (pp. 3–18). Boston: Allyn & Bacon.

Patterson, G. R., Reid, J. B. & Dishion, T. J. (1992). *Antisocial boys*. Eugene, Oregon: Castalia.

Peterson, C. & Seligman, M. (2004). *Character strengths & virtues: A handbook and classification*. New York: Oxford University Press.

Resnick, M., Bearman, P. S., Blum, R. W., Bauman, K. E., Harris, K. M., Hones, J., Tabor, J., Beuhring, T., Sieving, R. E., Shew, M., Ireland, M., Beariner, L. H. & Udry, J. R. (1997). Protecting adolescents from harm. *Journal of the American Medical Association*, *278*, 823–832.

Rigby, K. (2001). *Stop the bullying. A handbook for schools*. Melbourne: ACER.

Rigby, K. (2004, December). *What can be done to make anti-bullying programs more effective?* Paper presented at National Coalition Against Bullying Symposium, Melbourne.

Rigby, K. & Bagshaw, D. (2005). Helping students to counteract bullying by the use of educational drama and bystander training. In H. McGrath & T. Noble (Eds.), *Bullying solutions. Evidence-based approaches to bullying in Australian schools*. Frenchs Forest: Pearson Education.

Rigby, K. & Slee, P. T. (1999). Suicidal ideation among adolescent schoolchildren, involvement in bully/victim problems and perceived low social support. *Suicide and Life-Threatening Behaviour*, *29*, 119–130.

Ruddick, J., Day, J. & Wallace, G. (1997). Students' perspectives on school improvement. In A. Hargreaves (Ed.). *Rethinking educational change with heart and mind. The ASCD Yearbook* (pp. 73–91). Alexandria: ASCD.

Schaps, E., Battistich, V. & Solomon, D. (1997). School as a caring community: A key to character education. In A. Molnar (Ed.), *The construction of children's character, Part II, 96th Yearbook of the National Society for the Study of Education*. Chicago: University of Chicago Press.

Scheckner, S., Rollin, S. A., Kaiser-Ulrey, C. & Wagner, R. (2002), School violence in children and adolescents: A meta-analysis of the effectiveness of current interventions, *Journal of School Violence*, *1*(2), 5–32.

Seligman, M. (1995). *The optimistic child: A revolutionary approach to raising resilient children*. Milsons Point: Random House Australia.

Seligman, M. E. P. (2002). *Authentic Happiness*. Milsons Point: Random House Australia.

Severson, H. H. & Walker, H. M. (2002). Proactive approaches for identifying children at risk for sociobehavioral problems. In K. L. Lane, F. M. Gresham & T. E. O'Shaughnessy (Eds.), *Interventions for children with or at risk for emotional and behavioral disorders* (pp. 33–53). Boston: Allyn & Bacon.

Shechtman, Z. (1999). Bibliotherapy: An indirect approach to treatment of childhood aggression. *Child Psychiatry and Human Development*, *30*(1), 39–53.

Slavin, R. (1990). *Cooperative learning: Theory, research and practice*. Englewood Cliffs, NJ: Prentice Hall.

Slavin, R. (1995). Enhancing intergroup relations in schools: Cooperative learning and other strategies. In W. Hawley & A. Jackson (Eds), *Toward a common destiny: Improving race and ethnic relations* (pp. 291–314). San Francisco, CA: Jossey-Bass.

Stanley, M. & McGrath, H. (2005). Buddy systems: Peer support in action. In H. McGrath & T. Noble (Eds.). *Bullying solutions: Evidence-based approaches to bullying in Australian schools*. Frenchs Forest: Pearson Education.

Tolan, P. & Guerra, N. G. (1998). *What works in reducing adolescent violence: An empirical review of the field*. Boulder, CO: Institute of Behavioral Science, Regents of the University of Colorado.

Trent, F. (2001, August). *Aliens in the classroom or: The classroom as an alien place?* Paper presented at the Association of Independent Schools NSW Sex, Drugs & Rock 'n' Roll Conference.

Walker, H. M., Severson, H. H., Feil, E. G., Stiller, B. & Golly, A. (1998). First step to success: Intervening at the point of school entry to prevent antisocial behavior patterns. *Psychology in the Schools*, *35*(3), 259–269.

Weissberg, R. P. & Allen, J. P. (1986). Promoting children's social skills adaptive interpersonal behavior. In B. A. Edelstein & L. Michelson (Eds.), *Handbook of prevention* (pp. 153–175). New York: Plenum Press.

Weissberg, R. P. & Greenberg, M. T. (1998). School and community competence-enhancement and prevention programs. In Damon, W. (Ed.), *Handbook of child psychology* (Vol. 4) (5th ed.) (pp. 877–954). New York: Wiley.

Werner, E. (2000). Protective factors and individual resilience. In J. Shonkoff & S. Meisels (Eds.), *Handbook of early childhood intervention* (pp. 115–132). New York: Cambridge University Press.

Wilson, D. B., Gottfredson, D. C. & Najaka, S. S. (2001). School-based prevention of problem behaviors: A meta-analysis. *Journal of Quantitative Criminology*, *17*, 247–272.

CHAPTER 5

The P.E.A.C.E. Pack: A whole-school program for reducing school bullying

Phillip Slee

Introduction

In recent years there has been increasing global concern with school bullying and violence. A range of publications and international conferences have highlighted the concern in Europe (e.g. European Commission CONNECT Project on Violence in Schools, http://www.gold.ac.uk/connect), North America (e.g. Nansel, Overpeck, Pilla & Ruan, 2001), Canada (e.g. Pepler, Craig, Ziegler & Charach, 1994) and the Asia-Pacific Rim (e.g. Keeves & Watanabe, 2003). In Australia, the issue of school bullying, in particular, is presently attracting much media, research and government policy attention. There is no doubt that bullying is an all too prevalent feature of Australian schools and that it needs to be seriously addressed. Views on the issue range from rather idealistic, overly optimistic claims of 'bullyproofing' schools and students to the idea that the 'problematising' and sensationalising of child/youth violence is simply a symptom of 'ephebiphobia', or fear and loathing of young people.

What students say

The human misery of bullying is strongly conveyed in this story of an eleven year old boy referred to me by his doctor for counselling. As the boy described it: 'One thing that happened to me was that I was bashed up at school by one of the kids in my class. This kid kicked me in my legs and body. The teasing and bullying started in the first week of term one. It started with name-calling – Idiot, Carrot head, Freckle-face, Stuff-head, Dickhead, Loser. The kids excluded me from groups ... If I tried to play basketball with them at school they would tell me to "get lost". I hated that so much I spent more and more time in the library.'

What parents say

'If I were to find out that my child was being "bullied" by others at school and that the staff/teachers were aware of this but hadn't intervened – I would be both angry and disappointed and also disillusioned with the school.'

What teachers say

'Fairness, consistency, and transparency in policy and practice are needed to address school bullying effectively.'

Definition of school bullying

Bullying is widely regarded as a particularly destructive form of aggression. It can be defined as physical, verbal or psychological attack or intimidation that is intended to cause fear, distress or harm to the victim, where the intimidation involves an imbalance of power in favour of the perpetrator. Typically, there are repeated incidents over a period of time. There are variations in the definition of bullying (Slee, Ma, Hee-og, Taki & Sullivan, 2003; Smith, Cowie, Olafsson & Liefooghe, 2002). Taki, Slee and Murray-Harvey (2002) have argued that bullying is behaviour characterised by a power imbalance within a relationship context, involving repetition of the bullying behaviour, where the deliberate intent is to inflict mental suffering on the individual. While school bullying can assume the form of physical, verbal or indirect behaviour, the significant focus in this definition is on the intention to humiliate or embarrass the other in a group context.

International research into school bullying

The pioneering research of Dan Olweus in Norway and Peter Smith in England, and the outcomes of their successful practical intervention programs, heralded an international focus on the problem of school bullying. Outcomes of further international efforts to understand the nature of school bullying have been described in publications such as that by Smith et al. (1999), who have edited and drawn together the findings of research into bullying from over 22 countries.

Research of the last 25 years confirms the widespread nature of bullying and that it is particularly likely to occur in a group from which the potential victim cannot escape, e.g. schools. In particular, research highlights that children with special needs are particularly vulnerable to school bullying (Bottroff, 1998; Hugh-Jones & Smith, 1999). The international research suggests that there are cultural differences and similarities. For example, recent Australian and Japanese research has identified sex differences, with Australian boys using more verbal and direct means of bullying, while in Japan it is the girls who bully in this fashion (Murray-Harvey, Slee & Taki, article in preparation).

Research into bullying in Australian schools

In 1991 Rigby and Slee published the first Australian research on the incidence of bullying among students based on a sample of South Australian schools. In 1994 an Australian Federal Senate inquiry into school bullying resulted in the publication of an influential paper, 'Sticks and Stones: A Report on Violence in Schools'. This inquiry heralded a nationwide movement to address the issue of school violence, particularly bullying. One such move was the Alannah and Madeline Foundation's establishment of the National Coalition Against Bullying.

Australian research based on a sample of 25 000 indicates that over 20 per cent of males and 15 per cent of females report being bullied 'once a week or more often' (Rigby & Slee, 1999). A body of research has also focused on the relationship between bullying and gender (e.g. Owens, Shute & Slee, 2000; Shute, Owens & Slee, 2002).

Association of bullying with health and psychosocial and antisocial outcomes

In a study of the health of high school students the students reported on their experience of school victimisation and their level of physical health (Slee, 1995). The results showed that students who were most frequently bullied ('once a week or more often') were significantly more likely to suffer poorer health. Indications of suicidal ideation and attempts at self-harm were significantly associated with self-reports and peer reports of school bullying (Rigby & Slee, 1999). In this longitudinal study of adolescents over three years it was found that male and female students who reported a relatively high incidence of physical health complaints (e.g. headaches, stomachaches) in their first two years at high school had been victimised more frequently by their peers in the first two years at school. The links between bullying and poor health and suicidal ideation found in the Australian studies are consistent with the overseas research. In a meta-analytic review of 20 years of research, Hawker and Boulton (2000) concluded that it was clear that victimisation was positively associated with depression, loneliness, anxiety and low self-esteem, as well as poor social self-concept. They concluded by noting that cross-sectional studies '. . . demonstrate that victims of peer aggression suffer a variety of feelings of psychosocial distress. They feel more anxious, socially anxious, depressed, lonely and worse about themselves than non-victims' (p. 453).

In a summary of research Rigby and Slee (1999, p. 331) have noted that adolescent bullies were 'more likely than others to be absent from school, scrawl graffiti, shoplift and get into trouble with the police'.

Bullying and the law

In the last few years in Australia the legal aspect of bullying has been increasingly referred to in the press and in research (Slee & Ford, 1999). As Fehring (1998) concludes, there are rising community expectations that schools are required to deal with complex emotional and psychological problems which are part of the overall school experience. He goes on to note that:

> . . . teachers and schools are acting *in loco parentis* while a student is in their care. I believe that this requires teachers and schools to in fact actively intervene in any situation which comes to their knowledge which may involve significant risk of injury to a student in their care. This includes the risks of psychological injury so long as that injury is reasonably foreseeable. (p. 9)

Connell (2000, p. 68) notes 'A positive duty of care on the part of the school also arises in relation to bullying. The failure of a school to intervene may be a breach of that duty.'

The National Safe Schools Framework <http://www.ncab.org.au/> has set in place a procedure for addressing the issue of providing a safe learning environment. Schools are now being asked to develop anti-bullying policies, grievance procedures and intervention programs. The question raised here is: what best policy and practice will inform this imperative?

Value of intervention in reducing school bullying

As Eslea & Smith (1998, p. 203) have noted 'Most, if not all, children experience bullying at some time in their lives: they may be the victim, they may be the bully, or they may witness the suffering of others'. It has already been determined that up to a quarter of the Australian school population may be caught up at any one time in the cycle of bullying and victimisation, which begs the question of what the other three-quarters of the school population are doing (Salmivalli, Lagerspetz, Bjorkqvist, Osterman & Kaukiainen, 1996). There is now a significant body of research being conducted in Australia by Ken Rigby on the 'bystander' effect (Rigby, 2002).

Intervention to reduce school bullying has met with varying levels of success. There is a body of evidence which indicates that school-based intervention programs can be effective in reducing the level of school bullying (Attorney-General's Department, 2002; Smith, Pepler & Rigby, 2004). Widely known and well-documented evaluations include those by Olweus (1993), Smith (1996) and Pepler et al. (1994). Approximate effect sizes of intervention programs range from a 50 per cent reduction reported by Olweus (1993), 30–40 per cent reported by Clearihan et al. (1999) to a 30 per cent reduction reported by both Pepler et al. (1994) and Smith & Sharp (1999). Roland (1989) failed to find any reduction at all in the level of school bullying. However, one cannot easily compare the various intervention programs given the range and type of methods used and the procedures employed (Stevens, Bourdeaudhij & Van Oost, 2000).

A key element of intervention is the adoption of an *evidence-based approach*. This approach warrants that rigorous evaluation be integrated into decisions about intervention by policymakers and practitioners (Commonwealth of Australia, 2000). Adapting a model described by Mrazek and Haggerty (1994), cited in Commonwealth of Australia (2000), interventions may be targeted:

(a) universally at whole populations
(b) selectively at a population at risk

(c) indicatively at 'high-risk' individuals.

(a) and (b) are usually identified in terms of 'prevention' whereas (c) encompasses 'early intervention'.

Developmental differences should be taken into account in considering interventions. Knowledge about the specific ways in which children's understanding of violence changes as they mature is critical in designing effective programs for prevention and intervention (Buckley, 2000).

Countering bullying in the school community: The P.E.A.C.E. Pack program

A number of broad concepts underpin the P.E.A.C.E. Pack program including the idea that bullying is a wider community issue (Slee, 2001). This outlook is reflected in the growing number of organisations expressing some concern about this issue. Groups such as Safety House, Child Help-Line, and the Department of Community Services through Parenting South Australia and the National Coalition Against Bullying are just a few examples of where the issue of bullying is being addressed in the broader community context. The movement toward the wider community initiative is underpinned by the writing of authors such as Etzioni (1995) and Tam (1996). Etzioni (1995) describes the social webs of communities as binding individuals into groups of people who care for one another and who work together to help maintain a civic, social and moral order. A related facet of communitarianism is that of 'social capital'.

Social capital refers to features in a social organisation such as social networks, expectations and trust that facilitate coordination and cooperation for mutual benefit (Coleman, 1988; Putnam, 1999). It is derived from interpersonal relationships and an array of obligations, expectations, information channels and norms within families and communities. According to Hetherington (1999, p. 177), 'Social capital resides in relationships and social organizations that individuals may use to achieve their interests and that promote positive adjustment'. It is a resource and like other forms of capital can be drawn on or accessed as needed.

While limited research has examined possible links between social capital and child wellbeing, evidence exists for a link between social capital and school drop-out and an increase in child behaviour problems (Hetherington, 1999; Parcel & Menaghan, 1993; Runyan et al., 1998). And the National Mental Health Strategy (2000) identified school bullying as a significant risk factor in the development of mental health problems in children.

The P.E.A.C.E. Pack

The P.E.A.C.E. Pack is a systemically based intervention program (Slee, 2001). The program itself provides a framework for schools to assess the status of their anti-bullying policy in relation to policy and grievance procedures, curriculum initiatives and student social support programs. These components are organised and grouped under the acronym of P.E.A.C.E., which represents the orderly stages in the process of initiating, conducting and evaluating a program for reducing school bullying (Preparation, Education, Action, Coping and Evaluation). The actual pack provides practical resources, such as examples of policy and grievance procedures and lesson plans, as part of a comprehensive package for schools to develop their own intervention program.

Theoretically it draws on essential systemic principles (Slee & Shute, 2003) whereby the issue of school bullying is nested within relationships and understood in terms of social constructivist thought. Systemic thinking is sharply at odds with more conventional Western scientific thinking with its emphasis on remediation, deficits and weaknesses in the individual (Slee & Shute, 2003). In contrast to this 'deficit' approach, systemic thinking emphasises the active role of the individual in socially constructing meaning and has a strong focus on competency, success and individual strengths. It embraces the idea of the 'social', whereby meaning is constructed within the social setting of relationships, interactions and communication.

Broadly, interventions can involve 'first-order' change where individuals caught up in the bully-victim cycle may need some assistance and strategies to deal with bullying. The school system remains the same with the bully viewed as the 'bad' student in need of control and change and the victim viewed as an individual needing help and protection. If the view of the situation is accurate and constructive, and if in fact the students do simply need to acquire some new skills, then 'first-order' interventions have a place in an intervention program. There is certainly a well-documented body of evidence which attests to the value of such interventions (e.g. Owens, Shute & Slee, 2001).

'Second-order' change will occur when the system itself begins to change. For example, the school may gain some insight through a review of policy and practice as to how the current school procedures maintain and even amplify or encourage bullying. The school community in modifying attitudes, perceptions and beliefs may choose to approach the issue of bullying from a very different perspective. In shifting focus, and thinking in more systemic terms, change will resonate throughout the school system. Instead of concentrating on changing the 'bad' or problematic behaviour of the bully and on 'helping' the victim, consideration will be given to relationships, roles and interactions, and communication within the system, which encourage or discourage bullying. When the system itself begins to change or realign, second-order change has occurred.

First-order and second-order change and 'socially constructed' meaning are just some of the basic fundamentals underpinning systemic thinking, which provides the foundation for the P.E.A.C.E. program. Further details are to be found in Slee (2001).

The framework for interventions using the P.E.A.C.E. Pack is presented in Figure 5.1 and further details are available at <http://www.caper.com.au>.

Figure 5.1 P.E.A.C.E. Pack framework for intervention

PREPARATION

In this first stage emphasis is on gathering information regarding the nature of school bullying.

Summary: Lessons gleaned from national and international research

- The level of bullying is as high if not higher in Australian schools than overseas schools.
- Bullying is an identifiable form of violent behaviour.
- Bullying is part of the social fabric of the school and community which detracts from the social capital of the community.
- Schools and communities have a 'duty of care' to protect students from bullying.
- Bullying is associated with later antisocial behaviour and criminal activity amongst the perpetrators and poor mental health.
- outcomes for the victims

Action to take: Identify written resources, e.g. books, websites, video material addressing the issue of bullying. Establish a small working party including teachers, parents, students and community representatives.

EDUCATION

At this next stage information is provided to staff, students and parents regarding the impact of bullying on the school community.

Summary: Lessons gleaned from national and international research

- Child/youth bullying is a serious public health problem with far-reaching impact and consequences for the community.
- Bullying is a psychologically harmful, physically damaging and socially isolating feature of an unnecessarily large number of Australian children's school lives.
- Bullying inculcates a climate of 'fear' in the community.

Action to take: Conduct a school, parent or teacher survey on the issue of bullying, involving the students in preparing, conducting, analysing and presenting the findings.

ACTION

For teachers this means in-service; for students, lessons/programs; for parents information.

Summary: Lessons gleaned from national and international research

- Effective behaviour support is needed that bases interventions on the identification of functional relationships between bullying and environmental events or contextual variables rather than on punishment or aversive consequences. There is no evidence that sanctions suppressing aggressive behaviour help to reduce antisocial behaviour (Slee, 2002). Similarly, action which increases surveillance must be balanced against the feelings of vulnerability engendered by such interventions.

Figure 5.1 P.E.A.C.E. Pack framework for intervention *continued*

- Secondly, a graduated system of intervention to meet the needs of all students is warranted. At the first level are 'universal' interventions including the development of policy and grievance procedures and the use of effective teaching practices, e.g. creating 'safe' play areas. At the next level, 'targeted' interventions developed around the student's unique strengths, needs and behavior patterns are implemented, e.g. direct instruction in behavioural social skills.

Action to take: Audit your school regarding the development of policy/grievance procedures and the existence and effectiveness of programs (e.g. peer support) and practice (e.g. school security) to address bullying (see also <http://www.caper.com.au>*).*

Coping

In the PEACE Pack 'coping' is considered in terms of 'A B C'. Research into schools conducted by the author with a low incidence of bullying will be cited here.

Attitude

The longer term aim is the development of an attitude/ethos within the school/community which openly and directly addresses the issue of bullying. In the P.E.A.C.E. Pack schools with a low incidence of bullying had a vision/mission statement which captured a positive vision for the school, with an emphasis on creating a safe, caring community where bullying was sanctioned against. Policy statements in these schools:

- were developed and often driven by the students
- reflected student, staff and parent views
- emphasised the responsibility of the whole community in addressing bullying
- clearly defined bullying in simple terms
- were actively communicated to the community, e.g. through school newsletters
- were subject to regular review and evaluation.

Behaviours

Schools with a low incidence of bullying had clear behavioural strategies in place in terms of:

- grievance procedures for recording, reporting on and following up incidents
- clearly identified sanctions against bullying
- positive reinforcement for pro-social behaviour
- specific strategies for monitoring 'hot spots' where students felt 'unsafe' from bullying
- specific programs in place for teaching social skills, e.g. peer mediation, Student Representative Council activities
- training for staff members who received credit for addressing the issue.

Curriculum

Australian research indicates that constructive discussion of the topic of bullying is relatively easy to initiate amongst primary students and even amongst secondary students. About one-third are eager to discuss the issue (Rigby & Slee, 1999). To that end lessons may be developed around:

- Language arts – designing posters, writing/reading stories
- Maths – developing and evaluating school surveys
- Health/PE – examining the impact of bullying on student wellbeing
- Class meetings – running class discussions which address student concerns and action which can be taken; presenting at school assemblies on the issue.

Action to take: Use the P.E.A.C.E. Pack flow chart to evaluate the state of current school practice (see The P.E.A.C.E. Pack: A program for reducing bullying in our schools *or the website* <http://www.caper.com.au>).

continues

Figure 5.1 P.E.A.C.E. Pack framework for intervention *continued*

Evaluating (and celebrating)
It is important to find opportunity to celebrate the accomplishments of the whole school intervention program.

Action to take:
- announcements of progress at school assemblies
- class letters identifying ideas and accomplishments
- school newsletters
- parent information nights
- open days and displays at the school and local community shopping centres.

In relation to policy development, there is strong evidence to suggest that school bullying is a significant element of students' learning environments, which directly impinges on their health and wellbeing. While schools have a duty of care to fulfil, the issue of intervening to reduce school bullying is best understood within a broader community context. Bullying is seen as detracting from the social capital of the community.

P.E.A.C.E. Pack evaluations

A range of interventions using the P.E.A.C.E. Pack have been made in a number of schools in Australia and overseas at junior primary, primary and secondary school level and evaluations reported on (Slee, 1994, 1996). Recent one-year and three-year school interventions involving 954 students, comprising 458 males and 496 females ranging in age from 5 years to 13 years old, evaluated the effectiveness of the P.E.A.C.E. Pack program. For junior primary students 17 per cent of boys and 19 per cent of girls reported being bullied 'less' after the year-long intervention. Gains were generally made across the junior primary population with an increase in young students reporting:
- they could not join in bullying others (+ 4 per cent)
- knowing more about how to stop bullying (+ 18 per cent)
- knowing more about who to talk to if they were being bullied (+ 13 per cent), and
- they felt safer from being bullied (+ 22 per cent).

Overall, for the primary school students (aged 8–12 years), 29 per cent of boys and 20 per cent of girls reported being bullied 'less' after the year-long intervention. Gains were generally made across the primary school population with, on average, students reporting that they would know more about how to stop being bullied and who to talk to. And the gains were generally equivalent for males and females.

In a separate three-year study involving primary school students, on average 32 per cent and 33 per cent of students reported being 'bullied less' across the three-year period respectively. Findings from this study support the value of involving the Student Representative Council (SRC). The suggestion is that it is the ownership of anti-bullying initiatives by the student body and the broader community which enhances the impact of the P.E.A.C.E. process. In the schools where the SRC was actively involved significant improvements were made regarding student knowledge about who to talk to if they were being bullied and in the level of students feeling safe from bullying. This school had entered the program because of specific concerns by teachers regarding the level of school bullying. The school had no policy or grievance procedure in place regarding school bullying. Students were actively involved by teachers in developing and launching policy and grievance procedures and the school adopted a community-wide intervention program involving parents and community services such as the police. For example, the police community liaison unit ran sessions for the students on protective behaviours.

On launching its policy to the community, the school had helium balloons released carrying anti-bullying messages far and wide. The symbolism of this particular component was that school bullying is indeed a community issue. As an interesting aside, several of the balloons were carried up to 100 kilometres and messages of support for the school's initiative were sent in by members of the public upon finding the balloon messages.

Internationally, aspects of the P.E.A.C.E. Pack have been translated into Japanese and the program implemented in a number of Japanese middle schools (Slee & Taki, 1998). In the Japanese year-long school-based interventions, the implementation of the program has produced:

- positive changes in 'happiness at school' across Years 7 (3 per cent) and 8 (27 per cent)
- positive changes in attitude in the view that bullying is wrong in Year 7 (12 per cent) and Year 8 (4 per cent)
- a reduction in bullying (exclusion) of 13 per cent in Year 7 and 29 per cent in Year 8.

The preliminary findings from the Japanese intervention study using the P.E.A.C.E. Pack suggest that it is possible to adapt it cross-culturally to successfully intervene to reduce school bullying.

Overall, as noted by Stevens et al. (2000), outcomes of school anti-bullying intervention programs have produced effects ranging from very strong to almost negligible. The P.E.A.C.E. Pack interventions resulted in approximately one-fifth of students in the overall sample reporting that they were being bullied 'less' as a result of year-long interventions. In developing the resource, the explicit intention was not to provide a rigid, lock-step process for addressing school bullying. Rather, the purpose was to provide a resource that was adaptable to the socio-cultural background of the school.

Much remains to be done in order to understand the dynamics underpinning a successful intervention program, particularly in a cross-cultural setting. The experience of working to adapt the program cross culturally leads the author to conclude that historical, social and cultural factors impact significantly on the understanding and awareness of the issue of school bullying. To that end significant implications emerge in relation to the development of intervention programs in that they should be contextualised and not simply replicated from one school, or from one country, to another. Significantly, more research into the topic is needed to better inform 'best practice' intervention programs and avoid embracing ill-founded programs designed to meet a short-term political or social agenda.

Increasingly, school communities are taking up the challenge of examining bullying in a broader systemic sense (Slee, 2002). This involves more of a 'bottom up' approach aiming to engage both students and parents and reaching out to the wider community, including welfare and law enforcement agencies, and involving them in the development of community-based anti-bullying programs. Schools are also taking up the challenge of carefully examining their ethos and culture in the context of a socially critical curriculum as a means for reducing bullying.

Conclusion

School bullying is an issue that crosses individual, school, community, state and national boundaries. Its impact and effects are indeed far-reaching and now well documented and substantiated in the psychological research. Significantly, it has now crossed the boundary of what was once regarded by some, if not many, as 'acceptable' social behaviour. Outpourings in the media may thus be regarded as simply reflecting the significant voice of current individual and community concern regarding the issue. In the light of available evidence-based research the P.E.A.C.E. Pack provides guidelines for setting in place a program which would enable a community to argue that it had indeed more than fulfilled its duty of care to prevent bullying. In acting in the best interests of those deemed to be most vulnerable, the community would be seen to be fulfilling broader civic, social and moral imperatives.

REFERENCES

Attorney-General's Department (2002). A *meta-evaluation of methods and approaches to reducing bullying in pre-schools and early primary school in Australia*. Ken Rigby. Canberra: Commonwealth of Australia.

Bottroff, V. (1998). The development of friendship and the puzzle of autism. In P. T. Slee & K. Rigby (Eds.), *Children's peer relations* (pp. 91–106). London: Routledge.

Buckley, M. A. (2000). Cognitive-developmental considerations in violence: Prevention and intervention. *Professional School Counseling*, *4*, 60–70.

Child and Adolescent Psychological and Educational Resources (CAPER) (2001). P. T. Slee, *The P.E.A.C.E. Pack: A program for reducing bullying in our schools* (3rd ed.). Retrieved December 24, 2004, from <http://www.caper.com.au>

Clearihan, S., Slee, P. T., Souter, M., Gascoign, P., Nichols, A., Burgan, M. & Gee, J. (1999, May 25–26). *Antiviolence bullying prevention project*. Paper presented at Victimology Conference, Adelaide.

Coleman. J. S. (1988). Social capital in the creation of human capital. *American Journal of Sociology*, *94*, 95–120.

Commonwealth Department of Health and Aged Care (2000). *Promotion, prevention and early intervention for mental health: A monograph*. Canberra: Mental Health and Special Programs Branch, Commonwealth Department of Health and Aged Care.

Connell, S. (2000, February 26). Legal duties of teachers. *The Advertiser*, p. 68.

Eslea, M. & Smith, P. (1998). The long-term effectiveness of anti-bullying work in primary schools. *Educational Research*, *40*(2), 203–218.

Etzioni, E. (1995). *New communitarian thinking, persons, virtues, institutions, and communities*. Virginia: Virginia University Press.

Fehring, I. (1998). *Responsibility for supervising students: School law*. Sydney: LAAMS Publications.

Hawker, S. J. & Boulton, M. (2000). Twenty years' research on peer victimisation and psychosocial maladjustment: A meta-analytic review of cross-sectional studies. *Journal Child Psychology & Psychiatry*, *41*(4), 441–455.

Hetherington, M. (1999). Social capital and the development of youth from non-divorced, divorced, and remarried families. In W. A. Collins & B. Laursen (Eds.), *Relationships as developmental contexts*. New Jersey, Lawrence Erlbaum Assoc.

Hugh-Jones, S. & Smith, P. K. (1999). Self-reports of short and long-term effects of bullying on children who stammer. *British Journal of Educational Psychology*, 69, 141–158.

Keeves, J. & Watanabe, R. (Eds.) (2003). *The handbook on educational research in the Asia Pacific Region*. The Netherlands: Kluwer Academic Publishers.

Murray-Harvey, R., Slee, P. & Taki, M. Article in preparation.

Nansel, T. R., Overpeck, M., Pilla, R. S. & Ruan, W. J. (2001). Bullying behaviours among US youth: Prevalence and association with psychosocial adjustment. *Journal of American Medical Association*. *16*, 2094–2100.

National Coalition Against Bullying. Retrieved December 24, 2004, from <http://www.ncab.org.au/>

National Mental Health Strategy (2000). Retrieved February 5, 2005, from <http://www.mentalhealth.gov.au/resources/reports/pdf/nmhr2000>

Olweus, D. (1993). *Bullying in schools: What we know and what we can do.* Oxford: Blackwell.

Owens, L. Shute, S. R. & Slee, P. (2000). I'm in and you're out: Explanations for teenage girls indirect aggression. *Psychology, Evolution & Gender, 2*, 19–46.

Parcel, T. L. & Menaghan, E. G. (1993). Family social capital and children's behavior problems. *Social Psychology Quarterly*, 56, 120–135.

Pepler, D., Craig, W., Ziegler, S. & Charach, A. (1994). An evaluation of an anti-bullying intervention in Toronto schools. *Canadian Journal of Community Mental Health, 13*, 95–110.

Putnam R. D. (1999). Bowling alone: America's declining social capital. *Journal of Democracy*, 6, 65–78.

Rigby, K. (2002). *New perspectives on bullying.* London and Philadelphia: Jessica Kingsley Publisher.

Rigby, K. & Slee, P. T. (1991). Bullying among Australian school children: Reported behaviour and attitude towards victims. *Journal of Social Psychology, 131*, 615–627.

Rigby. K. & Slee, P. T. (1999). Suicidal ideation among adolescent schoolchildren, involvement in bully/victim problems and perceived low social support. *Suicide and life-threatening behaviour, 29*, 119–130.

Roland, E. (1989). Bullying: The Scandinavian tradition. In D. P. Tattum & D. A. Lane (Eds.), *Bullying in schools* (pp. 21–32). London: Trentham Books.

Runyan D. K., Hunter, M. H., Socolar, R. R., Amaya-Jackson, L., English, D., Landsverk, J., Dubowitz, H., Browne, D. H., Bangiwala, S. I., Mathew, R. M. (1998). Children who prosper in unfavorable environments: The relationship to social capital. *Pediatrics, 101*, 12–18.

Salmivalli, C., Lagerspetz, K., Bjorkqvist, K., Osterman, K. & Kaukiainen, A. (1996). Bullying as a group process: Participant roles in their relation to social status within the group. *Aggressive Behavior, 22*(1), 1–15.

Shute, R., Owens, L. & Slee, P.T. (2002). You just look at them and give them daggers: Adolescent girls use of nonverbal aggression. *International Journal of Adolescence, 10*, 353–372.

Slee, P. & Taki, M. (1998). The PEACE Pack evaluations of interventions to reduce school bullying in Japan. A paper presented at ISSBD, Berne, Switzerland.

Slee, P. T. (1994, January). I'm a victim – stop bullying. In K. Oxenberry, K. Rigby & P. T. Slee (Eds.), *Children's peer relations: Cooperation and conflict* (pp. 19–22). Adelaide: University of South Australia.

Slee, P. T. (1995). Bullying: Health concerns of Australian secondary school students. *International Journal of Adolescence and Youth, 5*, 215–224.

Slee, P. T. (1996). The P.E.A.C.E. Pack: A program for reducing bullying in our schools. *Australian Journal of Guidance and Counselling*, 6, 63–69.

Slee, P. T. (2001). *The PEACE Pack: A program for reducing bullying in our schools* (3rd ed.). Adelaide: Flinders University.

Slee, P. T. (2002). *Child, adolescent & family development* (2nd ed.). Melbourne: Cambridge University Press.

Slee, P. T. & Ford, D. (1999). Bullying is a serious issue – it is a crime! *Australian & New Zealand Journal of Law and Education*, 4(1), 23–39.

Slee, P. T. & Murray-Harvey, R. (2001). A comparative study of Australian and Japanese student's school lives. Unpublished study.

Slee, P. T. & Shute, R. (2003). *Child development: Thinking about theories*. London: Arnold.

Slee, P. T., Ma, L., Hee-og, S., Taki, M. & Sullivan, K. (2003). School bullying in five countries in the Asia-Pacific Region. In J. Keeves & R. Watanabe (Eds.), *The handbook on educational research in the Asia Pacific Region*. The Netherlands: Kluwer Academic Publishers.

Smith, P. K. (1996). England and Wales. In P. K. Smith, Y. Morita, J. Junger-tas, D. Olweus, R. Catalano and R. & P. Slee (Eds.) (pp. 68–90). *The nature of school bullying: A cross-national perspective*. London: Routledge.

Smith, P. K & Sharp, S. (Eds.) (1999). *School bullying: Insights and perspectives*. London: Routledge.

Smith, P. K., Cowie, H., Olafsson, N. & Liefooghe, A. P. D. (2002). Definitions of bullying: A comparison of terms used, and age and gender differences, in a fourteen-country international comparison. *Child Development*, *73*, 1119–1133.

Smith, P. K., Morita, Y., Junger-tas, J., Olweus, D., Catalano, R. & Slee, P. (1999). *The nature of school bullying: A cross-national perspective*. London: Routledge.

Smith, P. K., Pepler, D. & Rigby, K. (2004). *Bullying in schools: How successful can interventions be?* Cambridge: Cambridge University Press.

Stevens, V., Bourdeauhij, I. D. & Oost, P. V. (2000). Bullying in Flemish schools: An evaluation of anti-bullying interventions in primary and secondary schools. *British Journal of Educational Psychology*, *70*, 195–210.

Taki, M., Slee, P. T. & Murray-Harvey, R. (2002, August). *Life at school in Australia and Japan: Modeling the impact of stress and support on school bullying amongst girls*. Paper presented at symposium on International Society Study of Behavioural Development, Canada.

Tam, H. (1996). Education and the communitarian movement. *Pastoral Care in Education*, *14*(3), 1-10.

CHAPTER 6

Buddy systems: Peer support in action

Maree Stanley and Helen McGrath

Introduction

Peer support systems are increasingly being used in schools to promote a pro-social culture and prevent bullying. At the same time research is confirming that social and emotional learning is just as important as academic learning in its impact on student achievement and wellbeing (Schaps & Battistich, 2002; CASEL, 2003; Child Development Project, <http://www.devstu.org/cdp/index.html>). Cotton (1995) has identified the preparedness of teachers to promote respect and empathy and to create opportunities for students to serve as peer resources for one another as key aspects of school effectiveness.

As part of the movement towards incorporating social and emotional learning in schools, there has been a particular emphasis on those school initiatives that have the most potential to reduce the likelihood of student bullying and other forms of violence. These directions include:

- *Creating caring, safe and supportive learning environments* where students are affirmed rather than put down. A safe school environment fosters learning.

- *Fostering student connectedness* (i.e. feelings of belonging, being known, being affirmed and being accepted) in the school and classroom.
- *Teaching pro-social values* such as cooperation, respect for the rights and feelings of others, friendliness, acceptance of difference and compassion (McGrath & Noble, 2003).
- *Developing students' social competencies* (Ballard, Argus & Remley, 1999; McGrath & Francey, 1991; McGrath & Noble, 2003).
- *Developing responsible and ethical behaviour* not just compliance with rules because of adult supervision, rewards or punishment. Social and emotional cognition is the most important factor in the development of responsible behaviour (Bear, Manning & Izzard, 2003).
- *Implementing peer support systems* such as buddy programs, peer mediation, peer counselling and peer tutoring (Cowie & Wallace, 2000).

As schools begin to acknowledge the significance of students' social and emotional needs, a variety of exciting intervention programs for schools have emerged that have the potential to change bullying cultures in schools to ones of respect, care and support (Elias & Weissberg, 2000). These interventions can help schools to educate their students to become responsible, socially skilled, healthy, caring and contributing citizens who treat each other decently (Weissberg, Kumpfer & Seligman, 2003).

Reducing bullying by promoting care, cooperation and respect contributes to the development of schools which are high in community and connectedness and have a positive school climate (Schaps & Lewis, 1999). School climate reflects students' perception of a school's environment. It can be considered the 'personality' of a school and it distinguishes one school from another. A school's emotional and social climate influences the behaviour of its students (Hoy & Miskel, 1991). A sense of community and a positive school climate predispose students to adopt the goals and values of the school (Schaps & Lewis, 1999) and contribute to students' later development of:

- intrinsic academic motivation and high aspirations
- compassion and concern for others
- preparedness and skilfulness in resolving conflicts fairly
- altruistic behaviour
- intrinsic pro-social motivation
- inclusive rather than exclusive attitudes toward others
- positive interpersonal behaviour in class and in the playground (Battistich et al., in press; Bryk & Driscoll, 1988; Hawkins, Catalano, Kosterman, Abbott & Hill, 1999; Schaps, 1999).

Peer support systems offer one effective way to produce a connected, respectful and supportive school community.

Peer support systems

Cowie and Sharp (1996) have categorised peer support systems into three broad categories: befriending systems, conflict resolution systems (peer mediation) and counselling-based systems (peer counselling). However, they also note that there is some overlap between these categories.

In *befriending peer support*, students are asked to act as a temporary friend towards another student and offer support and friendship. This is the easiest approach to implement in a school because it is not as structured and complex as the other forms of peer support (Gini, 2004).

In *conflict resolution peer support*, nominated or self-nominated students are trained to mediate disputes between peers. Although mutual conflict is different from bullying, a school where conflict is managed well is more likely to be a school where there is less likelihood of bullying because of the positive and pro-social ethos that is created.

In *peer counselling support*, nominated or self-nominated students are trained to assist students in distress (e.g. because they are being bullied) through the use of simple counselling skills such as listening, showing understanding and support, and helping with problem solving.

Peer support systems always involve the participation of students in rejecting bullying behaviour (Hobden, 2003). They can contribute to positive peer pressure, improving young people's relationships with their peers and empowering them to take increased responsibility for themselves within the school community (Hobden, 2003). Many educational writers have suggested that there is a desire on the part of most young people to care for and support younger peers and/or peers in distress, despite not feeling confident that they have the skills to do so (e.g. Cowie & Sharp, 1996; Rigby, 1997). Luxmoore (2000) asserts that this is an intrinsic motivation which probably stems from sibling experiences.

Positive benefits from peer support systems

Cowie and Wallace (2000) have demonstrated that peer support programs can help students to feel more empowered to protect themselves from negative behaviour, such as bullying. A number of research studies have also shown that there are benefits not only to the students who are being supported, but also to the students who provide the support and to the school as a whole (Ames, Charlton, Leo & Indoe, 1991; Cowie, 2000; Cowie & Sharp, 1996; de Rosenroll, 1989; Sharp, Sellars & Cowie, 1994; Sprinthall, Hall & Gerber, 1992).

Cowie (1998) surveyed and interviewed peer supporters and teachers in two primary and seven secondary schools in the UK. A variety of peer support systems had been well established in these schools for at least 12 months as part of a school anti-bullying policy. The peer support systems that had been used included informal befriending schemes, peer mediation of conflict, and schemes in which selected students acted as peer counsellors, by request, for students who had problems with bullying or related issues. Both students who had been bullied and teachers reported that peer support systems had helped them to deal with the bullying (Naylor & Cowie, 1999). The peer supporters (older students) reported an increase in self-confidence and an enhanced ability to see things from other people's viewpoints. Peer supporters and the teachers in charge were all in agreement that the peer support schemes had provided an opportunity for them to learn useful interpersonal and helping skills, enhanced their sense of responsibility and given them an effective approach against bullying in their school. For peer supporters, the two most frequently mentioned benefits were the acquisition of skills and the opportunity to demonstrate that they cared. Following the introduction of the peer support systems across the schools, it became more acceptable for bystanders to report bullying incidents. There was a higher rate of 'telling' in peer support schools than in schools where no peer support system was in place (Naylor, Cowie & del Rey, 2001). The study suggested that the existence of peer support systems not only benefits those involved, but can also promote a climate of caring within the school that may ultimately facilitate the reporting of bullying and reduce its frequency.

In a larger similar study of 51 secondary schools that had an established peer support system in place, Naylor and Cowie (1999) interviewed not only peer supporters and teachers but also the recipients of the peer support in Year 7 (aged 11–12 years) and Year 9 (aged 13–14 years). They reported that 82 per cent of the 60 students who had used the services of peer supporters said they had found the schemes to be either *very helpful* or *helpful*. Peer support users mostly commented that the systems had provided someone they could talk to who would listen to their concerns, that this gave them the strength to deal with the problem, and that they felt that somebody cared about what was happening to them. Many of the peer supporters commented that they appreciated having a chance to make a difference to a real problem in the school.

One of the difficulties with research into the effectiveness of real-life peer support systems (such as was conducted in these studies) is that there is usually a mixture of different types of peer support systems in place. This means that it is impossible to ascertain which *kind* of peer support system is more or less effective. It is not uncommon, especially in secondary schools, to find that peer support systems evolve over time into different forms anyway (ACRO, <http://www.acro.com.au/buddy.html>). Cowie, Naylor, Talamelli, Chauhan & Smith (2002) carried out follow-up research into how the peer support schemes that they had studied three years beforehand had evolved over time. They found that they had become more flexible and incorporated features from several peer support categories. Overall there had been a shift away from formal, counselling-based models to a more informal, befriending approach to peer support. Peer supporters were more likely to be proactive and visible in the playground in order to advertise their service. They also began to socialise with younger students, whether they had a problem with bullying or not. This meant that peer support was more available and salient to more students than before. There was widespread support for the systems and a strong sense that both teachers and peer supporters were increasingly confident about the value of their service. The schemes were not without their problems, however, including some difficulties in the recruitment and retention of boys as peer supporters because of peer pressure to conform to a 'macho' image (Cowie, Naylor, Talamelli, Chauhan & Smith, 2002). A peer support program in a middle school in Tuscany (Menesini, Codecasa, Benelli & Cowie, 2003) also found that peer support models were more effective with girls than with boys (Naylor & Cowie, 1999).

Similar positive outcomes were identified by the Mental Health Foundation (UK) <www.mentalhealth.org.uk/peer/> in their evaluation of a number of funded peer support programs across five secondary schools in 1998. The programs focused more on peer counselling and mentoring of younger students by older students, but there were mixed elements. The older students who acted as peer supporters reported improved confidence and social skills, a greater understanding of other people's feelings and behaviour, more open-mindedness and a stronger sense of responsibility. Younger students who had received peer support reported that they had developed more skills in expressing their feelings, had increased their sense of trust, felt safer and had a sense of being listened to. The coordinators of the programs across the five schools believed that the program had helped to create a friendly environment and reduce bullying in the school.

Baginsky (2004) evaluated a peer support system implemented in seven primary schools and seven secondary schools. The goals of the schools involved in the project were mostly focused on the reduction of negative playground behaviour such as bullying, conflict and aggression, the development of respect and positive relationships, and improved behaviour (Baginsky, 2004). The main focus was on older students being trained and available for peer counselling of younger students. At the end of 12 months, only 8 of the 14 schools were still using the programs but participants in those 8 schools reported being satisfied with the positive outcomes.

The power of the peer group can also be used to stop bullying (Salmivalli, 2001). Salmivalli (1999) evaluated the effects of a slightly different peer support initiative. The program was very short and involved a peer-led intervention campaign against school bullying carried out by 8 'peer counsellors' over 1 week in 12 classes of seventh and eighth grade students in a high school in southern Finland. The peer counsellors emphasised in their campaign and class visits that each student in the school had a role to play in either encouraging or discouraging bullying. The campaign was especially effective among girls, with a decrease in bullying among girls and an increase in self-reported willingness to influence bullying problems in their class. There was a slight decrease in self-reported bullying by boys, but this was not confirmed by peer reports. Nevertheless, most students who had reported being bullied before the campaign were satisfied with the campaign and thought it had been helpful.

Cross-age peer tutoring

One very distinctive and well-researched form of peer support is that of cross-age tutoring, in which an older student both befriends a younger student and works with them on a regular basis to teach and revise academic content. Hundreds of evaluations of cross-age tutoring studies indicate that cross-age tutoring can contribute to positive academic gains and affective growth for both the tutors and the younger students (Benard, 1990; Fletcher, 2000; Gaustad, 1993; Kalkowski, 1995; Topping & Ehly, 1998). Topping and Bryce (2004) demonstrated that even a very brief cross-age peer tutoring program, in which 11-year-olds taught 7-year-olds, significantly improved their learning and use of thinking skills. Cross-age tutoring increases enjoyment and engagement of both students, increases requests for assistance, and creates more positive attitudes to the content being taught (Utay & Utay, 1997). Studies have also shown that cross-age peer tutoring can also reduce absenteeism and disciplinary referrals (Maher, 1982). Gaustad (1993) argues that cross-age tutoring is advantageous for the older tutoring students because they have more opportunities to review and rework material, reflect on the purpose of a task and practise organisational skills.

Many studies also attest to the affective and social gains for both younger and older students from being involved in cross-age peer tutoring, such as improved social skills (Gaustad, 1993; Topping & Ehly, 1998; Utay & Utay, 1997) and enhanced self-respect and pride (Fitzsimons-Lovett, 1998; Gensemer, 2000; Goodlad & Hirst, 1989). Older tutors benefit from being a role model and being looked up to by another student. Both feel a sense of personal accomplishment and competence, and they grow in their understanding and compassion for each other (McAllister, 1990). In her evaluation of a combined cross-age tutoring and 'big buddy' program in a secondary setting, Gensemer (2000) also found that the use of derogatory language (put-downs) had reduced for both tutors and younger students after three months involvement with the program.

Buddy programs

Research suggests that it is possible for schools to empower students to help and care for younger students by the adoption of buddy systems, which facilitate a cooperative and caring climate (Foot, Morgan & Shute, 1990; Hertz-Lazarowitz & Miller, 1992). Buddy systems promote intimacy between older and younger peers through regular collaboration between their classes, and this fosters a sense of whole-school community (Schaps & Lewis, 1999). Rigby (1997) has noted that programs such as buddy systems that contribute to the building of positive peer relations also have the potential to reduce school bullying.

The essential characteristic of a buddy system is that it involves older students participating in positive, supportive, structured and facilitated one-on-one relationships with younger students. In most cases the formal buddy relationship continues for one year. Buddy programs would be categorised under Cowie and Sharp's (1996) scheme as a 'befriending' peer support system.

A buddy system can strengthen school community and help to challenge stereotypes, misconceptions or fears that students hold about younger or older age groups. A buddy system can also help students to feel valued and supported, teach important social skills and create a caring ethos in the school (Schaps & Battistich, 2002). They can create feelings of connectedness that enable both older and younger 'buddies' to bond more closely with their school within a psychologically safe environment, thereby increasing the likelihood of more positive school behaviour (Schaps & Battistich, 2002; Schaps & Lewis, 1999). When students feel connected to their school, they also feel valued and safe and are less likely to either bully or be bullied. A buddy system can also help schools to cultivate respectful and supportive relationships between students and teachers as they share a common purpose and common goals, incorporating fairness, empathy, responsibility and concern for others (Developmental Studies Center, <http://www.devstu.org>).

Buddy systems have been used extensively in Australian schools to create caring, friendly and safe communities, and to reduce bullying. They can have several different components and can be categorised according to the combination of these components.

There are four main combinations of components:

- The Friendship Only Buddy Model
- The Mentoring Buddy Model
- The Friendship + Mentoring Buddy Model
- The Friendship + Tutoring Buddy Model

Friendship only

In this model the focus is totally on friendship and organised social interaction between the older and younger students in a one-on-one context. As part of the interaction, the older student is available for emotional and social support as needed in the playground. This model is more commonly used in primary schools, most often with older buddies from the two oldest year levels in the school and younger buddies from the two youngest year levels of the school. Students in the first year of school entry (aged 5–6 years) are more commonly in the role of younger buddies and the system facilitates the transition process from pre-school into formal primary school.

Mentoring

In a mentoring buddy model, the focus is more on emotional and social support and, in some cases, the teaching of social and personal skills. It is more a 'show the way' model, and the older student's role is to pass on their knowledge, experience and judgment, and provide guidance and friendship (Powell, 1997). Mentoring buddy programs are more commonly used in secondary schools, usually with a student in Year 11 (aged 16–17 years) mentoring a student in Year 7 or 8 (aged 12–14 years). However, this can vary from school to school. There is usually some friendly organised social interaction at the beginning of the year with a 'get-to-know-you' focus. If the younger students have just made the transition from primary school, then the older mentors support and facilitate this process. For the rest of the year, the contact is more on the basis of older buddies being available to emotionally and socially support their younger buddy as requested. Sometimes there is a regular meeting time in small groups or in a whole-class setting where the purpose is for the older mentors to teach and facilitate discussions about personal or social issues such as bullying, values, conflict or friendship.

Friendship plus mentoring

This model integrates friendship, support, organised social interaction and the teaching of personal and social skills as outlined above.

Friendship plus tutoring

This model is characterised by friendship, support, organised social interaction and regular sessions in which the older buddy helps their younger buddy to learn or revise academic content, usually in the areas of literacy or numeracy.

Examples of the four buddy models

Schools using one of the four buddy models are described below.

School A (Primary): Friendship Buddy Model

All students in Year 6 are paired with one of the students who is entering their first year of primary school. If the numbers are uneven, some younger students have two buddies or some older students share a younger student. Older buddies first meet their younger buddy at the end of the previous year when the younger students attend an orientation session at the school while on a pre-school visit. The older buddies spend a lot of time with them in the first three weeks of the school year to assist them to understand where things are and how things work. After that, weekly buddy sessions of one hour's duration are held. These mostly involve socialisation activities such as playing games, reading stories, etc. In the playground it is very common for buddies to seek each other out at some point to say hello. Younger students often seek out their older buddies if they have a problem in the playground, such as being bullied, feeling left out, losing their jumper, etc. Older buddies are asked to help with wet weather activities in the younger classrooms. At the end of the year there is a formal ceremony (plus certificates) to acknowledge the role of the older buddy.

School B (Secondary): Mentoring Buddy Model

Year 11 students are paired with Year 8 students to assist with their transition to high school (which begins in this school's state in Year 8). They meet their younger buddy in the previous year when they make a one-day visit to the high school. As a group, older mentors organise a 'Buddy Adventure Trail' for the younger students to help them to find and familiarise themselves with the locations of various places in the school. There is a lot of scheduled contact during the first few weeks. Weekly sessions are scheduled during which the older mentors meet individually with their younger buddy to 'debrief' the week. During the rest of the year, the mentors plan activities to discuss personal and social issues in small groups with their younger buddies (e.g. bullying, organisational skills, friendship, etc.). The mentors are given the topics but are expected to meet beforehand and plan these group sessions. It is assumed that younger students will contact their mentors if they have problems. For example, one Year 8 student contacted his mentor to talk about a situation in which he had, with the urging of another Year 8 student, stolen some money from another student. He felt guilty and didn't know how to handle it. The mentor acted as an advocate for him when he spoke to the year level coordinator.

School C (Primary): Friendship + Mentoring Buddy Model

School C uses the Alannah and Madeline's 'Buddy Bear' program <www.buddybear.com.au>. This program is very similar to the model used in school A. Additionally, a character called Buddy Bear is the focus of the program. A buddy week is held in the first two weeks of Term 1 during which there are buddy activities every day. There is a parent information night at which some of the older buddies present an outline of how the buddy program works and perform items related to the pro-social values of the school. Over the year, not only do they meet individually with their buddy at a regular time for social interaction and games, the older buddies also work in small groups to plan and deliver drama activities, games and presentations on pro-social values and bullying to their buddy classes. These are followed up with one-on-one activities on these topics with their buddies.

School D (Primary): Friendship + Cross-age Tutoring Buddy Model

School D uses a similar model to that of school A but Year 5 students are paired with Year 2 students. Additionally, each older buddy has two weekly half-hour teaching sessions with their younger buddy with a focus on spelling, word meaning and simple maths facts and processes. After being trained, older buddies also take turns to assist the Year 2 teachers by working with small groups of the younger students during the morning literacy and numeracy blocks.

School E (Primary and Secondary): Friendship + Cross-age Tutoring Buddy Model

Selected students in Year 9 at the local high school 'buddy' selected Year 6 students at the local primary school. The two schools are not very far apart and they meet twice weekly for an hour at the primary school. The main focus is on friendship, social interaction and support, but the older buddies also plan and implement teaching activities (individual or small group) on academic content as advised by the teachers of the Year 6 students. The relationship lasts for a year and for two months of the following year as the younger students are also 'buddied' (friendship and assistance only) when they make the transition to the high school in the following year. Each older secondary buddy makes a manual of 'how to survive high school' for their younger primary school buddy.

Positive aspects of buddy systems

A buddy system makes it easier for younger students to ask an older student for help with a problem. Several researchers have noted that many young people find it difficult to ask for help, viewing it as an admission of failure in their own and others' eyes (Garland & Zigler, 1994; Le Surf & Lynch, 1999). Others have speculated that young people may be more reluctant to seek assistance from adults and more receptive to the idea of approaching older students because the age and status gaps between themselves and adults may be too large (Baginsky, 2004). Those students most in need of support may also be the least likely to seek help from adults (Garland & Zigler, 1994) but may be prepared to ask for help from an older buddy or mentor.

Older students may be able to demonstrate more understanding of the particular concerns their younger buddies face, may have greater credibility and approachability, and may be more readily and regularly available (Baginsky, 2004). Older students have, in many cases, experienced some of the situations that the younger student is currently facing (De Paulo et al., 1989; Gensemer, 2000). A further advantage of a buddy system is that, when all students in the class or year level are involved as buddies or mentors (and this isn't always so), boys express less reluctance to become involved than they sometimes do in other types of peer support schemes where not every student is involved (Cowie, 2000; Sharp & Cowie, 1998).

Buddy systems, like most peer-led interventions, are very engaging (Tindall, 1995) as students are involved in behaviours they would naturally enjoy with each other, such as talking to one another, playing games, being recognised for their efforts and being actively involved (Topping & Ehly, 1998). After being in buddy roles, students report feeling proud of themselves, and say that they enjoy the opportunity to demonstrate that they care. Through their experience of the friendships of buddies/mentors children may be motivated to create similar relationships with other students (Kemple, 2004). Buddy systems can enable students to become more understanding of each other and more accepting of individual differences (Fletcher, 2000).

Buddy systems have been shown to lead to the development of stronger pro-social values and improved social skills in all students, especially the skills of listening and conflict management (Developmental Studies Center, 1996; Pierce, Stahlbrand & Armstrong, 1984). Older buddies accept some responsibility for the behaviours of their younger buddies and are more motivated to behave well and act kindly in order to impress their younger buddy and be a positive role model (Pierce et al., 1984).

Cross-age buddy relationships can provide students with opportunities to practise social skills without some of the threats and expectations that may accompany same-age socialisation. Older students may feel freer to adopt a warm and friendly manner with their younger buddies and this can have a positive modelling effect on the younger students (Developmental Studies Center, 1996).

The Child Development Project (CDP), which began in 1982, is a primary/secondary whole-school program that is designed to create caring school communities. A buddy system with peer tutoring is a key element of the program, which also includes class meetings, the use of cooperative learning strategies, school-wide activities and parent-school involvement (Schaps & Battistich, 2002). Several researchers (e.g. Battistich, Schaps, Watson, Solomon & Lewis, 2001; Solomon, Battistich, Watson, Schaps & Lewis, 2000) have evaluated the effects of the project over the last few years and have identified many positive outcomes for students such as:

- an increase in pro-social values and pro-social behaviour
- better social skills, and especially conflict-management skills
- reduced bullying, aggression and drug usage
- more positive attitudes towards school and their teachers.

Youngerman (1998) evaluated a successful but slightly unusual buddy program in a primary school which featured cross-age student buddies as well as cross-grade teacher buddies. The class teachers involved met weekly to plan two combined teaching sessions with both classes. The teachers identified an improvement in the level of respect in both classrooms after the buddy system was implemented. Greater respect of others leads to a psychologically safer environment which fosters learning. Problems with bullying decreased, students became more accepting of others and some parents reported that their children made fewer derogatory remarks about classmates (Youngerman, 1998).

Adam (1997) reported on the effectiveness of a friendship only buddy program in a primary school, in which Year 7 students (in their last year of primary) were paired with Year 1 students (in their first year of primary). Her conclusions were that the buddy program had been very effective and had helped to develop the values of responsibility, tolerance and sensitivity in the Year 7 students. Almost all of the older students had enjoyed being a buddy and felt that being given the responsibility of being a buddy had helped them develop a more tolerant attitude towards young children. Many students reported that they believed that the buddy program had reduced bullying in the school. Additionally, the Year 1 students felt the buddies had been instrumental in helping them settle happily into life in school. The Year 7 students also raised some concerns that they had with the system. Some felt they had little free time for themselves. Some experienced difficulties knowing how to respond to misbehaviour by their younger buddy, and some were concerned that their involvement may have hindered their younger buddies in making friends at their own age level. Their suggestions for change were that only students who wanted to be a buddy should take on the role, that they should work with a small group rather than one student to ensure that same-age friendships were not hindered, and that it would be better to have a more specific teaching role with their buddies.

A friendship only buddy program involving students from Year 10/11 and students from Year 8 was developed and trialled in 1994 in a Brisbane high school over a 12-month period. The program was a youth development/social justice initiative of the Australian Community Safety and Research Organisation (ACRO) <http://www.acro.com.au/buddy.html>. The buddy system was originally developed to reduce bullying and levels of fear amongst younger students. However, over time, it evolved into more of a mentor-style buddy program. Older buddies were trained in a two-day workshop. Each group of three Year 10/11 was allocated to a group of three Year 8 students. Older buddies/mentors met weekly to plan and debrief with a supervisor and twice weekly with their younger buddies. They also organised sporting activities for the younger students. Buddies were most active in the first two terms of the year. Evaluation was conducted through a questionnaire completed by all students involved and feedback was described as 'extremely positive'. However, the program was discontinued due to lack of funding.

Effective practices in buddy systems

Many features of buddy systems have been suggested by researchers and theorists as critical to success (e.g. Flaxman, Ascher & Harrington, 1988; Powell, 1997). These include:

- training and debriefing for the older students
- addition of peer tutoring
- optimal age difference between buddies
- voluntary participation only
- effective preparation

- commitment
- awareness within the school community
- teacher 'buddying'.

Each of these features will now be elaborated in more detail.

Training and debriefing for the older students

The importance of good training for older buddies/mentors has been stressed by many researchers (e.g. Cowie & Sharp, 1996; Hobden, 2003; Sharp, Sellars & Cowie, 1994). Some of the issues that need to be included in training are:

- Older buddies/mentors must understand the limits and boundaries of the system and their roles and expectations (Adam, 1997).
- Students need guidelines as to how quickly they should 'solve' a younger buddy's problem (Baginsky, 2004).
- Students need to have some skills in handling the misbehaviour of younger buddies (Adam, 1997) and knowing when and how to ask for teacher support in this situation.

There have also been some suggestions that teachers should debrief weekly with the older students about issues that arise and also offer encouragement and feedback (Bloom, 1978). Teacher monitoring has also been suggested as being crucial to the success of any buddy program that also involves cross-age peer tutoring. The teacher needs to be sure that the older buddy has a good grasp of the material or skills to be taught (Tansy & de Barona, 1996).

Addition of peer tutoring

The addition of peer tutoring has also been suggested as a factor which can increase the success of a buddy program (Adam, 1997; Bloom, 1978). Older buddies/mentors can be involved in teaching social skills and values, or about bullying (as in a mentoring program), or academic content and thinking skills (Gensemer, 2000; Topping & Bryce, 2004). By adding a component of teaching of any kind, there is more emphasis on the older student learning to take the perspective of another. However, Shariff (2003) asserts that research clearly directs that the emphasis in buddy systems that also include a component of teaching needs to be more on the development of support, respect and relationships than on specific methods of instruction or content.

Optimal age difference between buddies

Bloom (1978) has proposed that the most successful age difference between buddies is at least three years. De Paulo et al. (1989) found that buddy partners who were similar in age were the most threatened in a buddy peer tutoring relationship because of their social comparison, whereas those who had significant gaps in their ages were the least threatened by the buddy tutoring relationship.

Voluntary participation only

In one evaluation of a buddy system (Adam, 1997) the older buddies (aged 11–12 years) suggested that only students who wanted to be involved should be buddies and that not everyone wanted to. However, one could argue that, in some cases, those that might be less interested could well be those most in need of the experience.

Effective preparation

There is clear evidence from research that, to be effective, buddy systems need good preparation and that time and consideration needs to be given to systematic planning (Samway, Whang & Pippitt, 1995; Tansy & de Barona, 1996). This includes making decisions about partnerships, designing activities, training the older students, informing the younger students about what is happening, and developing ways of monitoring and evaluating the process. Consideration should also be given to accepting that a lot of time is required to set up buddy programs during the initial stages (Bloom, 1978). Buddy programs that consider such components as readiness, preparation, selection, implementation, supervision, and evaluation have been found to be more readily accepted by administrators, teachers, students and families (Ehly, 1986; Hawryluk & Smallwood, 1988). Well-planned programs are more effectively integrated into schools than programs that are not well-articulated from the outset (Greenwood, Carta & Maheady, 1991).

Commitment

There is evidence (e.g. Schaps, Battistich & Solomon, 1997) to suggest that teacher commitment is an important feature of successful buddy programs and that there needs to be a preparedness to give time to managing the process (Baginsky, 2004). It is a key requirement to have at least several members of staff who are enthusiastic about the scheme (Baginsky, 2004).There also has to be a real commitment of time and energy devoted to debriefing during teacher meetings and discussion (Baginsky, 2004). Effective buddy programs, like all peer support programs, also require the commitment of senior staff, especially the principal (Baginsky, 2004).

School commitment to a buddy system is also shown by staff acceptance that it is a long-term project and consideration being given to what happens when key members of staff leave and new staff arrive who are unfamiliar with the system (McGrath & Noble,

2003). Induction procedures, videos, program manuals and mentoring are all ways in which a buddy system can be maintained in a school over time (McGrath & Noble, 2003).

Student commitment to being an older buddy is also a crucial factor in a buddy program's overall effectiveness. Karcher (2005) found that buddy systems that involved tutoring created a stronger sense of connectedness for the younger buddy, who showed changes in self-esteem, social skills and behavioural competence that were related more to their relationship with their older buddy than to what they were being taught. However, when older buddies did not attend sessions or were inconsistent in their involvement, the impact on the younger buddies was negative rather than positive.

Awareness within the school community

Awareness of the school's buddy program by all students and staff in the school has been identified as a significant factor in program success (Schaps et al., 1997). Advance preparation of parents has also been shown as essential to a buddy program's acceptance (Tansy & de Barone, 1996).

Teacher 'buddying'

Teachers 'buddying up' with other colleagues to serve as role models for students can contribute to more effective buddy programs (Pierce et al., 1984; Schaps et al., 1997; Youngerman, 1999).

Conclusion

Buddy programs have enormous potential to assist schools to create respectful, connected and supportive school cultures in which bullying is less likely to occur and where students who are bullied are more likely to receive support and care from peers. They help develop empathy, social skills, trust, self-esteem and a strong sense of community. However, such programs are not a simple panacea and cannot be successful in isolation (Baginsky, 2004). They are more likely to produce these positive outcomes for students and school communities if they are part of a broader plan which is both multi-year and multi-focused (Baginsky, 2004; Catalano, Berglund, Ryan, Lonczak & Hawkins, 2002; Greenberg, Domitrovich & Bumbarger, 2001; Schaps & Lewis, 1999; Weissberg et al., 2003). Peer support systems such as buddy programs work best in settings where there are already established structures for working together cooperatively and a strong emphasis on empathy and respect.

REFERENCES

Adam, D. (1997). How the buddy system came to be a vital and integral part of the school's induction procedure. *Observations, 10*. Glasgow: The Scottish Council for Research in Education. Retrieved March 9, 2005, from <http://www.scre.ac.uk/tpr/observations/obs10/obs10adam.html>

Ames, J., Charlton, T., Leo, E. & Indoe, D. (1991). A peer to listen. *Support for Learning*, 6(4), 165–170.

Baginsky, M. I. (2004). Peer support: Expectations and realities. *Pastoral care in education*, *22*, 1, pp. 3–9.

Ballard, M., Argus, T. & Remley, T. P. Jnr (1999, May). Bullying and school violence: A proposed prevention program. *NASSP Bulletin*, 38–47.

Battistich, V., Schaps, E., Watson, M., Solomon, D. & Lewis, C. (2001). Effects of the Child Development Project on students' drug use and other problem behaviors. *Journal of Primary Prevention*, *21*, 75–99.

Battistich, V., Solomon, D., Kim, D., Watson, M. & Schaps, E. (1995). Schools as communities, poverty levels of student populations, and students' attitudes, motives, and performance: A multilevel analysis. *American Educational Research Journal*, *32*, 627–658.

Battistich, V., Solomon, D., Watson, M. & Schaps, E. (1997). Caring school communities. *Educational Psychologist*, *32*(3), 137–151.

Bear, G., Manning, M. & Izzard, C. E. (2003). Responsible behavior: The importance of social cognition and emotion. *School Psychology*, *18*(2), 140–157.

Benard, B. (1990, December). *A case for peers*. National Resilience Resource Center, University of Minnesota. Retrieved March 24, 2005, from <http://www.cce.umn.edu/pdfs/NRRC/THE_CASE_FOR_PEERS.pdf>

Bloom, S. (1978). *Peer and cross age tutoring in schools: An individual supplement to group instruction*. Hawthorn, Vic.: Australian Council for Education Research.

Bryk, A. & Driscoll, M. (1988). *The high school as community: Contextual influences and consequences for students and teachers*. Madison: University of Wisconsin, National Center on Effective Secondary Schools.

Carr, R. (1988). The city-wide peer counselling program. *Children and Youth Services Review*, *10*, 217–232.

CASEL (2003). *Safe and sound: An educational leader's guide to evidence-based social and emotional learning programs*. Chicago: Collaborative for Academic, Social, and Emotional Learning. Retrieved May 13, 2005, from <www.casel.org/safeandsound.htm.>

Catalano, R. F., Berglund, M. L., Ryan, J. A. M., Lonczak, H. C. & Hawkins, J. D. (2002). *Positive youth development in the United States: Research findings on evaluations of positive youth development programs*. Washington, DC: US Department of Health and Human Services.

Cotton, Kathleen (1995). *Effective schools research practices: A research synthesis 1995 Update*. Retrieved February 5, 2005, from <http:www.nwrel.org/scpd/esp/esp95.html>

Cowie, H. (1998). Perspectives of teachers and pupils on the experience of peer support against bullying. *Educational Research and Evaluation*, *4*(2), 108–125.

Cowie, H. (2000). Bystanding or standing by: Gender issues in coping with bullying in English schools. *Aggressive Behaviour*, *26*, 85–97.

Cowie, H. & Sharp S. (1994). Tackling bullying through the curriculum. In P. K. Smith & S. Sharp (Eds.), *School bullying: Insights and perspectives*. London: Routledge.

Cowie, H. & Sharp, S. (1996). *Peer counselling in schools: A time to listen*. London: David Fulton.

Cowie, H. & Wallace, P. (2000). *Peer support in action*. London: Sage.

Cowie, H., Naylor, P., Talamelli, L., Chauhan, P. & Smith, P. K. (2002). Knowledge, use of and attitudes towards peer support. *Journal of Adolescence*, *25*(5), 453–467.

Cowie, H., Smith, P. K., Boulton, M. & Laver, R. (1994). *Co-operation in the multi-ethnic classroom*. London: David Fulton.

De Paulo, B. M., Tang, J., Webb, W., Hoover, C., Marsh, K. & Litowitz, C. (1989). Age diffeences in reactions to receiving help in a peer tutoring context. *Child Development*, *60*, 423–439.

de Rosenroll, D. (1989). A practitioner's guide to peer counselling research issues and dilemmas. *Canadian Journal of Counselling*, *23*(1), 75–91.

Developmental Studies Center (1996). *That's my buddy! Friendship and learning across the grades*. Oakland, CA: Developmental Studies Center.

Ehly, S. (1986). *Peer tutoring: A guide for school psychologists*. Washington, DC: National Association of School Psychologists.

Elias, M. J. & Weissberg, R. P. (2000). Primary prevention: Educational approaches to enhance social and emotional learning. *Journal of School Health*, *70*(5), 186–190.

Elias, M. J., Zins, J. E., Graczyk, P. A. & Weissberg, R. P. (2003). Implementation, sustainability, and scaling-up of social-emotional and academic innovations in public schools. *School Psychology Review*, *32*, 303–319.

Elias, M. J., Zins, J. E., Weissberg, R. P., Frey, K. S., Greenberg, M. T., Haynes, N. M., Kessler, R., Schwab-Stone, M. E. & Shriver, T. P. (1997). *Promoting social and emotional learning: Guidelines for educators*. Alexandria, VA: Association for Supervision and Curriculum Development.

Fantuzzo, J., Riggio, R., Connelly, S. & Dimeff, L. (1989). Effects of reciprocal peer tutoring on academic achievement and psychological adjustment: A component analysis. *Journal of Educational Psychology*, *81*, 173–177.

Fitzsimons-Lovett, A. (1998). *Enhancing self-respect: A challenge for teachers of students with emotional/behavioral disorders*. ERIC Document 412676.

Flaxman, E., Ascher, C. & Harrington, C. (1988). *Youth mentoring: Programs and practices*. New York: ERIC Clearinghouse on Urban Education at Columbia University.

Fletcher, S. (2000). *Mentoring in schools: A handbook of good practice*. London: Kogan Page.

Foot, H., Morgan, M. & Shute, R. (1990). *Children helping children*. Chichester: Wiley.

Garland, A. F. & Zigler, E. F. (1994). Psychological correlates of help-seeking attitudes among children and adolescents. *American Journal of Orthopsychiatry*, 64(4), 586–593.

Gaustad, J. (1993, March). Peer and cross-age tutoring. *ERIC Digest*, *79*.

Gensemer, P. (2000). *Effectiveness of cross-age and peer mentoring programs*. ERIC Document Reproduction Service No. ED438267.

Gini, G. (2004). Bullying in Italian schools: An overview of intervention programmes. *School Psychology International*, *25*(1), 106–116.

Goodlad, S. & Hirst, B. (1989). *Peer tutoring: A guide to learning by teaching*. London: Kogan Page; New York: Nickols Publishing.

Greenberg, M.T., Domitrovich, C. & Bumbarger, B. (2001). The prevention of mental disorders in school-aged children: Current state of the field. *Prevention and Treatment*, *4*, Article 1. Retrieved May 8, 2005, from <http://journals.apa.org/prevention/volume4/pre0040001a.html>

Greenberg, M. T., Weissberg, R. P., O'Brien, M. U., Zins, J. E., Fredericks, L., Resnik, H. & Elias, M. J. (2003). Enhancing school-based prevention and youth development through coordinated social, emotional, and academic learning. *American Psychologist*, *58*, 466–474.

Greenwood, C. R., Carta, J. J. & Maheady, L. (1991). Peer tutoring programs in the regular classroom. In G. Stoner, M. R. Shinn & H. M. Walker (Eds.), *Interventions for achievement and behavior problems* (pp. 179–200). Washington, DC: National Association of School Psychologists.

Hawkins, J. D., Catalano, R. F., Kosterman, R., Abbott, R. & Hill, K. G. (1999). Preventing adolescent health-risk behaviors by strengthening protection during childhood. *Archives of Pediatric and Adolescent Medicine*, *153*, 226–234.

Hawryluk, M. K. & Smallwood, D. L. (1988). Using peers as instructional agents: Peer tutoring and cooperative learning. In J. L. Graden, J. E. Zins & M. J. Curtis (Eds.), *Alternative educational delivery systems: Enhancing instructional options for all students* (pp. 371–389). Washington, DC: National Association of School Psychologists.

Hektner, J. M., August, G. J. & Realmuto, G. M. (2003). Effects of pairing aggressive and nonaggressive children in strategic peer affiliation. *Journal of Abnormal Child Psychology*, *31*(4), pp. 399–412.

Hertz-Lazarowitz, R. & Miller, N. (Eds.) (1992). Interaction in cooperative groups: The theoretical anatomy of group learning. Cambridge: Cambridge University Press.

Hobden, J. (2003). Bullying and peer support: Peer Support Forum Briefing Paper. Retrieved March 15, 2005, from <http://www.ncb.org.uk/aba/res_detail.asp?id=378>

Hoy, W. K. & Miskel, C. W. (1991). *Educational administration: Theory into practice*. New York: Random House.

Kalkowski, P. (1995). Peer and cross-age tutoring. School Improvement Research Series. Northwest Regional Educational Laboratory, Portland, OR. Retrieved February 1, 2005, from <http://www.nwrel.org/scpd/sirs/9/c018.html>

Karcher, M. J. (2005). The effects of developmental mentoring and high school mentors' attendance on their younger mentees' self-esteem, social skills, and connectedness. *Psychology in the Schools*, *42*(1), 65–78.

Kemple, K. M. (2004). *Let's be friends: Peer competence and social inclusion in early childhood programs.* New York: Teachers College Press.

Kessler, R., Schwab-Stone, M. E. & Shriver, T. P. (1997). *Promoting social and emotional learning: Guidelines for educators*. Alexandria, VA: Association for Supervision and Curriculum Development.

Konet, R. (1991). Peer helpers in the middle school. *Middle School Journal*, *23*, 13–15.

Le Surf, P. & Lynch G. (1999). Exploring young people's perceptions relevant to counselling: A qualitative study. *British Journal of Guidance and Counselling*, *27*(2), 231–244.

Luxmoore, N. (2000) *Listening to young people in school: Youth work and counselling*. London: Jessica Kingsley.

Maher, C. A. (1982). Behavioral effects of using conduct problem adolescents as cross-age tutors. *Psychology in the Schools*, *19*, 360–64.

McAllister, E. (1990). *Peer teaching and collaborative learning in the language arts*. ERIC Clearinghouse on Reading and Communication Skills, Bloomington.

McGrath, H. (1997). *Dirty tricks: Classroom games which teach students social skills*. Melbourne: Addison Wesley Longman.

McGrath, H. (2004). Directions in teaching social skills to students with specific emotional and behavioural difficulties. In P. Clough, P. Garner, J. T. Pardeck & J. & F. Yuen. *Handbook of emotional and behavioural difficulties*. London: Sage.

McGrath, H. L. (1998). An overview of prevention and treatment programs for developing positive peer relations. In K. Rigby & P. Slee (Eds.). *Children's peer relations*. London: Routledge.

McGrath, H. & Francey, S. (1991). *Friendly kids, friendly classrooms*. Melbourne: Longman.

McGrath, H. & Noble, T. (2003). *BOUNCE BACK! A Classroom Resiliency Program*. Frenchs Forest, NSW: Pearson Education.

Menesini, E., Codecasa, E., Benelli, B. & Cowie, H. (2003). Enhancing children's responsibility to take action against bullying: Evaluation of a befriending intervention in Italian middle schools. *Aggressive Behavior*, *29*(1), 10–14.

Mytton, J. A., Di Guiseppi, C., Gough, D., Taylor, R., Roberts, I., Logan, S. (2002). School based violence prevention programme: Systematic review of secondary prevention trials. *Archives of Pediatrics and Adolescent Medicine*, *156*, 752–762.

Naylor, P. & Cowie, H. (1999). The effectiveness of peer support systems in challenging school bullying: The perspectives and experiences of teachers and pupils. *Journal of Adolescence*, *22*, 467–479.

Naylor, P., Cowie, H. & del Rey, R. (2001). Reported reactions to being bullied of a sample of UK secondary school girls and boys. *Child Psychology and Psychiatry Review*, *6*, 114–120.

Pierce, M., Stahlbrand, K. & Armstrong, S. (1984). *Increasing student productivity through peer tutoring*. Austin, TX: Pro-ed.

Powell, M. A. (1997). *Academic tutoring and mentoring: A literature review*. California Research Bureau.

Rigby, K. (1997). Peer relations at school and the health of adolescents [Electronic version]. *Youth Studies, Australia, 17*(1), 13–17. Retrieved April 4, 2005, from <http://www.education.unisa.edu.au/bullying/youthstudies.html>

Salmivalli C. (1999). Participant role approach to school bullying: Implications for interventions. *Journal of Adolescence, 22*, 453–459.

Salmivalli, C. (2001). Peer-led intervention campaign against school bullying: Who considered it useful, who benefited? *Educational Research, 43*, 263–278.

Samway, K., Davies, Whang, G. & Pippitt, M. (1995). *Buddy reading: Cross age tutoring in a multicultural school*. Portsmouth, UK: Heinemann.

Schaps, E. (1999). The Child Development Project: In search of synergy. *Principal, 79*, 22–24.

Schaps, E. (2003), The heart of a caring school. *Educational Leadership*, 60(6), 31–33. Retrieved May 13, 2005, from <http://www.devstu.org/about/articles/heart_of_caring_school.html>

Schaps, E. & Battistich, V. (2002, June 19). *Community in school: Central to character formation and more*. Paper presented at the White House Conference on Character and Community. Retrieved March 23, 2005, from <http://www.devstu.org/about/articles/CharacterandCommunity.html>

Schaps, E. & Lewis, C. (1999). Perils on an essential journey: Building school community [Electronic version]. *Phi Delta Kappan, 81*(3), 215. <http://www.devstu.org/about/articles/perils_essential.html>

Schaps, E., Battistich, V. & Solomon, D. (1997). School as a caring community: A key to character education. In A. Molnar (Ed.), *The construction of children's character, Part II, 96th Yearbook of the National Society for the Study of Education*. Chicago: University of Chicago Press.

Shariff, S. (2003). *A system on trial: Identifying legal standards for educational, ethical and legally defensible approaches to bullying in schools*. Unpublished doctoral dissertation. Simon Fraser University, British Columbia.

Sharp, S. & Cowie, H. (1998). *Counselling and supporting children in distress*. London: Sage.

Sharp, S. & Smith, P. K. (Eds.) (1994). *Tackling bullying in your school: A practical handbook for teachers*. London: Routledge.

Sharp, S., Sellars, S. & Cowie, H. (1994, June). Time to listen: Setting up a peer-counselling service to help tackle the problem of bullying. *Pastoral Care in Education, 12*(2), 3–6.

Smith, C. (2002). *B.E.S.T. buddies: A comprehensive training programme introducing a peer buddy system to support students starting secondary school*. London: Paul Chapman Educational Publishing.

Solomon, D., Battistich, V., Watson, M., Schaps, E. & Lewis, C. (2000). A six-district study of educational change: Direct and mediated effects of the Child Development Project. *Social Psychology of Education*, 4, 3–51.

Sprinthall, N., Hall, J. & Gerber, E. (1992). Peer counselling for middle school students experiencing divorce: A deliberate psychological education model. *Elementary School Guidance and Counselling*, 26, 279–294.

Tansy, M. & de Barona, M. S. (1996). Peer and cross-age tutoring programs. *Guidance & Counseling*, *12*(1), 21–25.

Tindall, J. A. (1995). *Peer programs: An in-depth look at peer helping – Planning, implementation and administration*. Bristol, PA: Accelerated Development.

Topping, K. & Bryce, A. (2004). Cross-age peer tutoring of reading and thinking: Influence on thinking skills. *Educational Psychology*, *24*(5), 595–621.

Topping, K. J. & Ehly, S. (Eds.) (1998) *Peer-assisted learning*. London: Lawrence Erlbaum Associates.

Utay, C. & Utay, J. (1997). Peer-assisted learning: The effects of cooperative learning and cross-age peer tutoring with word processing on writing skills of students with learning disabilities. *Journal of Computing in Childhood Education*, 8(2), 165–185.

Weissberg, R. P., Kumpfer, K. L. & Seligman, M. E. P. (2003). Prevention for children and youth that works: An Introduction. *American Psychologist*, 58(6/7), 425–432.

Youngerman, S. (1998). The power of cross-level partnerships. *Educational Leadership Abstracts*, 56(1), 58–60.

CHAPTER 7

The 'Willy Kids Are Friendly Kids' Program: One school's whole-school approach

Tilly Barger

Our history

Williamstown Primary School opened in 1873 and the stunning blue stone building which houses the main office and senior school classrooms is a landmark in the district and classified by the National Trust. The Junior School is housed in a red brick building which opened in 1906. In 1892, the number of students enrolled in our school was an amazing 1283. Enrolments have fluctuated over the years, as happens in many old schools as areas undergo ageing then regeneration. In 1991, the school experienced a low point of 224 students, whilst neighbouring schools were struggling to cope with large numbers of enrolments. The community had obviously lost confidence in the school and parents were driving past our school to take their children to other local schools. This is a worrying situation for any school. There were many reasons for this downturn in enrolments, but the most significant of these related to the general behaviour of our student body. Our students were seen to be unruly, with bullying rife. Teachers were spending most of their time on a small number of children who were very dominant and badly behaved.

Fortunately we were able to reverse this trend very quickly, so much so that in 1995 an enrolment policy had to be introduced to 'cap' the burgeoning enrolments to 420 students. For the past ten years we have been forced to adhere to this policy, even though we face the continuing pressure of excessive enrolments.

How was this turnaround achieved?

In 1993 a new leadership team was appointed at the school. This team identified that there was a huge problem with the 'tone' of the school and the behaviour of the children. It was obvious that a very small number of children were taking up most of the time and energy of the teachers. It was acknowledged that there was a majority of children who were well behaved and trying to do the 'right thing', but they were being influenced or dominated by the few with uncooperative and anti-social behaviour.

So in 1994 we introduced 'Willy Kids Are Friendly Kids', a program designed to teach social competencies and create a respectful, safe and cooperative school climate. Our aims were to provide awareness of and training in social skill issues for the staff and to develop in children appropriate pro-social skills and attitudes to enable them to deal with a complex and dynamic social situation. It was also recognised that we all needed common understandings in regards to behavioural expectations as well as a common language.

The birth of the program

One of the major motivating factors for the initial introduction of the program was the staff's disappointment and frustration with the prevailing code of conduct and apparent 'tone' in the school in the previous years. Teachers were feeling powerless and a little disenchanted as a result of this. On an individual level, most of the students were actually quite pleasant, but as a group they demonstrated behaviours that indicated a lack of awareness of the social skills required to establish and maintain a cooperative, respectful and satisfying school environment for everyone. There were some major issues of fighting and bullying, but also some more simple issues of courtesy, responsibility and cooperation that were making the school a less pleasant place to be for all.

As leaders, our biggest challenge was convincing the staff that we could in fact change the situation and implement our vision of how the school culture *could* be. We knew we needed a respected professional in this area, so psychologist Dr Helen McGrath (author of 'Friendly Kids, Friendly Classrooms') was invited to present a professional development session to all staff. Helen was a convincing and inspiring speaker who intuitively understood the problems we were experiencing in our classrooms and in the playground. As a former classroom teacher herself, she understood the role and motivation of teachers in the change process that we wanted to implement. She was also aware that the change we were proposing had to clearly articulate for teachers and students 'what's in it for me'. Therefore she spoke to the staff about their skills and knowledge and how teachers had rights, such as the right to teach and impart their knowledge, as well as the right to expect a respectful, cooperative and friendly environment in which they *could* teach. By the end of the presentation, Helen had a large number of staff motivated and believing that *we could* initiate changes to the school to improve the social environment for all.

As a result of the presentation, a committee was formed to design a program that would address our concerns. The specific aims of the program, as communicated to the whole school community, were to:

- create a cooperative, respectful and friendly atmosphere that supported learning
- increase student awareness and use of specific social skills
- improve the general social and behavioural climate of the school
- introduce and follow a set of consistent whole-school expectations about the importance of positive social interaction
- create shared understandings and a common language about social behaviour for the entire school community.

We decided to call our program 'Willy Kids Are Friendly Kids' and this 'slogan' has been used throughout the program and in response to specific situations.

Initially we invited the staff to brainstorm all the issues and behavioural concerns we had in relation to our students. This produced a long list of behaviours that reflected the children's poor social skills as well as issues that could be attributed to the age and style of the buildings in which the children coexisted.

From this list we classified the issues into four major categories – courtesy, respect, cooperation, and responsibilities. As we have a four-term year, it was clear that the most efficient way to proceed was to design a new whole-school program with a specific focus on one of these four categories for each term of the school year. Each category was further divided into ten weekly topics that supported each term's focus.

The committee recognised that the key to making this program a success was to get the support of the whole staff. It was pointless to have one or two teachers trial this in a few classes only, as the interactions in the playground and classroom would continue as they always had and the overall culture wouldn't change. This would not achieve our goal of common understandings and a common language. As a result we went back to the staff with the proposed program and asked that everyone trial the program for one term. Whilst some took some convincing, we were able to gain the support of the entire staff despite their initial reluctance.

The program was introduced at the beginning of first term in 1994. The impact was startling, and by the end of Term 1 the staff was convinced that this program could in fact achieve our initial aims. Unsolicited positive feedback was received from parents and visitors to the school. The school's 'tone' was changing for the better – and rapidly!

What was in our program (and still is!)

The Welfare and Discipline Committee had a significant role to play in organising and preparing the components of the program. After reading a range of materials, consulting with the rest of the staff on a regular basis and brainstorming ideas at staff meetings, they listed the social skills to be taught and sorted them into the four categories of courtesy, respect, cooperation, and responsibilities. (Further details are provided in the appendix at the end of the chapter.) Multiple copies of appropriate resources, such as Helen McGrath's *Friendly Kids*, *Friendly Classrooms*, were purchased for teachers.

The following steps are still a key part of our program. At assembly on Monday morning the skill of the week is introduced by the Principal. This is done through defining the skill and giving a brief description of how to do it. After assembly, each class conducts discussions where children further explore the issues, and these are followed by planned age-appropriate activities. Consideration is also given to the specific needs of each class. For instance, if children in one class have shown poor use of the social skill of 'taking turns', then this particular skill may require more discussion and activities for it to be learnt. If the children are showing good manners and using polite language and voice tone ('please' and 'thank you'), then just a simple discussion and review session would be held. There is no set time or activity during the week for further discussion and there is no designated duration of an activity. Therefore teachers have the opportunity to adapt the weekly focus skills to the needs of the children in their class. The only requirement is that each skill be given some consideration each week and that, when necessary, some skills are further elaborated and reinforced. Teachers are encouraged to 'teach to the moment' and identify 'real' opportunities to discuss and improve skills that have been a focus in previous weeks when appropriate situations arise.

To gain parental support the school newsletter publishes information for parents about the topic and specific social skill to be addressed in the following week with suggestions on ways parents can teach and reinforce the skill with their children at home. Weekly

'Willy Kids Are Friendly Kids' awards are presented at Friday assembly to celebrate and acknowledge the children who have best demonstrated the particular social skill during the week.

Outcomes of our program

The school continues to use the program because of student, teacher and parent satisfaction with the outcomes it consistently achieves. It works: our students are now friendly and respectful towards their classmates and teachers and our teachers can get on with teaching. There is very little bullying and, when it does occur, it can be quickly dealt with. Instances of physical aggression between students are now rare. There is an overall friendly tone in the school and students and teachers have very positive relationships. We think that the program produces the results we want because it works in the following ways:

- It establishes and communicates clear and consistent whole-school expectations about social behaviour and interactions. One example of this is the number of times students have been overheard saying to a new student to the school 'but we don't do that in this school'.
- It allows staff and students to use their common and shared language for discussing social issues.
- It increases the awareness of social issues in all children and develops their social competencies.
- It encourages children to think about, define and apply concepts such as 'respect' and 'responsibility'.
- It provides children with the opportunity to learn, practise and refine the skills to cope with difficult social situations (such as conflict or loneliness).
- It helps children to understand that they are not the only people who are upset and angry in a conflict situation and others may also be feeling upset. This contributes to empathy and resilience.
- It lets children know that their problems are being taken seriously.
- It encourages students to challenge the stereotypes they hold. For example, there has been a shift in the students' perceptions of those who bully. They now recognise different forms of bullying behaviour, rather than focusing on the 'stereotypical' size and appearance of a 'bully'. They understand that anyone can behave in a bullying manner – even the smallest child in the grade if they have power over other students.

- It empowers students and helps them to become more socially resilient through their acquisition of social skills such as assertiveness.
- It encourages children to include others rather than leave them out. As one student said, 'It's good to practise how to get into groups and if someone's left out we have to figure out how to include them'.
- It enables easier communication between teachers, students and parents about problem behaviour.
- It assists parents to further develop social skills and understanding with their children in the family context.

The program works for our school, whose student population is predominantly English-speaking and middle class. It is maintained both by the positive results it achieves for all of us and by parent and teacher commitment. We continue to use our slogan, 'Willy Kids Are Friendly Kids', and we continue to operate under the following guiding principles:

> *Everybody has the right to learn.*
> *Everybody has the right to be safe.*
> *Everybody has the right to be respected.*

APPENDIX 7A: COMPONENTS OF THE 'WILLY KIDS ARE FRIENDLY KIDS' PROGRAM

Term 1	**Courtesy**
Week 1	Smile Week
Week 2	Listening
Week 3	Playing together
Week 4	Please and thank you
Week 5	Give way
Week 6	Excuse me/sorry
Week 7	Taking turns
Week 8	Being helpful
Week 9	Punctuality
Week 10	Good winners/good losers

Term 2	**Respect**
Week 1	Body language
Week 2	Voice
Week 3	Using appropriate language
Week 4	Respecting adults
Week 5	Respecting the opposite sex
Week 6	Respecting differences
Week 7	Respecting property – yours and others
Week 8	Respecting our school
Week 9	Respecting our environment

Term 3	**Cooperation**
Week 1	What is bullying?
Week 2	Being assertive
Week 3	Saying 'No'
Week 4	Negotiating
Week 5	Suggesting and persuading
Week 6	Making decisions in a group
Week 7	Respecting the opinions of others
Week 8	Sharing
Week 9	Including others
Week 10	Team work

Term 4	**Responsibility**
Week 1	Doing your best
Week 2	Setting goals
Week 3	Who can help me?
Week 4	Consequences
Week 5	Rights
Week 6	Seeing it through
Week 7	Fixing things up
Week 8	Having a go
Week 9	Leadership
Week 10	Being positive
Week 11	CELEBRATE!!!

Sample newsletter items for parents

Willy Kids Are Friendly Kids!

This term we are working on **COURTESY**. Next week we will be looking at **LISTENING**.

Welcome back to school. I hope you have all enjoyed a good break and are ready for a great year at Willy. A special welcome to all our new families. As many of you know, our 'Willy Kids Are Friendly Kids' program is one of our most successful and enduring programs through which we aim to develop in children the social skills necessary to deal with the many issues that confront us all, not only at school but throughout our lives. Each week we publish the social skill that we will be teaching the following week. Hopefully these weekly lessons will be reinforced at home as well during the week.

With all classes now well underway, one of the most important skills any child or adult can develop is the skill of listening. Listening involves a lot more than hearing. Listening means concentrating on what the other person is saying, showing that you are listening by looking at the speaker and responding in some way – perhaps by nodding your head and certainly by responding to what they say with a question or statement.

Some do's and don'ts:

Do look at the person speaking.

Do stand still while you're listening.

Do respond to the speaker.

Do concentrate on what you want to say.

Don't ignore the speaker or change the subject unless that is appropriate.

Don't fidget or look at the ground.

Willy Kids Are Friendly Kids!

This term we are working on **COURTESY**. Next week we will be looking at **PLAYING TOGETHER**.

As you are no doubt aware our school has had some difficulties with playground space over the last few years and this highlights the need for us to be able to play together cooperatively. Playing together does not just mean playing happily with our friends, although that is important. Playing together means sharing our space and our games sensibly so that everyone can enjoy their playtime. It means thinking about other people and their games and making sure we are playing in a way that means everyone can enjoy themselves. In past years it has been amazing to see two football matches and a soccer game playing together practically in the same space on the oval. This shows real cooperation (and imagination!).

Some do's and don'ts:

Do play in sensible places. For example, footy for the big children should be played on the oval.

Do look to see if other children are involved in a game or an area before you set up your game.

Do play safe games, particularly in small spaces.

Don't run through other children's games.

Don't interfere with other children's games.

Don't take over other children's areas.

CHAPTER 8

Using educational drama and bystander training to counteract bullying

Ken Rigby and Dale Bagshaw

Introduction

Much of the work in countering bullying in schools is undertaken by teachers and counsellors who deal directly with students involved in bully/victim problems that require urgent attention. This important work, however, has limitations. Many of the problems of bullying never come to the attention of school staff. Those that do are usually the most serious and are addressed only after they have been going on for some time and have become quite difficult to resolve. Rarely are teachers present when issues first emerge. On the other hand, students as observers are commonly present. The work of countering bullying need not be left entirely to school staff. Students can often take effective action to prevent themselves being victimised by peers. Students can also help others who become involved in bully/victim problems, especially if they have been trained in some way in the requisite skills, both cognitive and behavioural.

A number of anti-bullying programs have included work designed to help students to improve their proficiency in taking action to prevent or reduce bullying in schools.

Some of these programs are directed towards helping students embroiled in conflict situations that may include or lead to bullying. Examples include peer support programs (Cowie & Olaffson, 2000) peer mediation structures (Cohen, 1995) and peer counselling training (Price & Jones, 2001). In some schools students have worked closely with school counsellors on anti-bullying committees aimed at coordinating staff and student initiatives (Petersen & Rigby, 1999). Attempts have also been made to guide and empower selected students to investigate cases of suspected bullying and take part in so-called 'Bully Courts' to 'try' those accused who, if found guilty, have passed judgment on them. Not all such programs have found favour in schools or produced high levels of success (Mahdavi & Smith, 2002) The kind of training required and the roles students can play in countering bullying is currently a matter of intense debate.

In this chapter we examine two promising methods of training that can help students to acquire the necessary understanding and skills to assist in reducing bullying in schools. The first involves the use of drama as a means of helping students to understand and appreciate the ways in which conflict develops and the options that are available to them to avoid the emergence of relatively intractable bully/victim problems. The second focuses on helping students to understand the behaviour of bystanders in the presence of bullying, and how they can become effective agents in discouraging the bullying they observe at school.

Value of educational drama

Educational drama can be used to enable students to develop skills that can help them to handle conflict more constructively, as opposed to using force to impose their will on others (as bullies do) or withdrawing from conflict situations if possible (as victimised children often do). The use of educational drama to address bullying can be illustrated by work undertaken in an international research project called DRACON International (Drama and Conflict) which has involved ongoing collaboration between four teams of researchers from universities in Sweden, Malaysia and Australia since 1996 (DRACON International, 2004).[1] The overall purpose of this project is to trial and evaluate drama-in-education as a method for assisting adolescents to handle conflicts and bullying at school in the three national contexts. The DRACON project is interdisciplinary and requires competence in two fields: drama-in-education and conflict resolution. In many ways the separation of drama and conflict resolution is artificial. Effective conflict resolution requires experiential knowledge about the nature of conflict, and this can be acquired by reliving or exploring conflict in all its dramatic intensity. This is precisely what is done in drama-in-education.

There are differences in the aims, concepts, theories and procedures of the four DRACON teams, but we have found that the underlying similarities and complementarities between the two fields of drama-in-education and conflict resolution are striking. The following section illustrates the activities of our Adelaide team in relation to verbal bullying and abuse in one school.

The Adelaide DRACON project

In the mid 1990s we conducted an extensive study of conflict and bullying in a wide and varied range of secondary schools in South Australia, involving focus groups and surveys with Year 9 students aged 13–15 years (Bagshaw, 1998). Some schools were located in communities where there were high levels of bullying and violence. Our findings suggested that adolescent students use a variety of conflict-handling styles – some constructive, such as problem-solving and compromise, and others that are likely to produce negative outcomes for individuals, groups and the school community at large, such as forcing and withdrawing. We were concerned that substantial numbers of students were predominantly using negative styles, such as forcing, often where there were imbalances of power (bullying) (Rigby & Bagshaw, 2001).

In 1996, four members of our Adelaide DRACON team[2] conducted a research project in a large school located in a low socioeconomic area in the suburbs of Adelaide. During planning meetings with teaching staff, the students in the assigned Year 9 drama class were described as 'difficult' – often uncooperative, seemingly disinterested in drama, boisterous and at times hostile. Initially there were 19 students in the class – 8 boys and 11 girls. They had already been in this drama class for one term and during this time the teacher had been unable to engage them in any meaningful way. The teacher indicated that some students in the class had chosen drama as an 'easy' option.

Verbal bullying and abuse was considered to be an appropriate focus for the educational drama sessions, as it had been identified as a problem by Year 9 students. Indeed, our previous research in a range of secondary schools had indicated that verbal bullying between adolescents at this and other schools was common, was often ignored by teachers, was often more hurtful than physical bullying and continued for long periods of time, and was difficult to handle (Bagshaw, 1998). It is important to reflect that in a subsequent large domestic violence study also conducted in South Australia (Bagshaw, Chung, Couch, Lilburn & Wadham, 2000) verbal bullying was also identified by many victims interviewed as being the most destructive form of violence in the long term.

Educational drama approaches that we tested included a range of drama exercises, improvisations and role-plays involving bullying and conflict situations typically experienced by students at school. The emphasis was on enabling students to develop their own conflict scenarios and to practise different styles of handling conflict, drawing on their own experiences and creativity. An action research framework was employed over 8 weeks for two 100-minute sessions a week. This allowed the researchers and drama teachers to work collaboratively with the participants and to constantly evaluate the process and modify activities. Each session was designed to introduce drama activities that facilitated the exploration of key concepts linked to conflict management. Most of the concepts introduced in the earlier stages, however, were also centrally important to the development of the group – in particular trust, cooperation, listening, empathy, nonverbal communication, feelings and status/power. The key order of introduction of the concepts was contingent on the stage of the group's development. Simple handouts were supplied, either at the beginning or at the end of the session, along with a brief discussion of the concept explored and how it related to the students' experience.

Students were then introduced to five strategies for handling conflict identified by Johnson (1997) – withdrawing, smoothing, forcing, compromising and problem-solving. Drama activities were designed to facilitate student exploration of the effect of each strategy, and to identify the potential destructive and constructive elements of each. The final sessions were devoted to the preparation and presentation of role-plays that required each small group or pair to develop a scenario involving verbal forms of bullying or abuse and to demonstrate different conflict strategies to deal with them. Students were given simplified handouts and explanations in class to assist them to understand the concepts. Individuals in the class had experienced or used most of the strategies but had not previously been able to label them. However, they were initially unable to demonstrate an understanding of the strategy of 'problem-solving'. It was agreed that in most conflict situations between peers at school, the cooperative strategies of compromising and problem-solving have the potential to generate the most satisfactory outcomes for everyone involved, as they preserve the relationship(s) and attempt to satisfy everyone's needs and goals. Forcing or bullying styles, on the other hand, can be destructive to relationships and the needs or goals of the bully are satisfied at the expense of others. Students identified their own dominant conflict strategy or style by completing a simple exercise from Johnson (1997, pp. 230–232).

Outcomes for students

Towards the end of the project, participants all demonstrated a marked increase in self-confidence and were not afraid to present their ideas for public scrutiny. The students chose to work on developing their own role-plays in small groups. Each group developed its own sets, organised props, devised scripts and successfully demonstrated different styles of handling conflict in various scenarios. All the students, even those who consistently reported hating 'doing plays' and 'performing in front of the class', wrote in their journals that they enjoyed developing their play and rehearsing for their final performance. After several rehearsals each sub-group performed for the rest of the class. They performed with confidence. In addition, each scenario demonstrated that they had understood and responded to the requirements, which were to devise a typical scene to illustrate a situation involving verbal bullying or abuse, and to demonstrate various styles or strategies to handle the situation. The journal entries continued to reflect learning about conflict, cooperation, expressing feelings and 'how to work together and not stuff around'. In the final scenarios devised by the students, where conflict was the subject of the drama, they were each able to experience different aspects of conflict and to experiment with different strategies of conflict handling. Each small group performance was videotaped and the edited video was played back to the students on the last day. Following this, students were videotaped as they interviewed each other in pairs (*vox populi* style) asking two questions:

- What style of conflict did you demonstrate in your play?
- If you were to demonstrate a problem-solving style, what would you have done differently?

Responses to these questions demonstrated an improved understanding of key conflict management strategies and concepts. All students were able to identify the conflict strategies that they had used in their role-play. Those who had used withdrawal, forcing or smoothing strategies were also able to describe more cooperative approaches they could have used, involving the use of compromise or problem-solving. This ability had not been evident in earlier sessions. In this and the previous session, oral feedback given to the researchers by students (in front of their classmates) indicated that their confidence levels had increased and that they appreciated learning about conflict through drama, especially through devising their own scenarios. Their final journal entries illustrated the potency of drama as a medium for learning and spoke of growing confidence, having fun, learning different conflict-solving methods, improved acting skills and improved communication skills.

This project was ambitious given the time frame and the student group involved. However, the observed shift in levels of attentiveness, cooperation and self-confidence in the students was profound, given the high level of disruptive behaviour initially displayed. Action research strategies enabled the team to respond flexibly to the needs and interests of the students and to affirm their abilities, thereby gaining their respect and trust. They appreciated the confidence that was placed in their ability to be self-directed – 'I enjoyed having a choice on what we wanted to do – not having the teachers choose what we had to do'. This finding is not surprising, given the push for autonomy typically displayed by adolescents at this stage of their development.

Journal sheets were designed to elicit student feedback immediately after each session – what they liked and disliked about the activities engaged in and what they had learned. This was the most important action research tool used, as the students were often reluctant to verbalise their ideas and opinions in front of each other. Information gained from observations and the journal entries was used to modify and shape each session. Oral feedback in the final session indicated that the students' ability to influence the project was considered to be a very important aspect of their experience.

It was also valuable to record focused observations of each session, as evaluation of the student feedback in journals needed to take into account the context of the session. The use of the video as a tool for evaluation and feedback, however, was the most potent research tool with this age group. They encouraged its use and were very keen to view themselves performing.

This exploratory research project demonstrated the potential for drama-in-education to engage adolescents in problem-solving and cooperative action. Although the project was a case study, limited to one class in one school, there were strong indications that drama is an effective medium for introducing possibilities for change by widening the experiences of adolescents and allowing them to explore conflict, and its resolution, from a variety of perspectives. Our findings have since been reinforced by those of our Griffith University colleagues in their independent but related studies (O'Toole, Burton & Plunkett, 2004). In the broader international DRACON study we have also demonstrated in many different ways that educational drama can provide a creative medium for the teaching of constructive conflict-handling skills (DRACON International, 2004). Drawing upon the understandings derived from what 13–15-year-old students told us about their bullying experiences in a range of schools, we believe that educational drama is a potent medium to use with this age group, in particular for early intervention and prevention.

Implications for school anti-bullying programs

Although no formal assessment was made of any changes in the level of bullying as a consequence of students being involved in educational drama, the outcomes clearly point to an increased awareness of the options open to children in conflict and the behaviours necessary to effect change. As part of a general program in which policies and procedures are put in place by a school to encourage and reward pro-social behaviour, it is evident that educational drama can substantially assist in the development of cognitive and behavioural skills that can be used by children to handle conflict and deal with bully/victim problems constructively.

Importance of student bystanders in reducing bullying

Bullying in schools commonly occurs in the presence of student bystanders. Observational studies at Canadian primary schools have estimated that bystanders are present about 85 per cent of the time (O'Connell, Pepler & Craig, 1999; Pepler & Craig, 1995). It has been reported that only on a minority of occasions do bystanders seek to discourage the bullying. However, when they do, bullying actually stops some 50 per cent of the time (Hawkins, Pepler & Craig, 2001). Most bullying in fact goes unreported. Students, especially in secondary schools, are reluctant to tell a teacher about it (Rigby & Barnes, 2002).

Study of student bystanders observing bullying in South Australian schools

An Australian study conducted in 2003–2004 by Rigby and Johnson (2004a, 2004b) from the University of South Australia examined the reported behaviour of children from state coeducational schools in the metropolitan Adelaide region in South Australia. The respondents consisted of 200 primary school students (Years 6 and 7) and 200 secondary school students (Years 8 and 9). The mean age for primary students was 11.5 years and for secondary students, 13.5 years. From each type of school, data were available for 100 boys and 100 girls. In accordance with ethical requirements, parental permission was required for each child to participate.

The children were shown a video prepared by the researchers which included illustrations of verbal and physical bullying. Most respondents reported that they had personally witnessed such verbal and physical bullying at school as part of a group of bystanders at least once. Some 95 per cent reported that they had witnessed verbal bullying and 68 per cent reported witnessing physical bullying. The figures for those who reported each kind of bullying on a weekly basis are given in Table 8.1 on the next page. These results confirm that bullying behaviour is frequently observed by children in Australian schools and strongly suggest that Australian secondary school students in Years 7 and 8 observe more bullying than do students in the last two years of primary school.

Table 8.1 Percentages of students reporting observing bullying behaviour at their school on a weekly basis

	Primary students	Secondary students
Verbal bullying	%	%
Boys	60	78
Girls	40	62
Physical bullying	%	%
Boys	32	50
Girls	24	50

For each sub-group, 100 students provided responses.

How respondents thought they would respond as bystanders

Of particular interest in the South Australian study was how students thought they would respond as bystanders observing bullying at school. The children were asked to indicate anonymously on questionnaires whether they would (i) ignore what was happening (ii) support the person being attacked (iii) support the attacker or (iv) get a teacher. Given below is the picture presented to the students as depicting physical bullying.

Most students indicated that they would either ignore the bullying behaviour or directly support the victim. Relatively few students indicated that they would support the bully. This response was more commonly made by secondary school students. Informing a teacher was more likely to be indicated by the younger primary school students. There was also a tendency for more boys than girls to report that they would ignore the situation, and more girls than boys to get a teacher (see Table 8.2).

This study was replicated in a number of other countries, where children in comparable age groups viewed the same video. The children were from England, Italy, Israel, South Africa and Bangladesh. In general, similar results were obtained with one notable difference: Australian students, especially those in secondary schools, were less inclined than children in the other nation samples to tell the teacher. Previous studies had shown that Australian students, especially those in lower secondary, were often distrusting of teachers, believing that they would not know how to intervene effectively (Rigby & Bagshaw, 2003).

Why students respond as they do in bystander situations

It is useful to know what factors incline students as bystanders to support victims of bullying. Questions were included in the student questionnaires to reliably assess attitudes towards victims in general. In addition, respondents were asked to view once more the picture above depicting bullying and to indicate what they thought each of a number of persons would expect them to do in such a situation, i.e. if they were bystanders. These persons were: their mothers, their fathers, their friends and their teachers. Lastly, they were asked to indicate whether they had in the current year done something personally to try to stop a student from being bullied by another student or group of students.

Table 8.2 Respondents' indication of how they would respond as bystanders observing physical bullying at school (as percentages)

	Ignore it	Support the victim	Support the bully	Get a teacher
Primary students	%	%	%	%
Boys	34	48	5	13
Girls	19	38	0	43
Secondary students				
Boys	51	30	11	8
Girls	38	37	7	18

Students who were most inclined to give direct help to the victim of bullying were found to have these characteristics:

- They had positive and supportive attitudes towards victims.
- They believed that their friends expected them to help victims of school bullying.
- They were more likely than others to have actually acted helpfully in support of a victim in the current year.
- They were more likely to be attending primary than secondary school.

Notably, the perceived expectations of teachers were found to be unrelated to the expressed intentions of students to support victims of bullying. Parental expectations were of slight importance, but only for girls.

Factors that appear to disincline students from helping victims

In this study opportunity was given for students to elaborate on the reasons for the actions they believed they would take. From this a number of possible explanations for some students not helping emerged. These included the following:

- feeling that people should look after themselves – if they are bullied it's their own fault
- feeling that one has a responsibility to help one's friends – and nobody else – because they would help you
- a recognition that intervening could be dangerous or embarrassing
- wanting the conflict to continue, because it was fun to watch.

Despite the fact that some students did not feel any obligation to help the victim, a much larger proportion did feel that way. Here, as examples, are some comments made by students:

- Because it's the right thing to do.
- Because I don't want anyone to be hurt.
- Because I couldn't stand watching a person being bullied.
- Because I would hate to be in that situation so I'd try to help the person being bullied.
- Because I don't want to stand around doing nothing, letting the person suffer.
- Because the person being pushed doesn't deserve it and he or she will need morale (sic) support.
- I would support the person being pushed down because if I do it, some of my friends might do it, too.

Such responses from both girls and boys in primary and secondary schools give us hope that such positive thoughts can be translated into action.

What teachers can do to promote more positive bystander behaviour

Here are some suggestions for teachers that are consistent with the research findings:

1. Elicit from students how they think they would react if they were observers of a bullying incident. Teachers may like to make use of a short questionnaire which includes a picture of a bullying incident to get written responses from students. See the practical guide to bullying for schools, *Stop the Bullying* (Rigby, 2003).
2. Ask students to give a reason for their reaction.
3. At the next lesson, feed back to them the results, reading out what students have said about why they would help the victim. (Generally these responses are very common and can convey a great deal of normative influence.)
4. Pay attention to, and discuss, comments that call attention to the potential danger of intervening and whether obligations to help should be limited only to one's friends.
5. Discuss how students might distinguish between dangerous and non-dangerous situations – and take appropriate action.
6. Consider what forms of discouragement could be effective without inflaming the situation.
7. Discuss how students might get others to voice their disapproval together with their own.
8. Rehearse possible scenarios and actions using role-plays.
9. Monitor what happens by getting the class to report back periodically. This may lead to different advice being suggested and given.
10. Always bear in mind that a direct exhortation by a teacher that a student is expected to help the victim of school bullying is likely to be disregarded. But there are ways of indirectly mobilising positive action under the more persuasive influence of peer pressure.

Conclusion

As recent studies evaluating the effectiveness of existing anti-bullying programs have shown, progress towards reducing bullying in schools has been slow and limited in its achievements (Rigby, 2002; Smith, Pepler & Rigby, 2004). A great deal more needs to be done. Among the more promising contributions to effective management of bullying have been those which have focused on what can be achieved through the involvement of school children in educational drama aiming to develop skills that can prevent conflicts between students that can lead to serious bully/victim problems, as described in O'Toole, Burton and Plunkett (2004) and DRACON International (2004). Helping students to become more effective bystanders is now achieving greater prominence, thanks especially to the work of Pepler and others in Canada, Salmivalli (1999) in Finland and Rigby and Johnson (2004a, 2004b) in Australia. But without the conscientious application of these ideas by teachers and counsellors in schools, it is unlikely that they will have the desired effect. There are challenges ahead in the implementation of these and other approaches to ridding schools of the miserable practice of bullying.

REFERENCES

Bagshaw, D. (1998). What adolescents say about conflict in schools. *Children Australia, 23*(3), 17–22.

Bagshaw, D. (2004). *Verbal abuse and adolescent identities: Marking the boundaries of gender.* Unpublished PhD thesis. University of Melbourne Library.

Bagshaw, D., Chung, D., Couch, M., Lilburn, S. & Wadham, B. (2000). *Reshaping responses to domestic violence*. Canberra: Department of Human Services and Partnerships Against Domestic Violence.

Cohen, R. (1995). *Students resolving conflict: Peer mediation in schools*. Watertown, MA: Goodyear/Addison Wesley.

Cowie, H. & Olaffson, R (2000). The role of peer support in helping the victims of bullying in a school with high levels of aggression. *School Psychology International, 21*, 79–95.

DRACON International (2004). *Bridging the fields of drama and conflict management.* Malmo: DRACON International.

Hawkins, D., Pepler, D. & Craig, W. M. (2001). Naturalistic observations of peer interventions in bullying. *Social Development, 10*, 512–527.

Johnson, D. W. (1997). *Reaching out: Interpersonal effectiveness and self-actualisation* (6th ed.). Boston: Allyn and Bacon.

Mahdavi, J. & Smith, P. K. (2002). The operation of a bully court and perceptions of its success: A case study. *School Psychology International, 23*, 327–341.

Naylor, P. & Cowie, H. (1999). The effectiveness of peer support systems in challenging school bullying: The perspectives and experiences of teachers and pupils. *Journal of Adolescence, 22*, 467–479.

O'Connell, P., Pepler, D. & Craig, W. (1999). Peer involvement in bullying: Insights and challenges for intervention. *Journal of Adolescence, 22*, 437–452.

O'Toole, J., Burton, B. & Plunkett, A. (2004). *Cooling conflict: A new approach to managing bullying and conflict in schools*. Frenchs Forest, NSW: Pearson Education.

Pepler, D. J. & Craig, W. M. (1995). A peek behind the fence: Naturalistic observations of aggressive children with remote audiovisual recording. *Developmental Psychology, 31*(4), 548–553.

Petersen, L. & Rigby, K. (1999). Countering bullying at an Australian secondary school with students as helpers. *Journal of Adolescence, 22*, 481–492.

Price, S. & Jones, R. A. (2001). Reflections on anti-bullying peer counselling in a comprehensive school. *Educational Psychology in Practice*, *17*, 35–40.

Rigby, K. (2002). *A meta-evaluation of methods and approaches to reducing bullying in pre-schools and in early primary school in Australia*. Canberra: Commonwealth Attorney-General's Department.

Rigby, K. (2003). *Stop the bullying: A handbook for schools* (Rev. ed.). Melbourne: ACER.

Rigby, K. & Bagshaw, D. (2001, December). What hurts? The reported consequences of negative interactions with peers among Australian school children. *Children Australia*, *26*(4), 36–41.

Rigby, K. & Bagshaw, D. (2003). Prospects of adolescent students collaborating with teachers in addressing issues of bullying and conflict in schools. *Educational Psychology*, *23*, 535–546.

Rigby, K. & Barnes, A. (2002). To tell or not to tell: The victimised student's dilemma. *Youth Studies Australia*, *21*, 33–36.

Rigby, K. & Johnson, B. (2004a). Students as bystanders to sexual coercion. *Youth Studies, Australia*, *23*, 11–16.

Rigby, K. & Johnson, B. (2004b, September). Innocent bystanders. *Education: The National Education Magazine*, 38–40.

Salmivalli, C. (1999). Participant role approach to school bullying: Implications for interventions. *Journal of Adolescence*, *22*, 453–459.

Smith, P. K., Pepler, D. & Rigby, K. (2004). *Bullying in schools: How successful can interventions be?* Cambridge: Cambridge University Press.

ENDNOTES

1 DRACON International involves collaboration between two research teams from universities in Sweden and Malaysia and two research teams from Australian universities – Griffith University, Queensland, and our University of South Australia team in Adelaide.

2 The Adelaide DRACON team working in this school comprised Dale Bagshaw and Dianne Halliday as the conflict management teachers and researchers and Rosemary Nursey-Bray and Myk Mykyta as the drama teachers.

SECTION THREE

AN OVERVIEW OF MANAGEMENT SOLUTIONS FOR BULLYING

CHAPTER 9

An overview of approaches to managing bully/victim problems

Ken Rigby

Introduction

The question of what can be done to manage bullying in schools has over the last 20 or so years occupied the attention of numerous writers, including Olweus (1993), Rigby (1996, 2003), Rigby and Thomas (2003), Ross (1996), Smith and Sharp (1994), Suckling and Temple (2001) and Sullivan (2001). A growing number of websites have been devoted to describing what schools, parents and students can do to counter the problem (see, for example, <www.education.unisa.edu.au/bullying/>). Typically, the accounts point to a combination of actions that can be taken by schools rather than one single action. Commonly, a distinction is made between preventive action and action that may be taken if and when bullying has taken place.

Preventive methods rely for the most part on educational means. They assume that if members of the school community were adequately informed about the problem they would take steps to counter it. It is further assumed that students can be convinced of its harmfulness and undesirability, and acquire skills to prevent bullying from occurring.

However, it is generally acknowledged that not all bullying in schools can be prevented by such educational means. Hence actions are proposed to deal with cases that arise. These actions are expected to result in the discontinuation of the bullying behaviour; they may deter others from engaging in bullying, and provide an outcome that is regarded as just.

In seeking to manage bullying, schools typically develop an anti-bullying policy or program which outlines procedures that are expected to reduce peer victimisation among students. The following is a description of what is typically involved.

Educating school staff and parents about bullying

Anti-bullying programs purport to educate members of the school community about the phenomena of bullying and how bullying behaviour in schools can be prevented or reduced. Education about bullying is typically research based. It includes a description or definition of what is held to constitute bullying, an account of its prevalence and its consequences if left unchecked. Explanations are provided about why it occurs in schools. The implications of these are discussed insofar as they provide justification for anti-bullying measures to be taken or promoted by the school. In addition to providing general information about the nature of bullying, a school may be required to investigate bullying among its own students by carrying out a survey. Finally, methods of dealing with issues of bullying are explained.

Education about bullying in general and at one's school in particular is directed first and foremost towards the staff at the school. It may take the form of a 'whole day conference' following Olweus's (1993) proposal or a series of meetings, as in the Seville program undertaken by Ortega and Lera (2000) in Spain in the 1990s. Only on rare occasions is education about bullying incorporated into teacher training in a systematic manner (see Nickolaides, Toda & Smith, 2002). A welcome exception is that provided in a program for Finnish teachers conducted for three and a half days as part of a one-year teacher training course in Helsinki and Turku in 1999–2000 (Salmivalli, Kaukainen, Voetin & Sinisammal, 2004). Meetings with parents are sometimes arranged and issues of bullying discussed with them. In addition, parents may be involved in committees set up to draft school anti-bullying policies and/or be provided with information about how bullying is to be addressed through newsletters.

Working with children in classrooms

Anti-bullying programs require that teachers work with children in classrooms to help reduce bullying. Such work typically includes:

- Explaining to students what bullying is and why it is unacceptable in a school.
- Informing students of their rights and responsibilities as members of the school community: specifically the right not to be bullied by anyone (and to receive help from the school if they are victimised) and the acceptance of responsibility to abstain from bullying others and, moreover, to give assistance as far as possible to children who are being bullied at school.
- Encouraging students to devise agreed rules of behaviour which can serve as guidelines on how to behave with peers, such as those suggested by Olweus (1993): 'We shall not bully other students; we shall try to help other students who are bullied; we shall make a point to include students who become easily left out'. In his view such 'rules' should be elicited from students rather than imposed upon them.
- Increasing the capacity of students to resist being bullied. This typically requires instruction or training in how to become appropriately assertive or socially skilled in situations where one is under pressure from others (see Field, 1999). Improving skill in this area is seen as particularly desirable for children who are easily bullied by their peers.
- Encouraging students to seek help when needed. This approach receives strong support in a government publication supplied to schools in the United Kingdom called *Don't Suffer in Silence* (DfES, 2002). Children may be helped to develop good judgment about when they should seek help and from whom help should be sought (Rigby & Thomas, 2003).
- Providing exercises designed to improve children's understanding and awareness of ways of handling conflict more constructively, for example, through the use of role-play and educational drama (O'Toole, Burton & Plunkett, 2004). (See also Chapter 8.) Conflict isn't the same as bullying as there is no imbalance in power, but some of the skills learned as part of conflict management (e.g. assertiveness) can also be used in bullying situations. Additionally, schools in which students feel confident that they can handle conflict can develop more positive and supportive cultures which are less likely to promote bullying.
- Promoting the development of attitudes and skills that can lead children to recognise and effectively discourage bullying behaviour and give support to victims, for example, through actions taken when, as bystanders, they witness bullying incidents (see Chapter 8).

- Conducting classes in which learning is acquired through cooperative processes (see Cowie, Smith, Boulton & Laver, 1994). This approach is thought to encourage the valuing of fellow students, which is incompatible with bullying others.
- Promoting empathic feelings among students. Methods devised to increase the capacity for empathy in young children through story telling and role playing have been successfully employed by McMahon, Washburn, Felix, Yakin & Childrey (2000).
- Developing greater control over anger. Given that aggressive behaviour and bullying may sometimes occur when an impulsive child is unable to control feelings of hostility, anger-management programs have been employed as a means of reducing bullying in young children (McMahon et al., 2000).
- Modelling and rewarding pro-social actions. This includes teachers acting in respectful and helpful ways towards students and avoiding the use of threats to control classes (Roland & Galloway, 2002). In addition, schools may identify and reward children who have helped others.

Empowering students to act to counter bullying

While schools generally see the primary responsibility for managing bullying in the school environment as belonging to teachers and implemented through their direct actions, many anti-bullying programs involve students as collaborators in addressing bullying. Student action may take a variety of forms, including acting as peer supporters, mediators, peer counsellors, members of 'bully courts' or members of school anti-bullying committees.

The aptitude and required training of students carrying such roles tend to be similar, although the specific tasks may be different. The activities in which they engage in some respects are also similar. Peer supporters have a more generalised task in providing support and assistance to students in need of help over a wide range of areas besides peer victimisation. Students trained in peer mediation are concerned with helping to resolve conflicts. The relevance of this activity lies mainly in contributing to a more positive school ethos in which bullying incidents are less likely to occur. Students who receive training in peer counselling aimed at resolving bully/victim problems have a particularly demanding task and some authorities believe such work is more justifiably handled by school authorities. The same is true of 'bully courts' consisting of students who are expected to 'try' students accused of bullying others, and to recommend suitable penalties (see Elliott, 1998). More readily justified are anti-bullying committees composed of students who have volunteered to work closely with the school counsellor in advising and assisting in the process of developing good anti-bullying practices (see Petersen & Rigby, 1999).

Non-educational approaches to preventing bullying

The three most commonly used non-educational approaches are (i) school surveillance, (ii) provision of safe places and (iii) the introduction of activities during school breaks.

School surveillance

Close monitoring by teachers of playgrounds and places where bullying is known to occur during breaks has been seen as an effective way of reducing bullying (Olweus, 1993). Ensuring that adults in authority are on buses taking students to and from schools may have a similar effect. Selected students, appropriately trained, have also been employed to assist in discouraging bullying behaviour, for example, so-called 'peacekeepers' (Rigby & Thomas, 2003).

Providing and/or identifying safe places

Children who are particularly vulnerable to being bullied at school may be provided with opportunities to avoid contact with those who may bully them. School libraries sometimes serve this function. Clubs for children who prefer less physically active pastimes such as chess may be formed. In some countries, including Australia, 'Safety Houses' have been established to provide a haven for children who are being harassed to or from school (Rigby, 1996).

Providing activities for students at break times

It has been suggested that bullying may occur because students lack opportunities to take part in interesting, constructive activities during break periods. Boredom develops and bullying may be seen as a means of overcoming it. Some educationalists have proposed that providing an interesting and stimulating school environment can act to reduce bullying (DfES, 2002).

Dealing with incidents of bullying

The distinction between 'dealing with bullying' and 'prevention' is somewhat artificial. For example, if bullying is dealt with in such a way as to deter future acts of aggression, the procedure for dealing with it can also be preventive. In what follows we will focus primarily on those strategies that have been suggested and undertaken in schools to deal directly with incidents of bullying.

We may distinguish between actions taken by school authorities that take the form of sanctions or penalties to be imposed on children judged to have bullied another child or other children, and actions that do not involve the use of sanctions or penalties, that is, essentially non-punitive approaches. Both kinds of actions may be regarded as 'consequences' for engaging in bullying, but the former contains a punitive element that is absent in the latter.

The use of sanctions

The most commonly used method of dealing with bullying is to identify the person who has engaged in bullying and to apply a sanction that is linked with the breaking of rules that students have been told about and, ideally, complicit in their formulation and acceptance. The sanctions may take different forms, such as being detained by the school, deprived of certain 'privileges' such as taking part in a game, and given menial tasks to do. Olweus (1993) emphasises that the treatment of cases of bullying should invariably include conducting 'serious talks' with parents or guardians. In extreme cases, being suspended or excluded from attending school may be justified. This method of managing bullying is seen not only as a means of discouraging further acts of bullying on the part of the 'bully', but also as a means of 'sending a message' to other students who might otherwise engage in bullying. Typically, such disciplinary actions are seen as the responsibility of the school staff, although, as discussed above, the staff may delegate some responsibility to students functioning in 'bully courts'.

A somewhat different approach may be taken based upon the principles of restorative justice. This approach (see Chapter 11 for more details) has some features in common with that outlined above insofar as it involves the use of sanctions. However, restorative justice is concerned with 'violations against people' and the restoration of positive relationships rather than simply applying punishment for breaking rules (Thorsborne & Vinograd, 2004). It operates primarily through the use of Community Conferences at which victims and perpetrators (typically those responsible for serious abusive behaviour) meet, together with their respective friends and families. Victims are encouraged to express their sense of hurt while perpetrators listen, become contrite and agree to compensate the victim in some way. An important aspect of the process is the inducing of a sense of shame in the perpetrator under conditions in which he or she continues to receive the love and support of others present at the meeting. Ways of applying principles of restorative justice in less serious cases have been suggested by Morrison (2002) and Thorsborne and Vinograd (2004).

Non-punitive approaches

Some educationalists have urged that non-punitive measures may be taken in dealing with cases of bullying. These measures are sometimes called 'problem-solving methods'. They include the use of mediation processes, the No-Blame Approach and the Method of Shared Concern. Chapter 12 contains a detailed comparison of these two approaches.

Mediation

A popular approach supported by some educational jurisdictions is the use of mediation. This involves intervention by a third person in a case of conflict between persons to help the participants reach some mutually satisfactory outcome. This must be one that requires the abandonment of bullying tactics. The 'bully' needs to be convinced that a different, no-bullying way of relating to the 'victim' is preferable. The victim needs to be assured that the bullying will cease. Much may depend upon the level of skill of the mediator and his or her perceived neutrality. Whether teachers – powerful authority figures – can fulfil this role has been disputed. As previously discussed, doubts have been expressed regarding the suitability of students as mediators in cases in which there is an imbalance and abuse of power. The use of mediation may be justified more readily, especially in cases of conflict where power is not being abused. Importantly, intervention at an early stage in conflict may prevent a conflict developing into a bully/victim situation. Further, where a mediation approach to resolving conflict is practised, the school ethos is likely to be one in which bullying behaviour is less common.

The No-Blame Approach

The so-called 'no-blame' approach is an attempt to solve the problem of bullying without resorting to sanctions or penalties. The primary aim of this approach is to change the motivation of the bully or bullies and to induce them to behave responsibly.

An approach developed by two English educationalists, Maines and Robinson (1992; Robinson & Maines, 2000) has been called 'The No-Blame Approach'. An alternative term used to describe this general method is the 'peer-support approach' (Young, 1998). This method begins when a victim is identified, either through a teacher observing what has been happening or by being told about it by the victim, the victim's parent(s), other children or other adults. The victim is interviewed to discover what has happened and who was involved. It is not intended that there should be a detailed investigation of the incident, or incidents, or an attempt made at this, or any subsequent stage 'to get to the bottom of it'. The focus is on the feelings of the child who has been victimised. The interviewer seeks to get permission from the child to tell the bullies how he or she (the child) feels about it. It is emphasised that the bullies will not be punished and that there is no reason to be fearful of informing. To provide a graphic account the child is asked to describe his or her feelings, if possible, in the form of a piece of writing, a poem or a drawing.

Next a meeting is convened. This includes the bully or bullies, and also any colluders or bystanders. The group also commonly includes children who are specially selected because they are known to have pro-social attitudes and are likely to exercise positive peer influence. The victim is generally not included. At the meeting, the teacher or counsellor seeks to describe how the victim feels about the bullying, drawing upon the materials that have been provided by the victim. This may involve simply a description of how the victim feels or, alternatively, the reading of a poem. There is no interrogation and no blaming. The aim is simply to share information and produce an empathic response. It is pointed out by the convener that it is the children's joint responsibility to help by improving the situation for the victim. Specific suggestions may then be elicited as to how the victim can be made happier. No promises are required from the children regarding any proposals to help. The meeting ends with the teacher handing over to the group responsibility for deciding how the victim is to be helped and the situation put right. The teacher undertakes to meet with them about a week later to review progress. The teacher also meets with the victim and members of the group individually to monitor progress and to express appreciation for the positive things that are being done.

The Method of Shared Concern

This is a more complex approach similar in some respects to the No-Blame Approach. It was developed by the Swedish psychologist, Anatol Pikas (1989, 2002), and has been widely used in Europe and Australia. An extended and detailed description and evaluation of The Method of Shared Concern is given in Rigby (2005, in press). Its first step is to identify the problem. Unlike the No-Blame Approach, there is no attempt initially to interview the victim. Information may be gathered by direct observations or from reports of those who have witnessed the bullying. In this way the teacher or counsellor seeks to identify the persons who have been involved in the bullying, the perpetrator(s) and the victim(s), and to learn about how the victim is being treated. Next the suspected bullies are seen. Unlike the No-Blame Approach, the method is to interview each of the suspected bullies individually. No accusations are made. The meeting begins with the interviewer inviting the student to sit in a chair opposite (without an intervening desk) and waiting for eye contact before the interaction begins. The interviewer starts by sharing a concern for the person who is being victimised. Once the feelings of the interviewer have been clearly and sincerely conveyed, the student is asked to say what he or she knows about the situation. As soon as the student has acknowledged some awareness (not necessarily guilt) relating to what has been happening, the student is asked directly what he or she can do to help improve matters. The interviewer is not trying to 'get to the bottom of the matter' or to apportion blame but rather is trying to elicit a constructive response and change the situation. Commonly, the interviewees do make suggestions, but if they do not, the interviewer may make suggestions, which are positive, acceptable and not difficult to follow. The interviewer expresses strong approval for any constructive proposals and, importantly, arranges for another meeting (at an agreed time) to see how things have gone. At no time are threats made or warnings given.

Subsequently the victim is interviewed. The interviewer begins by expressing concern, sympathy and support for what has been happening. However, further questions need to be asked to find out whether the victim has been doing anything to bring on the bullying, i.e. by acting as a provocative victim. The interviewer discloses that he or she has actually talked with the bullies individually and that each of them agreed to cooperate. The interviewer undertakes to meet again with the victim to see how things develop.

Next a meeting with the whole group is organised. At this meeting, it is usually possible to (a) compliment the members on the progress that has been made and (b) to 'fall in with' (or elicit) a suggestion from members of the group that the victim be invited to join them for a final meeting to demonstrate that the problem of bullying has really been resolved. Reassurances are given by individual members that they will act positively towards the victim at such a meeting. The victim can normally be induced to join the group for a final meeting, with assurances that there will be no unpleasantness. Such a meeting, if well conducted, can demonstrate publicly that the bullying is well and truly over. However, in cases where the victim has behaved provocatively, the interviewer must seek to facilitate adjustments in the behaviour of both sides, i.e. play the role of mediator. The aim is to get the students to reach an agreement – ideally in writing and in an agreed form – relating to how each will behave in future.

The basic assumption here is that children who bully can be brought to appreciate the harm they are doing and begin to act responsibly – if they are approached in the right way. Unlike the No-Blame Approach, this method assumes that the best way to approach a bully is in a one-to-one situation. The interaction with the bully is intended to help him or her to become 'reindividualised' rather than continue to bully mindlessly under the influence of a group. This does not mean, however, that the Method of Shared Concern is aimed at destroying groups. It recognises that peer groups fulfil an important role in a child's development. Hence, those who use this method are advised to meet with the group of children who have engaged in bullying – after each has individually acted responsibly – and to share with them an appreciation of how as a group they are now functioning in a constructive way. It does not mean either that the victim is necessarily blameless. It is recognised that he or she may need to change and act in a less provocative manner to prevent further bullying. Finally, it places a good deal of emphasis upon the need to monitor progress and to react to changes in the situation as it develops. The originator of this method, Anatol Pikas, has recently likened his work with individuals involved in bully/victim problems to that of those who practise 'shuttle diplomacy' (Pikas, 2002).

Mixed approaches to interventions

The intervention approaches that have been described as 'rules and sanctions' and 'no-blame' are seen by some to be incompatible. The two Scandinavian researchers who have pioneered these approaches, Dan Olweus and Anatol Pikas, in fact, each regard the other's approach to dealing with bullying as totally misguided. While there are many who see these approaches in opposition, there are schools where both are in use. Typically, non-punitive approaches are used with less severe cases of bullying and punitive approaches (i.e. sanctions and punishments) are used with more severe cases and with cases that cannot be solved using a non-blaming approach (see Rigby, 2003).

Conclusions

It is clear that anti-bullying programs tend to contain similar elements, but there are significant variations, especially in the area of addressing and treating cases of bullying. A further area in which differences arise is in the thoroughness of the implementation of anti-bullying programs. It is evident that how the policy is implemented is at least as important as its specific content. There is now strong research-based evidence that bullying in schools can be substantially reduced in schools *only* when schools take their responsibilities seriously and respond whole-heartedly to the problem.

REFERENCES

Cowie, H., Smith, P. K., Boulton, M. & Laver, R. (1994). *Co-operation in the multi-ethnic classroom*. London: David Fulton.

DfES (2002). *Bullying: Don't suffer in silence – An action pack for schools*. London: DfES.

Elliott, M. (1998). *Bullying*. London: Hodder Children's Books.

Field, E. M. (1999). *Bullybusting*. Lane Cove, NSW: Finch.

Maines, B. & Robinson, G. (1992). *Michael's story: The 'No Blame' Approach*. Bristol, England: Lucky Duck Publishing.

McMahon, S. D., Washburn, J., Felix, E. D., Yakin, J. & Childrey, G. (2000). Violence prevention: Program effects on urban preschool and kindergarten children, *Applied and Preventive Psychology*, 9, 271–281.

Morrison, B. (2002). Bullying and victimisation in schools: A restorative justice approach. *Trends and Issues*, No. 219. Canberra: Australian Institute of Criminology.

Nickolaides, S., Toda, Y. & Smith, P. K. (2002). Knowledge and attitudes about school bullying in trainee teachers. *British Journal of Educational Psychology*, *72*(105), 118.

Olweus, D. (1993). *Bullying at school*. Oxford: Blackwell.

O'Toole, J., Burton, B. & Plunkett, A. (2004). *Cooling conflict*. Frenchs Forest, NSW: Pearson Longman.

Ortega, R. & Lera, M. J. (2000). The Seville Anti-Bullying in School Project. *Aggressive Behaviour*, *26*, 113–123.

Petersen, L. & Rigby, K. (1999). Countering bullying at an Australian secondary school. *Journal of Adolescence*, *22*, 481–492.

Pikas, A. (1989). The Common Concern Method for the treatment of mobbing. In E. Roland & E. Munthe (Eds.), *Bullying: An international perspective* (pp. 91–104). London: David Fulton in association with the Professional Development Foundation.

Pikas, A. (2002). New developments in the Shared Concern Method, *School Psychology International*, *23*(3), 307–326.

Rigby, K. (1996). *Bullying in schools – and what to do about it*. Melbourne: ACER.

Rigby, K. (2003). *Stop the bullying: A handbook for schools* (Rev. ed.). Melbourne: ACER.

Rigby, K. (2005, in press). The Method of Shared Concern as an intervention technique to address bullying in schools: An overview and appraisal. *Australian Journal of Counselling & Guidance*.

Rigby, K. & Thomas, E. B. (2003). *How schools counter bullying: Policies and procedures in selected Australian schools*. School Principal's Handbook Series. Point Lonsdale, Vic.: The Professional Reading Guide.

Robinson, G. & Maines, B. (2000). *Crying for help: The No-Blame Approach to bullying*. Bristol, England: Lucky Duck Publishing.

Roland, E. & Galloway, D. (2002). Classroom influences on bullying. *Educational Research*, 44, 299–312.

Ross, D. M. (1996). *Childhood bullying and teasing: What school personnel, other professionals and parents can do*. Alexandria, VA: American Counseling Association.

Salmivalli, C., Kaukainen, A., Voetin, M. & Sinisammal, M. (2004). Targeting the group as a whole: The Finish anti-bullying intervention. In P. K. Smith, D. Pepler & K. Rigby (Eds.), *Bullying in schools: How successful can interventions be?* (pp. 251–275). Cambridge: Cambridge University Press.

Smith, P. K. & Sharp, S. (Eds.) (1994). *School bullying: Insights and perspectives*. Routledge, London.

Suckling, A. & Temple, C. (2001). *Bullying: A whole school approach*. Melbourne: ACER.

Sullivan, K. (2001). *The anti-bullying handbook*. Auckland, New Zealand: Oxford University Press.

Thorsborne, M. & Vinograd, D. (2004). *Restorative practices in schools*. Geelong: Margaret Thorsborne and Associates.

Young, S. (1998). The support group approach to bullying in schools. *Educational Psychology in Practice*, *14*, 32–39.

CHAPTER 10

A resilience-based approach to helping victims of bullying and their families

Andrew Fuller

Introduction

Bullying is both insidious and pervasive. Modern forms of communication, such as e-mail, chat rooms and text messages, enable bullying to be much more subtle and, at the same time, much more damaging to a victim's social reputation.

While we should never stop trying to prevent bullying, it is unlikely that we will ever get to the point where it is eliminated. Therefore, we cannot just rely on bullying prevention and intervention programs. We need to find ways to support the victims of bullying and to help them recover and retain their resilience. Resilience can be viewed as the happy knack of bungy jumping through the pitfalls of life. Research indicates that three factors predominate in predicting resilient outcomes for young Australian people: family connectedness, having a diversity of friendships and knowing that there is a trustworthy adult outside the family who can provide support (Fuller, McGraw & Goodyear, 1999).

A treatment protocol is outlined in this chapter that can be used by school counsellors or student welfare coordinators when they are working with young people and their families who have experienced bullying. It is designed both to stop the bullying and to assist in the building of protective factors in the young person being bullied so that bullying is less likely to recur.

The treatment protocol has its origins in the area of solution-focused therapy (de Shazer, 1988; Fisch, Weakland & Segal, 1982; Haley, 1973), which has been shown to be an effective form of intervention for many conditions, including bullying (Young & Holdorf, 2003). It was initially developed at a university psychology clinic in Melbourne and has been refined over the past 10 years into the current format.

Format of the family-focused program

Being bullied is a family business. It often shatters the confidence of the direct victim and also traumatises the parents. The parents of victims often describe feeling helpless, angry and powerless. Most parents were educated at a time when there was less awareness of effective approaches to bullying prevention. This has resulted in many parents having experienced bullying at school without an effective resolution. One father told me, 'There wasn't much you could do about bullying – you could biff them back if you were big enough, or try to form your own gang, or just put up with it. Most of us just put up with it.'

Young people respond to being bullied in different ways. Some attempt counter-aggression either towards the bully or more often towards someone else in their school or family (Salmivelli, Karhunen & Lagerspetz, 1996). Some victims spend more time alone at recess, feel sadder in the school environment and feel less safe in the playground (Slee, 1995). Others feel helpless, unable to respond in any effective way. Yet others try nonchalance or ignoring the bullying. Unfortunately, this is very difficult in a school situation, and students who have been repeatedly told to 'just ignore it' often report feeling stuck and unheard.

In the initial trial carried out at the university, five sessions were offered to bullied students and their families over approximately one school term. A summary of the five sessions follows.

Session 1: A pact for joint communication

At the outset, families were told that if the bullying could not be stopped within one school term, then it was too big an issue to allow to continue and they should consider either class or school change. This was done for two reasons: firstly, to inform the victims that we were serious about stopping them being bullied; and secondly, to alleviate the fears many young victims express – that adults are going to stomp in, try to fix it all in a few days, and then move on in the belief that all has been resolved but, in reality, leaving the young person vulnerable and isolated.

An assessment of the situation was conducted in which the students and their families were asked to describe the bullying problem and outline what they had tried to do to deal with it. Often families described a series of ineffective solutions that increased in intensity and desperation as the bullying continued. Care needed to be taken to ensure that all attempts to solve the problem were covered in order to be clear about what had not worked.

Students were asked questions such as:

- How long has the bullying been happening?
- Have there been times in the past when you've been picked on or bullied and, if so, how did you manage to stop that?
- What have you already tried to do to stop the bullying?
- What advice have you received from parents/friends/teachers?
- What have your parents and teachers done or suggested you try?
- What have your social experiences been like in other social settings outside school?
- Do you have friends who don't go to your school? How do things go when you're with them?

It was clear that the diversity of advice received by young people who are bullied at school can be quite staggering.

It can also be beneficial to tap into victims' fantasies about stopping the bullying. It is not uncommon for bullied students to harbour quite violent thoughts towards the perpetrators.

Questions were also asked of the parents, including:

- Are there any specific things that you have tried to help stop the bullying?
- Have you contacted the school to discuss the issues? If yes, what happened?
- If you haven't contacted the school, what made you decide not to?
- Who is the best person to contact at your school regarding this?

The first intervention was to ask parents to contact their child's school to explain their concerns and to establish a joint monitoring system whereby the adults in the system, teaching staff and parents, unite to monitor and record what is happening.

At this stage a joint parent-school monitoring system was outlined to the parents in the following way:

> As a first step we suggest you contact the school and discuss setting up a system whereby you keep a record of any incidents you hear about and they do the

> same and that then you meet to compare notes. We don't expect this in itself will solve the problem but it's important that everyone begins to work together to stop this problem.

At the completion of the first session each bullied student was asked to draw a map of their school indicating safe places with a tick and unsafe places with a cross. They also completed a School Safety Survey (Fuller, 1998) (see also Appendix 14B for more details of this survey).

Family permission to contact the schools was then sought and the schools were contacted to explain the monitoring system and to obtain additional information regarding the students' academic and social skills. A check was also made that the schools had access to evidence-based bullying intervention strategies such as the No-Blame Approach and the Method of Shared Concern discussed in Chapters 9 and 12.

Session 2: Invisibility training

The second session, usually held two weeks later with the bullied young person and their family, focused mainly on the following aspects.

Review of map and monitoring system

Safe and unsafe places in the school were reviewed and a careful analysis undertaken of what made particular places safe or dangerous. At this point, we discussed the concept of invisibility training. While we didn't want the bullied young person to begin an avoidance program, temporarily altering their position in the school grounds can be beneficial.

Children and adolescents are creatures of habit, but if the routine of the young person is changed, even for a few days, the extent of the bullying also alters. Changes include the time of catching public transport to and from school and use of locker areas.

Meeting between parents and school

If the parents had already met with the school, a discussion was held about the outcome – whether they had felt heard and whether the school seemed prepared to act. If they hadn't met with the school, barriers to this were explored. Sometimes, at this point, parents expressed reservations about the school or the seriousness with which they believed their concerns would be received. If this appeared to be a major issue, we would contact the school after the second session to assess the likely accuracy of the parents' perceptions.

Cognitive reframing of negative beliefs possibly caused by the bullying

A discussion was held with the parents and the bullied young person that incorporated some of the following questions:

- Have you ever been tempted into believing that any of the insults are true?
- Do you ever forget the friends that you do have when you get picked on?
- Who likes to spend time with you? How come they like you?
- What do they know about you that the bullies don't?
- If bullies bully to make themselves feel good, why do you think they are so insecure?

Check of parents' own school experiences

Parents' own experiences of bullying at school often shape their responses to the situation with their child as well as the extent to which they feel powerless to help their child. Questions were asked such as:

- Were you ever picked on or bullied at school?
- If yes, how did you cope?
- How did it get resolved?
- How did your school help (or not help) you?
- If the bullying didn't get resolved, does that make it difficult for you to understand the strength of your daughter's/son's reaction?

Discussion on strategies for responding to incidents

Using the incidence diary, we then looked for patterns in the bullying. For some, it was a repeated pattern of being excluded or having rumours spread about them. We tried to discuss with many of these young people why they wanted to be friends with those who bullied them. In instances where exclusion was the main form of bullying, we asked the bullied young person to bring in a class list of all students. We then went through it, and with them highlighted students' names into one of three categories: hates or doesn't like me; neutral; likes me. Strategies for befriending some of the neutral people were then discussed. Generally, young people who had initially claimed 'nobody likes me' found that the majority of students were actually either neutral towards them or liked them. (A study by Smith, Talamelli, Cowie, Naylor and Chauhan, 2004, which followed up young people who had been victimised at school, found that those who were no longer victims two years later 'had more strenuously sought social support and tried to make other friends compared to those that were still being victimised'.)

In cases where physical bullying was the major problem, we carefully reviewed the young person's 'safe/unsafe' map and discussed their movements around the school.

A follow-up contact with the school was then made to discuss how the physical bullying could be stopped.

In instances where the bullying was in the form of verbal insults, an attempt was made to understand the power of these terms for the young person. The parents were also involved in a discussion about their own experiences of being insulted or teased.

Several tasks were requested at the end of the second session:

- The parents were asked to compare their monitoring with the school's, if they had not already done so.
- The young person was asked to continue keeping an incidence diary.
- The therapist wrote a therapeutic letter to the young person.
- The family was asked to watch some videos about bullying, such as *The Simpsons*' episode, 'Bart – The General', or the film, *Roxanne*.

The second session was followed up with a supportive letter to the young person. An example of one of these is given below:

> *Dear Harry,*
>
> *I just thought I'd write to you to let you know how impressed I've been with how you're coping with being picked on at school. Many people your age get sucked into believing that the insults are true and that it's their fault.*
>
> *I guess the people bullying you must either feel bad about themselves or are just bored. Still that's no excuse for picking on people.*
>
> *Just from talking to you I can tell that people would like to be with you and that you would be a good friend to have.*
>
> *Hopefully we can find a way to help these bullies stop what they are doing. I've talked to your school about this and we've got a few ideas about ways to handle them.*
>
> *Keep trying to work out different ways to handle what they do and we'll talk about these next time we meet. Remember if you get stuck for ideas you can always telephone or email me. Just remember to leave your number and I'll call you back as soon as I can.*

Session 3: Resilience training

The response many young people have to being bullied is one of shame and helplessness. Unfortunately, this appears to make victims of school bullying 'smell of fear' in that they almost appear to give off signals that suggest to other students that they are vulnerable in some way. Sadly, this all too often leads to them experiencing more bullying.

Resilience training begins with a review of progress since the last session. The young person's social contacts outside school are bolstered and parents are encouraged to ensure that their child sees friends outside school. In instances where there are no social contacts outside school, extended family members and local youth, sports, social and scouting clubs are investigated.

In the third session we went through the young person's incidence diary and picked out insults that could either be deconstructed or deflected. The young person was asked to say one of the insults from their incidence diary to the counsellor, using the same tone or gestures as used by the students who had been bullying them. It is important to be clear that the purpose of this is not to help a bullied young person to learn how to bully but rather to equip them with a variety of responses when they do get bullied. The counsellor then modelled a variety of responses from ignoring them, changing the topic, thanking them for their interest to using a few comeback responses. Humour is a powerful weapon for disempowering insults and some 'nice' stock responses are 'wastoid' and 'snot gobbler'. These were then rehearsed. The method of deflection equips the bullied student with one or two brief responses to common insults. These responses are not insulting to the bully but deflect or deconstruct the term, thereby reducing its hurtfulness. For example, does someone who calls you a 'smart-arse' actually mean that your bottom is clever? While it is important that the focus not be taken off changing the way bullies behave, it is also important to empower bullied students so that the insults directed at them are not believed.

Session 4: Consolidation

The fourth session aimed to consolidate the strategies suggested in the previous meeting. Interestingly, bullied students would often return to the fourth session and say that the strategies devised in Session 3 had not been used but, nevertheless, the bullying had abated and, in many cases, ceased all together. In talking to young people who have been bullied at school, the impression gained is that the deflection strategies are potent even if they are not stated, as the victim is aware that they *could* use them if they chose to. This appeared to lessen their 'smell of fear' to potential bullies.

Generally, Session 4 also involved further deconstruction of insults and refinements of the deflection method. If no improvement had occurred, the young person and their family discussed further strategies for invisibility training as well as additional ways of building up social contacts outside school. If the parents were themselves fairly socially isolated they were encouraged to increase the frequency of their own socialising in order to demonstrate this to their children.

Session 5: Final

During the fifth session the Safer Schools Survey was readministered to the young person. Together with the family, strategies were reviewed and the frequency of bullying was checked. If the process had not been effective in stopping the bullying, the parents were involved in a discussion about whether or not to continue in the same class or school. It was explained to the bullied student that many young people find that moving to a new school can help them to start again and not have to put up with being bullied.

If the process had been effective in stopping the bullying, the family were involved in a discussion on relapse prevention and future strategies. The importance of maintaining a second peer group was emphasised as was the importance of maintaining a high level of social activity for the whole family. The young person was asked:

- Would you be prepared to be a consultant to other young people who are being bullied in school?
- What would you suggest we do to help someone overcome similar problems?
- How would you know if bullying was becoming a problem for you again?
- If that happened, what would you do?

At the conclusion of the last session a therapeutic letter was again sent from the therapist to the young person and their family. An example of a letter that was sent if the process had stopped the bullying appears below:

> *Dear Harry and family,*
>
> *I thought I'd write again to make sure you realise the achievement you've made. It took a lot of courage to do what you did and to decide not to put up with being bullied at school. By doing this you've helped us to stop other people being bullied in schools.*
>
> *Clearly you have given a lot of thought to how not to let insults affect you so much and also how insulting people and putting them down can really be hurtful to people.*
>
> *We hope that you can continue to help us by keeping us informed of any new ideas you have about ways to stop bullying. If you get an idea please write to us.*
>
> *In the meantime we would like you to know you have been accepted as a certified bully buster! Please find your certificate attached.*
>
> *Kind regards,*

An example of a letter that was sent if the process had not stopped the bullying and the family had decided to change the child's school is given below:

> *Dear Harry and family,*
>
> *I thought I'd write again to make sure you realise the achievement you've made. It took a lot of courage to do what you did and to decide not to put up with being bullied at school. By doing this you've helped us to stop other people being bullied in schools.*
>
> *Even though we didn't manage to stop the bullying, we know that you will be able to find lots of friends in the future. Sometimes, it is better to move away from a situation that is not going to change.*
>
> *Clearly you have given a lot of thought to how to not let insults affect you so much and also how insulting people and putting them down can really be hurtful to people.*
>
> *If your parents decide to change your school, we hope you can get a new start where people will be able to see what a great person you are. We are happy to help you to settle in to a new school if this is what happens.*
>
> *We hope that you can continue to help us by keeping us informed of any new ideas you have about ways to stop bullying. If you get an idea please write to us.*
>
> *In the meantime we would like you to know you have been accepted as a certified bully buster! Please find your certificate attached.*
>
> *Kind regards,*

Format of the student-focused program within the school setting

This program has been adapted from the initial protocol, which focused on the student being bullied and their family, for use with students at school.

Session 1: Working together

1. Let the student know that it may take a few months for the situation to improve. Reassure the student that the approach will not be heavy-handed and that it will be a team effort.
2. Ask them to document what happens. They should write down who was there when the bullying occurred, what role they played, and the date, time and where it occurred.

Tell them that the school will also be monitoring and documenting what happens and that their notes will be compared with the school's observations to identify patterns.

3. Explain that you don't expect this in itself will solve the problem but it's important that everyone begins to work together to improve the situation.
4. Ask the student to outline what they have already tried to do to deal with the bullying using questions such as:
   - How long has the bullying been happening?
   - Have there been times in the past when you've been picked on or bullied and, if so, how did you manage to stop it?
   - What have you already tried to do to stop the bullying?
   - What advice have you received from parents/friends/teachers?
   - What have your parents and teachers done or suggested you try?
   - What have your social experiences been like in other social settings outside school?
   - Do you have friends who don't go to your school? How do things go when you're with them?
5. Ask the student to draw a map of the school indicating safe places with a tick and unsafe places with a cross. Ask them to complete the School Safety Survey (see Appendix 14B).

Session 2: Invisibility training

1. Review the student's perceptions and map of safe and unsafe places in the school and analyse what makes particular places safe or dangerous.
2. Discuss the concept of invisibility training. Talk about the possibility of the student changing their routines (e.g. use of locker areas, time for using the canteen, path used to walk to the toilets) in order to reduce the bullying.
3. Discuss thoughts that the student has about the bullying, using questions such as:
   - Have you ever been tempted into believing that any of the insults are true?
   - Do you ever forget the friends that you do have when you get picked on?
   - Who likes to spend time with you? How come they like you?
   - What do they know about you that the bullies don't?
4. Use the young person's record of bullying incidents and look at it together for patterns in the bullying.
5. If social exclusion is an issue, ask the student to bring to the next session a class list of the names of all students. Go through them and categorise students' names into one of three categories: hates or doesn't like me; neutral; likes me. Discuss strategies for befriending some of the students in the neutral category.

6. If verbal insults and putdowns are an issue, discuss what it is about each insult that is particularly upsetting for them.
7. Request that they continue keeping records of incidences in a notebook.
8. For homework, ask them to watch some videos about bullying, such as *The Simpsons*' episode, 'Bart – The General', or the film, *Roxanne*.
9. Consider writing a supportive letter to the student between this and the next session, such as the one below:

   Dear Sarah,

   I just thought I'd write to you to let you know how impressed I've been with how you're coping with being given a hard time at school right now. Many people your age get sucked into believing that the nasty things that people say about them are true and that it's their fault that they're being badly treated.

   I guess the people who are bullying you must be low on kindness or desperate to convince others about how popular they are (or tough). Still that's no excuse for picking on people.

   Just from talking to you I can tell that most people would enjoy spending time with you and that you would be a good friend to have.

   Hopefully we can find a way to help these kids stop what they are doing. The school has got a few ideas about ways to handle them but we are trying to sort things out without making things worse for you.

   Keep trying to work out different ways to handle what they do and we'll talk about these next time we meet. Remember, if you get stuck for ideas you can always telephone or email me.

Session 3: Resilience training

1. Discuss the importance with the student of looking like they don't have a 'smell of fear' or feel ashamed, and presenting confidently with a loud voice, firm eye contact and standing tall.
2. Review any social contacts that the student has had with others their age, to make the point that there are situations where the bullying doesn't happen and that there are other people who like them and treat them with respect.
3. Ask them how they are doing with getting to know some of the people in their class that they had categorised as 'neutral'.

4. Review the incidence diary again and select insults that can either be deconstructed or deflected. Ask them to say one of the insults from the diary using the same tone or gestures as used by the students who have been bullying them. Model for them a variety of responses from ignoring, changing the topic, thanking them for their interest to using a few humorous comeback responses which are not insulting but deflect or deconstruct specific terms.

Session 4: Consolidation

Review the current situation and continue with the same processes as were used in the first three sessions.

Session 5: Final

1. Readminister the Safer Schools Survey to the young person and review the current situation.
2. Help the student to write a simple story about a person such as themselves (but with a different name) who was bullied and who dealt with it. Ask for permission to use the story (without naming them) with other students.
3. Congratulate them if they report feeling more able to deal with the bullying.
4. Ask questions that will help prevent a relapse of the student's confidence, such as:
   - Would you be prepared to be a consultant to other young people who are being bullied in school?
   - What would you suggest we do to help someone overcome similar problems?
   - How would you know if bullying was becoming a problem for you again?
   - If that happened, what would you do?
5. Consider a supportive follow-up letter such as the one below:

   Dear Sarah,

   I thought I'd write again to make sure you realise the achievement you've made. It took a lot of courage to do what you did and to decide not to put up with being bullied at school. By doing this you've helped us to stop other people being bullied in the school.

   Clearly you have had to think a lot about how to not let insults affect you so much and also about how insulting people and putting them down can really be hurtful to people.

   I hope that you can continue to help me and the rest of the school by keeping us informed of any new ideas you have about ways to stop bullying. If you get an idea please come and see me or email them to me.

   Kind regards,

Note: If things have not improved as a result of the shared sessions and monitoring and warning steps taken by the school, consider using the next step of a non-punitive approach such as the No-Blame Approach or the Method of Shared Concern discussed in Chapters 9 and 12.

Conclusion

Becoming aware that a young person is being bullied at school is distressing for all concerned. It is tempting when we are threatened or distressed to become more primitive and more urgent in our responses. In the case of bullying this is not always the most effective way to intervene.

By methodically helping the young person to create alternative responses to bullying while also helping the parents to form an alliance with the school, and at the same time assisting schools to apply effective intervention strategies to help the students doing the bullying to stop, many thousands of young people have been assisted to stop bullying and being bullied.

REFERENCES

de Shazer, S. (1988). *Clues: Investigating Solutions in Brief Therapy*. New York: Norton.

Fisch, R., Weakland, J. H. & Segal, L. (1982). *The tactics of change*. San Francisco: Jossey-Bass.

Fuller, A. (1998). *From surviving to thriving: Promoting mental health in young people*. Melbourne: Australian Council for Educational Research Press.

Fuller, A., McGraw, K. & Goodyear, M. (1999). Bungy jumping through life: What young people say promotes well-being and resilience. *Australian Journal of Guidance and Counselling*, 9(1), 159–168.

Haley, J. (1973). *Uncommon therapy: The psychiatric techniques of Milton H. Erickson*. New York: Norton.

Salmivelli, C., Karhunen, J. & Lagerspetz, K. M. J. (1996). How do the victims respond to bullying. *Aggressive Behavior*, *22*(2), 99–109.

Slee, P. T. (1995). Bullying in the playground: The impact of interpersonal violence on Australian children's perceptions of their play environment. *Children's Environments*, *12*(3), 320–327.

Smith, P. K., Talamelli, L., Cowie, H., Naylor, P. & Chauhan, P. (2004). Profiles of non-victims, escaped victims, continuing victims and new victims of school bullying. *British Journal of Educational Psychology*, *74*(4), 565–581.

Young, S. & Holdorf, G. (2003). Using Solution Focused Brief Therapy in individual referrals for bullying, *Educational Psychology in Practice*, *19*(4), 271–282.

CHAPTER 11

Restorative responses to bullying

Margaret Armstrong and Margaret Thorsborne

> I find myself sometimes curious, often times irritated, and occasionally astonished by the whole concept of bullies, bullied, and those who are witness to the activity and remain silent. That we lack the skills of dealing with bullying in peacefully effective ways screams at us from the news headlines. And there is a line crossed all too often where the bullied becomes the bully. The idea that being excluded, shunned, ridiculed, ostracized, and physically assaulted by the bullying faction merits vengeance and violence is but one of those self-degrading ideas we embrace, creating a cure that is worse than the disease.
>
> Dianne Reeves letter to Barbara Colorosa, *The Bully, The Bullied and the Bystander* (2003), p. 1

Introduction

This chapter describes an approach that an increasing number of schools are finding effective in responding to incidents of bullying, from low-level teasing to more serious cases of assault and emotional violence. Such incidents create great challenges for school communities generally, and school senior and middle management in particular, when a response that satisfies the needs of all parties to the bullying is demanded. We will offer definitions for terms such as restorative justice (RJ) and restorative practice (RP) as they apply in schools. We will explain how such practice, supported by formal evaluation, has been instrumental in providing long-lasting solutions for individual cases of bullying and culture change in schools. We will draw on the work of leading restorative practitioners, writers and academics, and provide practical advice on the complex process of implementation of RP in schools. A case study will highlight a typical restorative response in a school which has embraced the RJ philosophy.

Restorative justice; restorative practice

Restorative justice applied in a school setting is underpinned by the following fundamental concepts (adapted from Zehr, 1990):

- Misconduct is viewed as a violation of people and relationships.
- These violations create obligations and liabilities.
- Problem-solving focuses on healing and making things right.

The term, restorative practice, refers to a range of processes which are underpinned by these concepts. These practices, ranging from proactive to reactive, involve development and enhancement of relationships in schools and teaching of conflict resolution and other problem-solving skills. They also involve classroom management that is participatory and democratic and focuses on problem-solving. These practices require a shift in philosophy from traditional punitive models of behaviour management to those relational models which, as well as holding wrongdoers accountable for their behaviour, provide support for the community affected by the wrongdoing. Restorative practices help students learn from their mistakes, reconcile and resolve problems with others. They can effectively address a wide variety of harm done in school settings, including bullying, as well as truancy, alcohol and other drug use, classroom problems and property damage.

The range of restorative practices includes community conferences, small group and individual conferences, and classroom conferences.

Community conferences

This is the most formal of all RPs and is the intervention used when significant harm has been done (as in a serious case of bullying). A community conference brings together, in the wake of a serious incident of harm, the wrongdoer (the bully) and his or her victim(s), along with their families and appropriate school personnel. Conducted by a trained facilitator, a series of scripted questions is directed to participants in order to understand the incident and its antecedents and the effects of the incident (i.e. the harm done) on the community. The school system (structures, policy, practice) is also subjected to scrutiny and is made accountable in this process. An agreement is reached whereby all participants feel that there has been some restitution and that relationships have been repaired. The agreement also reflects plans to meet identified needs of any of the participants (such as counselling or other educational support) and to implement necessary changes to school structures, policies and practices in order to minimise the chance of the behaviours being repeated. Follow-up is crucial for ongoing support and to ensure compliance with the agreement.

Small group and individual conferences

These are usually confined to a small group of students or an individual student and perhaps teacher(s) who have been involved in a less serious incident of harm. Typically, small group conferences might be used to deal with low-level bullying (such as social exclusion from group work in class) before matters escalate. Parents, while not directly involved, are informed of the process and its outcomes. Again, follow-up to ensure ongoing support and compliance with the terms of the agreement is essential.

Classroom conferences

These involve the whole-of-class group in addressing issues which have affected teaching and learning in the classroom and student wellbeing, such as classroom bullying and, more generally, classroom disruption. These conferences have also been used where teachers and students are in conflict over a range of matters: respectful treatment of each other, curriculum issues and teaching styles. In some, where teachers themselves have felt bullied by powerful groups of students, these conferences have produced very positive outcomes.

Other restorative processes which some readers will be familiar with include problem-solving circles and mediation.

Once schools have begun to adopt this relational approach to problem-solving, it becomes clearer that proactive processes, matched with appropriate curriculum, must be developed to ensure that students and staff have skills to manage relationships in healthy ways. A 'Learning Unit for Primary Schools: Responsible Citizen Program' developed at a primary school in Canberra is an example of such proactive work and its positive impact on incidents of bullying (Morrison, 2002, 2005). The reliance by some schools on anger-management programs for bullies and assertiveness training for victims as the major responses to incidents of bullying has significant limitations. It means that there has been a lack of understanding about the complexities of building a whole of school model where the major energies must be spent on social and emotional skill development, followed through with processes that are respectful, demand accountability for harm done, and offer support for both victims and wrongdoers.

This hierarchy of proactive to reactive processes is probably best illustrated by Morrison's (2005) model, which has been adapted slightly for this chapter (see Figure 11.1). Morrison, describing three levels of intervention: universal, targeted and intensive, likens the interventions to a health care model and continuum:

> Briefly, these levels of response form a continuum of responses, based on common principles. By way of analogy to a health care model, the universal level of intervention targets all members of the school community through an 'immunisation' strategy; such that, all members of the school community

Figure 11.1 Whole-school model of restorative justice

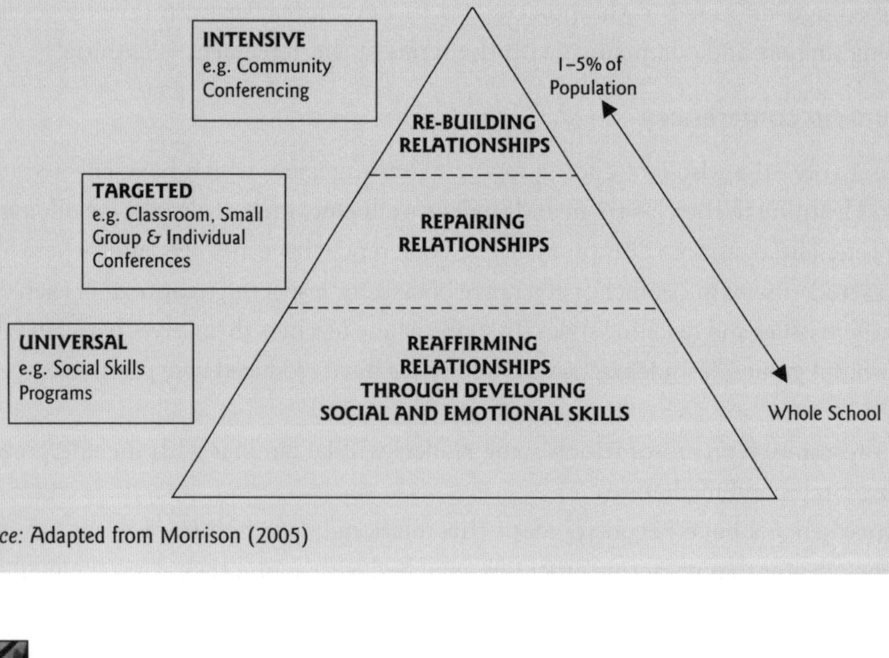

Source: Adapted from Morrison (2005)

> develop social and emotional skills to resolve conflict in caring and respectful ways. The targeted level of intervention addresses conflict that has become protracted such that it is affecting others within the school community, as such a third party is often required to help facilitate the process of reconciliation. The intensive level of intervention typically involves the participation of an even wider cross section of the school community, including parents, guardians, social workers, and others who have been affected or need to be involved, when serious offences occur within the school. A face-to-face restorative justice (community) conference is a typical example of this level of response. Taken together, these practices move from proactive to reactive, along a continuum of responses. Movement from one end of the continuum to the other involves widening the circle of care around participants. The emphasis is on early intervention through building a strong base at the primary level, which grounds a normative continuum of responsive regulation across the school community. (pp. 105–106)

Guiding principles of restorative practice

To develop such a comprehensive approach to relationship management in a school it is necessary to have a set of guiding principles based on a thorough understanding of restorative philosophy. The Restorative Justice Consortium, UK (2003) has developed a specific set of guiding principles which underpin restorative practice in schools. These include the following:

Principles relating to those who have sustained harm or loss

- respect for their personal experiences, needs and feelings
- acknowledgment of their harm or loss
- recognition of their claim of amends
- opportunity to communicate with the person who caused the harm or loss, if that person is willing
- entitled to be the primary beneficiary of reparation.

Principles relating to those who have caused the harm or loss to others

- the opportunity to offer reparation
- reparation to be appropriate to the harm done and within their capacity to fulfil it
- respect for the dignity of the person(s) making amends.

Principles relating to the interests of local community and society

- the promotion of community safety and social harmony by learning from the restorative processes, and so take measures that are conducive to the reduction of anti-social behaviour, crime or harm
- the promotion of social harmony through respect for cultural diversity and civil rights, social responsibility and the rule of law
- opportunity for all to learn mediation and other methods of non-violent resolution of conflict.

Principles relating to the school

- primary aim to be the repair of harm
- restorative requirements to be fair, appropriate and workable
- where a restorative requirement is appropriate, but victims decline to participate, there should be reparation to others who have suffered harm or loss
- voluntary offers to repair harm or loss, by those who have caused it, to be valued
- contents of restorative meetings to be considered confidential.

These principles and the continuum of restorative practice described above allow schools both an insight and a broadened perspective into the possibilities for the use of restorative practices in general and, in particular, restorative responses to bullying where all parties' needs for empowerment, support and procedural fairness are met. Included in Table 11.1 is a summary of the differences between traditional approaches to dealing with bullying behaviour and restorative practices (Blood, 2004). This table aligns with the core principles of teaching as described in Figure 11.2.

Case study

A vivid illustration of restorative practice at work is this case study of a Year 7 class in a metropolitan high school. It demonstrates how restorative practice can respond comprehensively to a long-term case of bullying, using first a community conference to repair the harm done to individuals, followed by a classroom conference to repair relationships between individual students and the classroom group (the need to restore relationships beyond the primary parties to the bullying is often overlooked).

A newly arrived student, Tess, was being bullied by her classmates, particularly one girl, Pam. The behaviours included excluding her from class activities, name-calling and teasing. Tess responded by retaliating in similar ways. These behaviours escalated until one day a note was sent around the class organising a physical fight between Tess and

Table 11.1 A paradigm shift: Retributive justice v. Restorative practices

Retributive justice – old paradigm		Restorative practices – new paradigm
Inappropriate behaviour defined as a breach of the school rules	1	Inappropriate behaviour defined as adversely affecting others
Focus on establishing blame or guilt and on the past (did he/she do it?)	2	Focus on problem-solving by expressing feelings and needs and how to meet them in the future
Authoritarian/power over adversarial relationship and process	3	Dialogue and negotiation – everyone involved in communicating and cooperating with each other
Imposition of consequence to punish and deter/prevent	4	Restitution as a means of restoring both/all parties, the goal being reconciliation
Attention to right rules, and adherence to due process	5	Focus on righting relationships and achievement of the desired outcomes
Conflict represented as impersonal and abstract: individual versus school	6	Inappropriate behaviour recognised as interpersonal conflict with value for learning
One social injury replaced by another	7	Focus on repair of social injury/damage
School community as spectators, represented by member of staff dealing with the situation	8	School community involved in facilitating restoration
Those affected by inappropriate behaviour not necessarily involved (victims/disempowering)	9	Encouragement of all concerned to be involved – empowerment
Accountability defined in terms of receiving an administered punishment	10	Accountability defined as understanding the impact of the action, seeing it as a consequence of choices and helping to decide how to put things right

Source: Adapted from Zehr (1990)

Figure 11.2 The core principles of teaching

Teaching is about Human Relationships	Teaching is about Control
Inevitability of conflict in relationships	Power
Hurt	Misbehaviour
Healing process	Punishment
Forgiveness & reparation	Revenge/retribution
Restoration of relationships	Battles/reputations
Learning & growing	Further conflict

Source: Harrison (2003). Reproduced with permission.

Pam at morning recess that day. The entire class was aware of the ongoing conflict. Some classmates had joined in, and it was common knowledge that the fight was to occur, as indeed it did. The fight was observed by a number of students in the yard at the time. It was eventually stopped by the teachers on yard duty and both students, who had sustained minor injuries, were referred to the office. In a traditional school, both students would more than likely have been suspended. This particular school decided to adopt a restorative approach which included the following.

A community conference was conducted which was attended by the two girls and their respective family members, their classroom teacher, the yard duty teacher, the assistant principal and a couple of classmates. The incident was discussed, the harm to both students and the class was explored by all participants, and an agreement was reached. Both students understood the impact on themselves and others and committed to ceasing the harmful behaviour and becoming role models for their classmates and other students. The class teacher and the assistant principal monitored this agreement and the behaviour ceased.

In recognition that the whole class was also accountable for failing to report the difficulties and the impending fight, and indeed their participation in the escalation, a classroom conference was convened where the general bullying behaviour of the class was explored. In this conference all class members were given an opportunity to say how they felt about the behaviour and its effects on them and were invited to take responsibility for their contribution to the conflict. A class agreement was reached whereby all class members agreed that their behaviour towards each other would, in the future, be respectful and caring. This agreement was revisited regularly as follow-up and ongoing problem-solving.

Both restorative processes, without the need for punishment, went a long way to changing the culture in the classroom to a more supportive, safe and friendly one.

Evaluations

Evaluations of the effectiveness of restorative practices in schools indicate a range of positive outcomes for individuals and the wider school community. As expected, all pilot studies revealed inherent challenges. These mostly focused around the conflict between traditional and restorative philosophy and practice, and misunderstandings about, and underestimation of, the complexity of culture change within the school. We have attempted to address these challenges later in the chapter in our discussion about implementation strategies. Despite these challenges, the pilots offered such hope, particularly in response to bullying incidents, that the results cannot be dismissed.

The Queensland experience

This study focused on the effectiveness of the community conference process as a response to serious incidents of harm.

During the course of the early Queensland study, 119 schools were involved across a range of regions, districts and settings (Cameron & Thorsborne, 2001). A total of 379 school and district personnel were trained as conference facilitators, although a significant number of those trained had never conducted a conference or had become 'accredited' according to departmental guidelines. A total of 89 conferences were conducted, and schools continue to use conferencing to deal with serious cases of harmful behaviour. The majority of conferences were in response to assaults and serious victimisation, followed by property damage and theft. Conferences were also used to address incidents involving drugs, damaging the reputation of the school, truanting, verbal abuse, persistent disruption in class, and in one case, a bomb threat.

Findings from this trial included:

- Participants were highly satisfied with the process and its outcomes.
- There was a high compliance rate with the terms of the agreement by offenders.
- There were low rates of reoffending.
- A majority of victims felt safer and more able to manage similar situations than before conferencing.
- The majority of conference participants had closer relationships with other conference participants after conferencing.
- All school administrators felt that conferencing reinforced school values.
- Most family members expressed positive perceptions of the school and comfort in approaching the school on other matters.
- Nearly all schools in the trial reported that they had changed their thinking about managing behaviour from a punitive to a more restorative approach.

The Victorian experience

During 2002, the Victorian Department of Education & Training embarked on a nine-month pilot of restorative practices/community conferencing. The pilot was designed to support and evaluate the application of restorative practices as a strategy in the management of incidents such as bullying and in reducing the number of young people at risk of being alienated from mainstream education. The experiences of staff, students and parents from 23 government and Catholic schools and from 16 regional support staff involved in this pilot provide sufficient evidence to suggest that restorative practices/community conferencing can be a highly effective way to manage incidents in Victorian schools.

Participants reported positively about the process and initial outcomes of 'mini-conferences' and community conferences. There were favourable reports about the scripted process as a guide to convening and structuring these conferences. Facilitators of conferences and those using mini-conferences reported favourably on the benefits of restorative practice compared to other means available to them. Most parents and students were also found to be satisfied with the outcomes of conferences. A majority of the cohort reported on their training with a high degree of satisfaction in both quality of teaching and course content.

The emergence of an ongoing network of trained facilitators in each of the pilot clusters was seen as a highly positive and important forum. There was strong support for the maintenance of these networks beyond the pilot phase. National and international literature suggests that the proactive role of education systems is critical in the uptake and imbedding of restorative practices. The pilot revealed that the intention and philosophy of restorative practices were consistent with the rhetoric of Victorian policy frameworks and that restorative practices have the potential to be an important strategy in terms of student wellbeing (Shaw & Weirenga, 2002).

The evaluation also highlighted a number of factors that contributed to the impact of the pilot and provides some indicators for future directions in restorative practice.

- **A whole-school approach works best.** Many participants reported on the need to adopt a whole-school approach to achieve more effective implementation of restorative practices. Tensions with traditional methods, contradictions in the management of incidents, and lack of staff awareness and understanding were cited as adversely affecting the impact of the strategy.
- **School leadership needs to be involved.** Where school principals and/or their assistants have been trained there appears to be more interest in and better uptake of restorative practices. Conversely, participants reported a perceived lack of interest or awareness in principals as a barrier to implementation.
- **Collegiate support is needed.** Pilot schools had between two and six staff trained as community conference facilitators. Most participants felt it was important to have other trained people in the school. This support was highly valued as was the opportunity to use a fellow participant to debrief following management of a serious incident.
- **Issues related to time are crucial.** One of the most significant challenges for pilot schools was that of time. The first issue was the lack of time available in the pilot to establish and implement a restorative approach in their schools. The second issue concerned the time required to run formal conferencing. Incident management using a traditional approach was also reported as time consuming. A consistent view expressed was that a conference could save time overall because it had a greater poten-

tial to resolve issues. It was felt that punitive approaches did not always deal effectively with other issues surrounding an incident particularly for the victims.

- **Staff readiness needs to be taken into account.** Many participants reported that they were in the early stages of developing expertise in using restorative strategies and were more confident practising mini-conferences or simply using restorative language and principles than running a 'formal' conference.
- **Conferences are not always appropriate and need to be matched to the situation.** Conferences were seen at the extreme end of restorative practices, to be used selectively for serious incidents. It was felt that not all incidents suited conferences and that conferences did not suit all people.

The Australian Capital Territory experience

At a recent Restorative Practices Forum conducted in the Australian Capital Territory (Blood, 2004), which was attended by 12 primary and secondary schools at varying stages of RP implementation, participants reported the following outcomes:

- a reduction of 70 per cent and higher in reoffending rates for students dealt with by a restorative response
- emerging cultural change in the student body
- increased reporting of incidents as students felt safer to self-disclose or raise other matters out of concern for what was happening in their school
- a change from a culture of 'dobbing' to one of seeking assistance
- improved problem-solving and conflict-resolution skills amongst students
- a gradual shift from a punitive to a relational approach
- a reduction in the need to use the formal conference process as interventions were occurring earlier before problems escalated
- a reduction in suspension rates.

Other evaluations of RP pilots in North America (Mirsky, 2003), Europe (Henskens-Reijman, Van Pagee & College, 2003) and the UK (Bitel, 2005), and our own experiences, have convinced the authors that restorative philosophy and practice is applicable across a wide range of cultures, ages, nationalities and educational settings.

Implementation

Given that restorative practice and its underlying philosophy represent a radical departure from traditional retributive behaviour-management practice, it is important to understand that the uptake of this new approach represents a culture change for most schools. In order to maximise the likelihood of sustainable change, we have included the following recommendations for reform, adapted from Blood and Thorsborne (2005):

- Build a case for change by determining the cost of current practice. Factor in high levels of detentions and suspensions, high levels of reported bullying and playground incidents, absenteeism, poor student wellbeing and safety data, and staff dissatisfaction with current practice, and align with system imperatives such as suspension reduction initiatives, curriculum reform, etc.
- Gain commitment from senior management and leadership. This is critical to the success of any implementation as evidenced in all management theory about culture change and in all restorative practice pilot studies and evaluations.
- Develop the vision and strategy by identifying what outcomes are sought and developing a three to five year strategic plan for implementation.
- Provide training and ongoing technical support for all members of the school community, including senior and middle managers, welfare staff, classroom teachers, behaviour specialists, parents and students. High-quality training ought to be sourced from experienced, respected practitioners who are familiar with the education setting.
- Monitor for quality standards both within the school (e.g. through peer feedback and support) and externally through the use of ongoing supportive consultancies.
- Collect data for ongoing evaluation, including measurement against stated outcomes, data collection of suspensions, exclusions, detentions, absenteeism and playground incidents, and measures of student and staff safety and wellbeing.
- Manage the transition from a traditional paradigm to a restorative philosophy carefully. Such a transition is fraught with confusion, frustration, anxiety and resentments, and must be managed strategically and sensitively, again from within the school community and by using external sources for support and coaching.
- Realign school policy with new practice. This does not necessarily require huge changes to the written policy, but rather changes in its execution.
- Establish a maintenance loop. Since whole of school organisation and cultural change cannot be achieved overnight, it is vital that ongoing and high-quality training and support be provided across the school community, including new staff, students and parents.
- Widen the lens. Once practitioners are familiar with the philosophy and guiding principles, experimentation and application of RP to case management, staff conflict, etc., they begin to see a different vision.

Finally, it is important to understand that some schools are more ready to embrace a restorative philosophy than others. In working with a variety of schools across a variety of sectors, our experience has been that schools which are explicit about their core values and practice around the importance of relationships are more likely to be successful in the implementation of this approach than those schools wedded to traditional notions of discipline in the form of punishment.

Conclusion

A punitive response to bullying behaviour does not necessarily reduce the risk of reoffending or meet the needs of the victim and the wider school community. In many cases it can make bullying situations worse. Restorative practice, with its focus on repair of relationships, healing of individuals and making things right, is more likely to deliver positive outcomes and meet the procedural, emotional and substantive needs of both wrongdoer and victim and their respective supporters. Restorative practice also demands accountability at the school system level and therefore increases the likelihood of positive culture change within the school community. Passionate and committed leadership and a willingness of those in senior and middle-management positions to reflect on their own attitudes and behaviours are critical factors for the success of this type of organisational transformation.

Our final comments are best represented in a quote from Morrison (2005).

> These practices, in their wide variety, are about empowerment through building relationships. They seek to empower victims, offenders and communities to take responsibility for themselves, and in doing so, for others. Through empowerment, the multiplicity of voices within school communities rise, and healthy deliberative democracies emerge. (p. 99)

REFERENCES

Bitel, M. (2005). National evaluation of the restorative justice in schools programme. Retrieved April 19, 2005, from <http://www.youth_justice_board.gov.uk>

Blood, P. (2004, October 22). ACT Restorative Practices Forum, Canberra. Unpublished document.

Blood, P. & Thorsborne, M. (2005, March). *The challenge of culture change: Embedding restorative practice in schools*. Sixth International Conference on Conferencing, Circles and other Restorative Practices.

Cameron, L. & Thorsborne, M. (2001). Restorative justice and school discipline: Mutually exclusive? In J. Braithwaite & H. Strang (Eds.), *Restorative justice and civil society* (pp. 180–194). Cambridge: Cambridge University Press.

Colorosa, B. (2003). *The bully, the bullied, and the bystander – from pre-school to high school: How parents and teachers can help break the cycle of violence*. Canada: Harper Collins.

Harrison, L. (2003). Unpublished training document. Marist Youth Care, Sydney.

Henskens-Reijman, J., Van Pagee, R. & College, T. (2003, August). *Restorative practices in a Dutch school*. Fourth International Conference in Conferencing, Circles and other Restorative Practices.

Mirsky, L. (2003, May 20). SaferSanerSchools: Transforming school culture with restorative practices. Restorative Practices E-forum. Retrieved April 19, 2005, from <http://www.iirp.org/library/ssspilots.html>

Morrison, B. (2002). Restorative justice for bullies and victims in schools: A program that fosters responsible citizenship. Retrieved January 10, 2005, from <www.crj.anu.edu.au/pubs.bm.restorativeprogram.pdf>

Morrison, B. (2005). *Building safe and healthy school communities: Restorative justice and responsive regulation*. Sixth International Conference on Conferencing, Circles and other Restorative Practices, Penrith, Sydney.

Restorative Justice Consortium (2003). A statement of restorative justice principles as applied in a school setting. Retrieved January 10, 2005, from <www.restorativejustice.org.uk>

Shaw, G. & Wierenga, A. (2002). *Evaluation of restorative practices/community conferencing pilot*. Melbourne: University of Melbourne.

Thorsborne, M. (1999, May). *School violence and community conferencing: The benefits of restorative justice*. Guidance Counsellors and the Law: A Conference for Best Practice, University of Queensland, Brisbane.

Wachtel, T. (1999, February 16–18). *Restorative justice in everyday life: Beyond the formal ritual*. In Reshaping Australian Institutions Conference: Restorative Justice and Civil Society, Australian National University, Canberra.

Zehr, H. (1990). *Changing lenses: A new focus for crime and justice*. Scottsdale, PA: Herald Press.

CHAPTER 12

A comparison of two non-punitive approaches to bullying

Helen McGrath and Maree Stanley

Introduction

Many schools are moving towards the use of non-punitive methods of responding to bullying situations. The basic assumption of non-punitive methods is that punishing students who are bullying a classmate can make things worse rather than better for the victim. This chapter looks at the two most significant non-punitive approaches and highlights their key features, their similarities and differences, their advantages and disadvantages, and the research support for each of them.

Punitive approaches

A punitive approach reflects a traditional model of 'crime and punishment' and is based on the assumption that students who bully deserve punishment and that punishment will deter them from bullying again. Rigby and Thomas (2002) conducted an Australia-wide research study into how schools at both primary and secondary levels responded to bullying situations in their schools. They found that the 40 schools in their study mostly used a punitive approach in which punishments or sanctions were imposed on students for breaking the school's 'no bullying' rule. Schools preferred to use the term 'consequences' rather than 'punishments' in their policies and programs. Sometimes the punishment was minor, such as not being allowed to continue playing in a sporting match. Sometimes it was major, such as detention, suspension or expulsion. Most schools believed that the consequences that followed physical bullying should be more severe than those relating to non-physical bullying.

Schools reported that they responded to the problem of bullying behaviour in exactly the same way as they did to students' violation of other school rules such as stealing, swearing or fighting. However, most schools reported that they found a punitive approach to be less effective in situations in which the bullying was subtle such as the use of ongoing insulting gestures or smirking, acts of deliberate social exclusion or repeated references to an embarrassing incident.

Arguments for and against punitive approaches

Many arguments in favour of adopting a punitive approach have been proposed. The main ones are:

- Justice is 'seen to be done' by teachers, other students and parents.
- It is easier to make clear statements about what will happen if students bully so that students are directly aware of what punishments bullying behaviour will incur.

However, there are also some strong arguments against the adoption of punitive methods, especially if they are used exclusively as the first (or only) approach, for example:

- It is difficult, or impossible, to specify rules to cover all the ways in which a person could bully someone, even though all bullying behaviour needed to be confronted (Rigby & Thomas, 2002).
- Teachers must investigate thoroughly and be very sure of the facts of a situation so that an innocent student is not punished. This can be time consuming and involve 'grilling' many students.
- A student who has been punished for bullying someone can 'pay them back' by persisting in bullying in more subtle and less detectable ways or encouraging friends to pay back the victim. Research suggests that this is the main factor which inhibits students from reporting to teachers that they are being bullied (Rigby & Barnes, 2002). Researchers such as Olweus (1993) and Tattum (1993) have identified that students who are involved in bullying on more than one occasion typically have low levels of empathy, are impulsive and inclined to retaliate if punished.

- Punishment usually makes recipients think only of themselves and their own resentment rather than about the consequences of their behaviour for another. In particular, rapid escalation to punishment can make young people more angry than thoughtful (Braithwaite, 1989; Thorsborne, 2000).
- Isolating a student who has bullied through suspension or exclusion does not help develop a sense of community and a focus on repairing relationships.
- Punishment can result in the 'demonising' of particular students, resultant damage to reputation and perhaps a downward behavioural spiral.

What evidence is there for the effectiveness of punitive approaches?

The results of early research into programs that were characterised by firm punitive responses to bullying behaviour (e.g. Olweus, 1993) looked very promising but later researchers have not been able to replicate the results (Smith, 2001). For example, Olweus reported a 50 per cent drop in victimisation in schools in Bergen, Norway, but a number of other researchers using similar procedures in England, Flanders, Germany, Canada and the USA have achieved much more modest results.

Non-punitive approaches

A non-punitive approach to bullying is one in which students who are taking part in bullying are not directly blamed and do not receive punishments or negative sanctions when the school becomes aware of their behaviour. Instead, the school puts into place a problem-solving approach which involves the students who have been involved in the bullying.

Non-punitive methods challenge the assumptions teachers make about children's problem behaviour in that they are not directly concerned with punishment, truth or control (Tyler, 1998). Rather they involve reframing bullying as a problem situation that needs to be improved through input from those involved (Tyler, 1998).

The two most significant non-punitive approaches that have been developed are:

- The No-Blame Approach (Maines & Robinson, 1992), which has been revised as the Support Group Approach by Young (1998) and contains some features which differ from Maines and Robinson's original model
- The Method of Shared Concern (Pikas, 1989, 2002).

The No-Blame Approach has some similarities with the Method of Shared Concern and they are often confused (Young, 1998). A chart which highlights the differences between the two approaches is presented in Appendix A at the end of this chapter. Full details of how to use each of these two approaches can also be found at the end of the chapter in Appendix B, and the flow chart in Figure 12.1 highlights the key steps in each approach. However, as Rigby and Thomas (2002) have noted, many schools employ hybrid or mixed versions of the two approaches.

Restorative justice (see Chapter 11) has sometimes been described as a non-punitive approach but, because there is a very strong focus on the importance of students accepting responsibility/blame for any bullying in which they have taken part and making amends, it also has some elements of a punitive approach. Schools still retain the right to apply a punishment if there is no agreed outcome as to how the student(s) involved in the bullying will make amends or if students do not honour their commitment to make amends. Restorative justice may be somewhere in the middle.

Arguments for and against non-punitive approaches

Many strong arguments have been proposed in support of non-punitive approaches, such as:

- Teachers don't have to build an airtight case before intervening as the focus is less on the precise truth and specific actions and more on the overall negative situation that needs to be changed (Tyler, 1998).
- Many schools recognise the reality that some students may not be aware of the degree of harmfulness and seriousness of their bullying actions (Rigby & Thomas, 2002). Therefore it makes more sense to take a problem-solving and awareness approach.
- In a non-blaming interview, students are more likely to privately accept personal responsibility for their role in the bullying rather than become defensive, resentful and retaliatory (Rigby & Thomas, 2002). Tyler (1998) has argued that any process which fails to engage students who bully and does not attempt to enhance their feelings of empathy and understanding is unlikely to bring about any fundamental change in behaviour.
- Non-punitive approaches are less likely than punitive approaches to place the victim at further risk from retaliation and more subtle bullying. Fear of retaliation and social exclusion as a result of others being punished for their bullying behaviour have been shown to be a major factor in preventing students from letting teachers know that they are being bullied (Rigby & Barnes, 2002). Most schools are not in a position to protect a student from these predictable reactions.
- Gamliel, Hoover, Daughtry & Imbra (2003) investigated young people's views about what schools should do about bullying and found that most of them clearly perceived that the best way for a school to respond to a bullying situation was to find a way

Figure 12.1 Key steps in the Support Group Approach and the Method of Shared Concern

1. The Support Group Approach (based on the No-Blame Approach)

Step 1

Information about the bullying situation is collected and then the victim is interviewed to obtain more information.

Empathy is expressed for their situation.

The victim's permission is sought to hold a support group meeting (without them) with the students involved, plus bystanders and supportive classmates. They offer suggesions on who to choose.

The victim is reassured that nobody will get into trouble.

Step 2

The support group meeting of between six and eight students is organised and held. The victim does not attend.

The facilitator makes it clear that 'no-one is in trouble' and no blame is allocated.

The victim's difficult and unhappy situation is described in order to elicit an empathic response from the group.

Everyone is asked to make suggestions for improving the situation for the victim.

Step 3

One week later, another support group meeting is held to review progress.

Step 4

The victim is interviewed again to see if there have been changes.

Step 5

A week later each student in the support group is interviewed individually about what they have been able to do.

2. The Method of Shared Concern

Step 1

Information about the bullying situation is collected by teachers independently and without discussion with the victim.

Step 2

The facilitator interviews all students involved in the bullying separately, starting with the ringleader.

Each student is asked what they know.

No-one is blamed.

They are asked to suggest ways to improve the situation for the victim.

Another interview is booked with each student.

Step 3

The victim is interviewed and concern is expressed for their situation.

They are told about the earlier interviews and the suggestions that were made for improving things.

They are asked about ways in which they can improve their own situation as well.

Step 4

Everyone (including the victim) is interviewed separately again a week later to monitor progress and give positive feedback for what they have done to improve the situation.

Step 5

After two weeks, and if there has been positive change, a group meeting (without the victim) is held to celebrate progress.

At the meeting, it is suggested that another group meeting be held, which includes the victim, in order to show that the bullying problem has been solved.

Step 6

The victim is interviewed separately again to check for improvements in their situation.

Their permission is sought for a group meeting, which would include them.

Step 7

If permission has been given by the victim, a group meeting is held which includes the victim.

Positive feedback is given to the students for their cooperation and the improvements they have made to the situation.

for students who are being bullied to rationally work through the problem with the aggressor.

- Because no negative sanctions are used, no student can be unfairly punished (Young, 1998).
- Non-punitive approaches utilise the considerable power of the peer group, which is empowered to intervene appropriately and effectively to support a classmate (Newton, Taylor & Wilson, 1996).

Many strong arguments against the use of non-punitive approaches have also been put forward, such as:

- Research has shown that students who are ringleaders in bullying situations tend to have lower levels of empathy than other students (Olweus, 1993; Tattum, 1993). This makes it less likely that empathic responses as a result of a small group student meeting to problem solve how to improve things for the victim will motivate them to change their behaviour, especially if the victim is a student they don't like or have no positive feelings for.
- Parents often react negatively to 'non-blaming' approaches, seeing them as unacceptable as they incorrectly perceive that the school is doing nothing and feel angry that no-one has to accept responsibility. Given the suffering of their child, this does not seem to them to be fair.
- Many teachers and parents also find the basic assumptions behind the model unacceptable; they believe that students who bully others should take the consequences of their actions.
- Rigby and Thomas (2002) found that many teachers did not believe that students would necessarily respond constructively and responsibly to the plight of the victim, even if they acted that way in group meetings. Negative reactions to the approach can undermine the effectiveness of non-punitive approaches.
- A non-punitive approach can take more time to use and seem less effective to teachers who are often 'time poor' (Rigby & Thomas, 2002).
- The success of a non-punitive approach depends to a great extent on the people using the technique, in particular the degree to which they can bring the quality of genuineness to the situation (Tyler, 1998).
- Given that a large number of victims are very anxious (Bernstein & Watson, 1997; Craig, 1998; Olweus, 1991) it may be very threatening to put pressure on them to take part in a group meeting that includes their attackers (as sometimes happens in the Method of Shared Concern) but they may have difficulties saying 'no' to the teachers' request to do so.

What evidence is there for the effectiveness of non-punitive approaches?

The arguments over the use of these approaches tend to be very emotional. Highly respected anti-bullying researcher Ken Rigby is positive about them (see Chapter 9) but well-respected Norwegian anti-bullying researcher Dan Olweus has been highly critical of them (Olweus, 1991, 1993, 2004). Another well-regarded anti-bullying researcher, Michelle Eliott (2000), now the director of Kidscape in the UK, is also highly critical of the No-Blame Approach. She describes receiving many complaints from parents who say that their experience of it has been that, although the students who bullied pretend to cooperate in the discussions, they still retaliate.

However, there is some research support for the effectiveness of both the No-Blame Approach and the Method of Shared Concern.

The No-Blame Approach

In their research into how Australian schools manage bullying, Rigby and Thomas (2002) noted that the No-Blame Approach was used with reported success in a number of primary schools. Most schools *offered* the approach to students who had been bullied and did not impose it on them if they didn't want to take part in the meeting. They stressed the importance of monitoring the situation closely after the process had been used. However, they also found that many primary schools often modified the approach with older students and added punitive elements.

Smith & Madsen (1997) asked teachers in 155 schools in the UK to rate their satisfaction with the No-Blame Approach which they selected to use within a system-wide adoption of an anti-bullying package. They were asked to rate the approach from 1 (not at all satisfied) to 5 (extremely satisfied). The average rating was 3.5.

An evaluation of the No-Blame Approach in UK schools that was part of the same project found that 45 out of 47 interventions in secondary schools and 7 out of 7 interventions in primary schools were successful (Smith & Sharp, 1994). However, it was concluded that independent replication and further rationale on how or why the approach was effective would be valuable.

Young (1998) evaluated teacher use over two years of a modified version of the No-Blame Approach which, as noted above, she called the Support Group Approach. The emphasis was less on the feelings of the victim and more on the unpleasantness of the situation for them. In 55 cases referred from 51 primary schools (over 70 per cent of the referrals), the Support Group Approach was used, usually by the Special Educational Needs Support Service anti-bullying coordinator or occasionally by a teacher in the school. She reported that the approach was 'successful' in the great majority of cases, as defined by the bullying stopping completely or the victim no longer feeling in need of support. In a small number of cases several extra weeks of meetings were required before the situation was resolved to the satisfaction of all involved, including the victim. Of the four cases from four secondary schools, two were immediate successes, one student changed school and one did not return to school at all.

The Method of Shared Concern

The Method of Shared Concern (Pikas, 1989, 2002) received an average satisfaction rating from teachers in 155 schools of 3.9 in the Smith & Madsen (1997) research mentioned above.

Smith and Sharp (1994) trialled the Method of Shared Concern in seven secondary schools in Sheffield and then trained 21 teachers to use it. They reported that 12 of the trained teachers were able to use the method and, in interviews, all reported that they had found it to be an appropriate and helpful response to bullying.

Rigby and Thomas (2002) found that many of the schools who claimed to be using the Method of Shared Concern were employing their own version of it. They reported that some schools used a version of the approach which had three steps and individual discussions with the students who were bullying were along the lines of:

- Someone's very unhappy. What can you tell me about it?
- The bullying must stop because it is making someone very unhappy.
- Someone's doing it to them. Could you make sure they're all right?

For three consecutive days the bullying students were required to come back and report on how things were going.

Increasing the effectiveness of non-punitive approaches

These recommendations for good practice have emerged from the research literature on implementing non-punitive approaches.

Take a positive but balanced approach

It helps if everyone in the school commits to taking an optimistic approach if they decide to adopt a non-punitive method. Senior staff and classroom teachers need to be positive in their endorsement of the approach when talking to colleagues, parents and teachers. The group facilitators need to be positive, convincing and optimistic: the problem *can* be addressed and *will* be solved by group efforts. However, although it is helpful to assure parents and students that a non-punitive approach can have a high success rate, it is also important to point out that it is not guaranteed (Young, 1998).

Explain the rationale behind the approach

Smith and Sharp (1994) suggest that it is sometimes not clear to teachers and parents why non-punitive approaches are often successful, and Young (2001) argues that if an approach is not open to plausible explanation it may be less likely to gain widespread adoption. Some of the positive arguments and evidence for the approaches that can be made to parents and staff are listed earlier in this chapter.

It is also helpful to explain that the Support Group Approach can be viewed as an example of Applied Brief Therapy (Young, 1998), which can be described as a number of short sessions which utilise a concentrated structure of questions designed to move people towards a solution, rather than concentrating on the problem. When working with a system, small changes can lead to profound changes (Young, 1998). Young argues that this approach has more potential to change bullying situations for the following reasons:

- The solution develops outside the direct influence of the teacher and students feel empowered to act (Young, 1998).
- Empathy for the victim is enhanced and this acts as a motivating force for self-change (Maines & Robinson, 1992).
- Social psychologists such as Baron, Kerr & Miller (1992), Brewer and Crano (1994) and Deaux, Dane, Wrightsman and Sigelman (1993) have identified the factors that motivate bystanders to help others in distress rather than ignore the victim's plight. Young (1998) asserts that these help-enhancing factors are part of a Support Group Approach:
  - They have been asked to help and have agreed.
  - They know that help is really needed; the situation is not ambiguous. They have witnessed harm, even if some were not an active part of it.
  - They have been given some responsibility to act and they have individual responsibility as well.
  - Their empathy for the plight of the victim has been aroused.
  - They know that they will receive feedback about the outcomes of their efforts to help.
  - They have a specific assigned task as part of the overall helping plan.
  - They feel guilty about what the victim has suffered.
  - They know that their suggestion for action will be considered.
  - Even if only one member helps initially, the others are likely to follow.
  - They have made their commitment to action 'public'.
  - Their anonymity is not reduced.
  - Identifying with a successful group increases their self-esteem.

- Continuing to act unhelpfully becomes unacceptable to the group.
- They receive a range of positive outcomes such as freedom from various levels of guilt, feeling good about their own altruism, and approval from the facilitator.

Take a whole-school approach

Non-punitive approaches, like most smaller components of an anti-bullying program, are most likely to be effective in the long term when they are part of a whole-school approach to bullying prevention (Smith, 1997).

Avoid the term 'no-blame'

The term, 'no-blame approach', has been replaced by the preferred term, 'support group approach', to make it more acceptable in the current political climate (Smith, 2001; Young, 1998). The Method of Shared Concern can be described as a 'problem-solving approach' rather than a 'no-blame' approach.

Educate parents about the approach

Parents may initially want punishment for the bullying students because they know of no other approach that could be successful. They need to be educated not only about the rationale behind non-punitive approaches but also about the details of what actually happens (Young, 2001; Young & Holdorf, 2003). As part of the overall process, parents can be asked to become involved by keeping the school informed of their child's progress. This can often help rebuild the parent's relationship with the school, which may have been strained beforehand (Young, 1998). If it is effective, parents are very happy that the nightmare for themselves and their child has ceased (Young, 1998).

Train teachers in the process

Tyler (1998) has argued that bullying in schools is such a regular event that, in order to be effective, teachers need to learn how to suspend their own feelings of anger and repugnance and endorse the most effective approach, not the one for which they feel the strongest emotional pull. This requires extensive training in and understanding of the rationale and use of the process, even for those in the school who may not be involved in the facilitation process themselves.

Ensure commitment by senior staff

Sharp, Cowie & Smith (1994) identified that commitment to non-punitive methods by senior management was essential.

Match the approach to the situation

Smith (2001) has pointed out that non-punitive approaches are not suitable for all circumstances and argue that a careful matching of approach and situation is vital. Approaches need to be not only matched to the situation but in some cases also adapted to local school conditions (Smith, 2001).

Conclusion

We still have a lot to learn about what does work and what does not in anti-bullying interventions and there is evidence that both punitive and non-punitive methods can work (Smith, 2004). The arguments for non-punitive methods are strong but the research evidence is only moderately persuasive so far. Non-punitive approaches, when used with aspects of good practice, have a lot of potential for helping schools to deal with bullying (Smith, 2001).

REFERENCES

Baron, R. S., Kerr, N. L. & Miller, N. (1992). *Group process, group decision, group action.* Buckingham: Open University Press.

Bernstein, J. Y. & Watson, M. W. (1997). Children who are targets of bullying: A victim pattern. *Journal of Interpersonal Violence, 12*(4), 483–499.

Braithwaite, J. (1989). *Crime, shame and reintegration.* Cambridge: Cambridge University Press.

Brewer, M. B. & Crano, W. D. (1994). *Social Psychology*. Minneapolis: West.

Craig, W. (1998). The relationship among aggression types, depression, and anxiety in bullies, victims, and bully/victims. *Personality and Individual Differences, 24*, 123–130.

Deaux, K., Dane, F. C., Wrightsman, L. S. & Sigelman, C. K. (1993). *Social Psychology in the 90s* (6th ed.). California: Brooks/Cole.

Duncan, A. (1996). The Shared Concern Method for resolving group bullying in schools. *Educational Psychology in Practice, 12*(2), 94–98.

Elliott, M. (2000, December 13). Extract from letter to Guardian Society. Retrieved February 14, 2005, from <http://www.kidscape.org.uk/press/131200NoBlameReasons.shtml>

Gamliel, T., Hoover, J. H., Daughtry, D. W. & Imbra, C. M. (2003). A qualitative investigation of bullying: The perspectives of fifth, sixth and seventh graders in a USA parochial school. *School Psychology International, 24*(4), 405–420.

Maines, B. & Robinson, G. (1992). *The No-Blame Approach.* Bristol: Lucky Duck Publishing.

Newton, C., Taylor, G. & Wilson, D. (1996). Circles of friends. *Educational Psychology in Practice, 11*(4), 4108.

Olweus, D. (1991). Bully/victim problems among school children: Some basic facts and effects of a school-based intervention program. In D. Pepler & K. Rubin (Eds.). *The development and treatment of childhood aggression* (pp. 411–438). Hillsdale, N.J.: Erlbaum.

Olweus, D. (1993). *Bullying at school: What we know and what we can do*. Oxford, UK: Blackwell.

Olweus, D. (2004). The Olweus bullying prevention programme: Design and implementation issues and a new national initiative in Norway. In P. K. Smith, D. Pepler & K. Rigby (Eds.). *Bullying in schools: How successful can interventions be?* (pp. 13–36). Cambridge: Cambridge University Press.

Pikas, A. (1989). A pure concept of mobbing gives the best results for treatment. *School Psychology International*, *10*, 95–104.

Pikas, A. (2002). New developments of the Shared Concern Method. *School Psychology International*, *23*, 307–326.

Rigby, K. (1996). *Bullying in schools – and what to do about it*. Melbourne: ACER.

Rigby, K. & Barnes, A. (2002). To tell or not to tell: The victimised student's dilemma. *Youth Studies Australia*, *21*(3), 33–36.

Rigby, K. & Thomas, E. (2002). *How Australian schools are responding to the problem of peer victimisation in schools*. Canberra: Criminology Research Council. Retrieved February 16, 2005, from <http://www.aic.gov.au/crc/reports/200001-10.html>

Sharp, S., Cowie, H. & Smith, P. K. (1994). Working directly with pupils involved in bullying situations. In P. K. Smith & S. Sharp, *School bullying*. London: Routledge.

Smith, P. (2004). Bullying: Recent developments. *Child and Adolescent Mental Health*, 9(3), 98–103.

Smith P. K. (1997). Bullying in schools: The UK experience and the Sheffield anti-bullying project. *The Irish Journal of Psychology*, *18*(2), 191–201.

Smith, P. K. (2001). Should we blame the bullies? [Electronic version]. *The Psychologist*, *14*(2). Retrieved February 14, 2005, from <www.luckyduck.co.uk>

Smith, P. K & Madsen, M. (1997). *A follow-up survey of the DFE Anti-Bullying Pack in schools: Its use and the development of anti-bullying work in schools*. London: DFE.

Smith, P. K. & Sharp, S. (Eds.) (1994). *School bullying: Insights and perspectives*. London: Routledge.

Smith, P. K. & Shu, S. (2000). What good schools can do about bullying: Findings from a survey in English schools after a decade of research and action. *Childhood*, *7*(2), 193–212.

Tattum, D. P. (Ed.) (1993). *Understanding and managing bullying*. London: Heinemann.

Thorsborne, M. (2000). *School violence and community conferencing: The benefits of restorative justice*. APAPDC National Online Conference. Retrieved February 12, 2005, from <http://www.apapdc.edu.au/archive/ASPA/conference2000/papers/art_2_13.htm>

Tyler, K. (1998). A comparison of the No-Blame Approach to bullying and the Ecosystemic Approach to changing problem behaviour in schools. *Pastoral Care in Education*, *16*(1), 26–32.

Young, S. (1998). The Support Group Approach to bullying. *Educational Psychology in Practice*, *14*(1), 32–39.

Young, S. (2001). Solution-focused anti-bullying. In Y. Ajmal & I. Rees (Eds.). *Solutions in schools: Creative applications of solution focused brief thinking with young people and adults*. London: B T Press.

Young, S. & Holdorf, G. (2003). Using solution focused brief therapy in individual referrals for bullying. *Educational Psychology in Practice*, *19*(4), 271–282.

APPENDIX 12A: DIFFERENCES BETWEEN THE SUPPORT GROUP (OR NO-BLAME) APPROACH AND THE METHOD OF SHARED CONCERN

	The Support Group (or No-Blame) Approach	The Method of Shared Concern
People associated with the approach	Developed by Barbara Maines and George Robinson in the UK (1991) Refined as the Support Group Approach by Sue Young (1998)	Developed by Anatol Pikas in Sweden (1989)
Basic assumptions underpinning the approach	It is more important to solve the problem than to punish the students who are doing the bullying. Punishment doesn't work as it invites defensiveness and retaliation and does not change the attitudes of those bullying. If the students who are involved with bullying are not being blamed for what they've done, they stop feeling threatened and can be part of finding a solution. If bystanders are included in the problem-solving process, they become more aware of their own role in the bullying when they do nothing and fail to speak up.	Many students who bully other students are unaware of the extent of the harm that they are causing to their victim. Bullying occurs in a group context, so changing the social dynamics and promoting empathy for the victim can change the situation. Punitive measures model and reinforce the use of power to meet needs and wants. A hostile punitive approach will increase the bullying and result in greater peer group unity among the bullying students and later retaliation.
Is there any parental involvement?	Parents are not directly involved in the process but they are asked to report on how their child is responding to changes made after the support group meetings.	Parents are not directly involved in the process but they can be asked to report on how their child is responding to changes made after the interviews.
Is training needed to use the approach?	Yes	Yes
How many staff members are involved?	Usually one staff member, who can be anyone who has been trained, e.g. classroom teacher, coordinator, assistant principal, school counsellor. However, all teachers can be trained.	Anyone who has been trained, but usually a coordinator, assistant principal, school counsellor.
Age suitability	Suitable for all ages, but used more often in primary settings.	Suitable for all ages, but used more often in upper primary or secondary settings.

(continued)

	The Support Group (or No-Blame) Approach	The Method of Shared Concern
What kind of bullying situations can it be used with?	Appropriate for bullying situations that: • haven't responded to simple interventions or warnings • have persisted for some time. Not suitable for situations where there is serious physical danger to a student or where the student involved in bullying has a strong history of violence or erratic behaviour. Especially suitable if the bullying is an after-effect of a friendship fall-out.	Appropriate for reasonably serious bullying situations but not those which involve physical assault nor those which a teacher can easily deal with by a simple intervention or warning.
How is information collected about the bullying situation?	The victim is interviewed at the start of the process and asked to describe what has been happening and how they feel about it. The focus is not on getting to the bottom of specific incidents, but more on the general picture and the distress of the victim.	All teachers are asked to provide information about the suspected bullying by observing, keeping notes, and informally and confidentially asking the victim about what has been happening. No prior meeting is held with the victim in order to reduce the likelihood that the victim will be seen to have 'told' and that there will be retaliation for having done so.
What is the first step?	To interview the victim to get a general picture of what has been happening and how they feel about it.	To individually interview each student involved in the bullying, starting with the ringleader.
How much is the victim involved in the process?	• At the start of the process they have an individual interview to provide information about what has been happening. • The support group meetings are only held if they give permission. • They don't attend any of the support group meetings. • They have a second individual interview to review the situation and identify any improvements.	They have at least two individual interviews with the facilitator during the process but after the bullying students have been individually interviewed. At the end of the process, they are invited to attend a meeting with all of the students who have been individually interviewed by the teacher. This may or may not occur.

(continued)

	The Support Group (or No-Blame) Approach	The Method of Shared Concern
How long does the process take?	The process may take several weeks. • There is one individual interview with the victim for about 15–20 minutes. • This is usually followed by at least two support group meetings of 20–30 minutes each. • There are usually four to five individual interviews with members of the support group of 5–10 minutes each and one interview of the same duration with the victim.	The process may take several weeks. The actual time taken depends on how many students are involved in the bullying. • The victim has at least two individual interviews of 10–15 minutes each. • Each student who has been involved in the bullying has at least two individual interviews of 10–15 minutes each. • The final group session if it is held takes about 10–15 minutes.

APPENDIX 12B: HOW TO USE TWO NON-PUNITIVE APPROACHES TO BULLYING – THE SUPPORT GROUP APPROACH AND THE METHOD OF SHARED CONCERN

The Support Group Approach (adapted from the No-Blame Approach) (Maines & Robinson, 1992; Young, 1998)

This non-punitive approach addresses a bullying situation by forming a support group of students who are encouraged to take responsibility for solving the problem of the bullying. It uses a non-judgmental problem-solving approach.

Step 1: Talk with the student who is being bullied

Interview the victim. Express empathy and support for their situation and reassure them that the situation will improve. Ask them to give you a general picture of what has been happening and how they feel about it. Don't focus on the details of specific events. Focus more on how any event they mention has affected them (e.g. 'So when they ran off without you for the third time that week, you felt miserable and excluded'). Accept what they tell you in a non-judgmental way and don't grill them with questions such as 'Did you do anything to them first?'

Tell them that you want to organise and run a support group meeting of about six to eight people which would include:

- the students who are involved in the bullying
- any bystanders who have watched and laughed or helped them
- any friends or other helpful students they would like to include.

Ask them for some suggestions of students who could be included at the meeting.

The student must agree to the meeting for it to happen. Stress that the purpose of the meeting will be to solve the problem, not to blame or punish anyone. Ask them if there is anything they have told you that they don't want you to mention at the meeting. Remind them that they can come and talk to you at any time during the process.

Step 2: Organise and run the first support group meeting

Start by explaining that you have called this support group meeting to explain a problem that is affecting one of their classmates and that they have been chosen as it was felt they were all able to help. Explain that (the victim) is very unhappy at school and that everyone has the right to be happy at school.

Ask 'Has anyone here ever felt unhappy at school?' in order to tap into empathy. Then, after hearing what some of them have to say about it, conclude with something like 'Well, I guess that (the victim) must be feeling very like you have described feeling when you were pretty unhappy'.

Do not detail specific incidents. Use non-judgmental and non-blaming responses. Try to avoid the word 'bullying'. Explain that no-one is in trouble or going to be punished and that everyone in the group has a shared responsibility to help (the victim) to feel included and safe. Emphasise your confident belief that the group can do something about what is happening. Say something like 'I guess you all have a better idea than anyone about why the victim is unhappy'.

Then invite suggestions about what could be done to improve the situation for (the victim). All students are asked to suggest one thing they could do using the sentence stem 'I could . . .' (e.g. 'I could include them more in conversation', 'I could make sure I don't use the nickname they don't like', etc.). Don't try to extract commitments to do what they suggest, just pass responsibility over to them (e.g. 'Okay, well, let's meet again in a week's time and see what we have been able to do by working together to improve things').

The students involved in the bullying need to feel part of a problem-solving group and not accused or blamed. Non-bullying students need to realise that by not speaking up or acting they are allowing the bullying to continue. Non-bullying students work alongside those who are causing the distress.

Step 3: Hold a second support group meeting

A week later, hold another support group meeting and review the changes the group has been able to make.

Step 4: Interview the victim again after the second support group meeting

Hold a brief individual meeting with the victim to see how things are going and what improvements there have been.

Step 5: Interview each member of the support group individually

A week later, hold brief individual interviews with each student who has been part of the support group. This allows you to continue to monitor progress and keep the students involved in the process. Individual interviews enable each student to non-competitively make a statement about their contribution to solving the problem. It does not matter if some have not followed through on their suggestion. What matters is that the victim reports that the bullying has stopped.

Hold as many review support group meetings or individual interviews as necessary.

The Method of Shared Concern (Pikas 1989)

All students involved in the bullying take part in a series of individual interviews with a staff member and are encouraged to see that the victim is having a very difficult time. They are all asked individually about what they could do to improve the situation for the victim. The victim also has two individual interviews with the staff member to brainstorm any changes they could make to improve their own situation and to check for positive improvements.

Step 1: Collect information about what is happening

Collect as much information as possible about the bullying situation through teacher observations, reports from other students, etc. This is to prevent repercussions for the victim for supposedly 'telling'.

Step 2: Individually interview each student involved in the bullying

Individually interview each student who is suspected of being involved in the bullying situation in some way. Start with the ringleader if known. Don't make any accusations. Share your concern for the distress felt by the victim. Ask the student to say what they know about the situation. As soon as the student has acknowledged some awareness of what has been happening (not necessarily guilt), ask directly 'What could *you* do to help improve the situation?' The purpose is not to get the facts straight nor to blame anyone, but rather to produce constructive responses that will help change the situation for the victim. Ask for any suggestions that the student can make for improving the situation. If they don't make any, offer some simple ideas of how they might help. Strongly approve of any constructive proposals. Don't make any threats or give any warnings. Arrange another one-on-one meeting with them for a specified time to see how things have gone.

Repeat this step with each of the students involved.

Step 3: Individually interview the victim

After all of the students involved in the bullying have been separately interviewed, interview the victim. Express concern, empathy and support for their situation. Tell them that you have spoken individually to everyone involved and that each of them has agreed to cooperate to improve the situation. Ask if they can think of any changes they could make that might help them to improve their own situation. Do not blame or judge, just elicit some ideas. Make an appointment for another follow-up interview to check on progress.

Step 4: Individually re-interview each student (including the victim) involved in the bullying

Re-interview each of the students (including the victim) involved in the bullying in order to monitor progress and give positive feedback for what they have done to improve the situation.

Step 5: Organise a group meeting without the victim

Organise a meeting that everyone, except the victim, attends. Congratulate them on any progress that has been made. Encourage the group to suggest that the victim join them at a second meeting to demonstrate that the bullying problem really has been resolved. Ask for reassurances from each student that they will act positively and respectfully towards the victim at such a meeting.

Step 6: Re-interview the victim

Re-interview the victim individually to check for improvements in their situation. Ask the victim if they are prepared to take part in a meeting with the other students and give them assurances that everyone will be respectful and positive at the meeting. Do not proceed to the next step if they are reluctant to do so.

Step 7: Organise a group meeting that the victim also attends

At the meeting, highlight the improvements that have been made and ask for a commitment to behave well in the future.

CHAPTER 13

Effective ways to work with parents

Evelyn Field and Pam Carroll

Introduction

Parents are an essential part of an effective approach to both preventing and managing bullying in schools. However, although there is some literature to inform schools about the most useful ways to do this, it is not at all extensive (Forgatch, 2003; Stevens, De Bourdeaudhuij & Van Oost, 2001).

In this chapter the issue of parent-school partnerships is explored, with a particular focus on how all parents can help with bullying prevention and why schools need to involve the parents of students who bully and are bullied in the management of the situation. There are also guidelines on involving parents in whole-school bullying prevention, how schools can work sensitively with parents in bullying situations, and how parents can collaborate with the school against bullying. The appendix contains a list of signs that may indicate to a parent that their child is bullying or being bullied.

Why involve parents in the issue of school bullying?

The implementation of any social innovation, such as programs for the prevention or management of school bullying, involves multi-level processes (Choi, 2003). The most effective means of intervention in relation to school bullying is for family and school systems to work together (Ahmed & Braithwaite, 2004). Schools that adopt a systems approach to altering a child's social environment by working with parents are more likely to produce positive outcomes for teachers, parents and students (Bastiani & Wolfendale, 1996; Ortega & Lera, 2005; Stevens, Van Oost & De Bourdeaudhuij, 2000; Sharp & Smith, 1991; Smith & Sharp, 1994). Australian research echoes the conclusion that where schools have adopted policies and programs that involve staff, parents and students, irrespective of how well or poorly resourced, the frequency of bullying is lower (*Sticks and Stones*, 1994).

The evaluation of the 1991–1993 Sheffield Anti-bullying Project in the UK (Sharp & Smith, 1991) demonstrated the importance of whole-school involvement in reducing bullying. Similarly, research into the effectiveness of the Friendly Schools Families Project in Western Australia (Cross, 2004; Cross et al., 2003) concluded that parent involvement was an essential part of any approach to reducing bullying. This program studied 20 randomly selected primary schools in an attempt to identify the program components that resulted in the greatest reduction of bullying. The researchers found that effective ways of consulting and communicating about bullying with the majority of parents was a vital ingredient in a program. This was best achieved through the use of a range of strategies such as students presenting items on bullying solutions during assembly, regular newsletter information, homework activities involving students and their parents and special communication with fathers to ensure their involvement. Practical ideas for parents on improving their child's social skills, resiliency and ability to handle bullying situations were provided in this program in a range of parent booklets (Cross et al., 2004; Griffiths & Weatherilt, 2004).

Parent workshops were also part of the project's concept of parent-school partnerships. Griffiths (2001) recommends that a variety of processes should be used in these workshops to ensure maximum parent participation, including individual and small group exercises, information sheets, visually presented information, role-plays, videos and demonstrations. Typically, parents were introduced to up-to-date research on bullying. Areas of focus included definitions of bullying, the effects of bullying, the incidence of bullying in schools, whole-school strategies, and a demonstration of unhelpful and helpful parental responses to bullying incidents using a series of scenarios. A summary of conciliatory non-punitive methods used by the schools in their initial response to bullying situations was also provided (Griffiths, 2001). Parent feedback indicated that the provision of written information helped them to reflect further and was often used as a talking point with staff at a later stage if their own child was bullied (Cross, 2004; Cross et al., 2003; Griffiths, 2004). Students, parents and staff can also be taught effective bystander responses to incidents of bullying (Cross, 2004; Cross et al., 2003; Griffiths, 2001; Smith & Sharp, 1994).

Working with parents of students who may have been bullied

All school staff need to be consistent in their use of careful, sensitive and supportive responses to parents who are concerned that their child is being victimised. Such parents may have strong emotional reactions to what they perceive as unfair and cruel mistreatment of their child, so it is essential that school staff respond with patience, support and understanding to the parents of students who have been bullied. These parents need to have a sense of having been fully heard and taken seriously. They need reassurances that the school will take the problem seriously.

Although parents claim to 'know' their children, they may not be aware that their child is being bullied as some students are very reluctant to tell them (or anyone) and may 'stay silent' for many years (O'Moore, 1998). However, when parents do become aware of the situation, they will differ in relation to how they approach the situation with the school and whether or not they are willing to work with the school.

The very angry parent

School staff need to be aware of what happens when a child returns home after a day of being bullied and tells their parents. Often parents become very upset and angry when they hear what has been happening to their child. These parents require patience, understanding and validation. Some parents are actually traumatised by their child's experiences and require professional assistance to deal with painful feelings. Schools need to understand that parents can remain extremely angry long after their child is no longer being bullied and the situation with their peers has greatly improved. It is always important to monitor the progress of a bullying situation that has been addressed but, when the parent(s) is very angry, it is particularly important to do this over an extended period.

When a parent is angry about how their child has been treated and feels that the school has not treated them with respect, or has acted indifferently to their child's plight, they may react in a number of ways. They may tell their child to 'fight back', remove their child from the school, spread angry comments to other parents or take legal action against the school and specific teachers.

One of the potential dangers in this situation is that the angry parent will attempt to take matters into their own hands and contact either the child (or children) whom they believe to be the bully or their parents. They may be acting on incomplete information, and there is a risk of their inflaming the situation and making things much worse by taking action which may cause alienation between members of the school community (who often take sides) or result in assault charges. It will certainly make the situation worse for the child who is being bullied. It is essential that all parents be asked not to approach other students or their parents. They need to work with the school to decide on the most appropriate and sensitive way in which to handle the problem so that their child is not further affected.

The parent who feels powerless

Some parents feel powerless about their child's situation and do nothing in response to their child's distress. Some of these parents have themselves experienced bullying at school or at work with unsatisfactory outcomes. In doing nothing and encouraging their students to 'just learn to live with it' they may be teaching the same powerless attitude to their own children. The school should consider making strenuous and optimistic efforts to involve parents who feel powerless and keep them informed of progress and outcomes.

The parent who focuses on punishment

Some parents are insistent that the bullying child (or children) should be punished. This is an understandable initial response. However, research suggests that in the early stages of a bullying situation, punishing young people who have been involved in bullying usually makes the situation worse for the victim. Many young people report that their reluctance to let someone know that they are being victimised is related to their fear that the students involved will be punished (Rigby & Barnes, 2002). They perceive that there is a risk of retaliation (by the punished students or their friends) and they are concerned that their social reputation and social acceptance will be damaged. Parents who believe that the bullying child should be punished are more likely to work alongside the school if they are given information about non-punitive methods and an explanation for their adoption as an initial approach to the problem (see Chapters 9 and 12 for more details about these approaches).

Some parents are unaware that they can assist their child more productively in the short and long term by enabling their child to learn more effective social survival skills, such as moving away from peers who are teasing, speaking assertively, acting in a neutral manner when 'picked on', using retorts, and using a strong voice and firm eye contact (Field, 1999). Implementing a whole-class program to teach these skills without focusing on any one student is well worth consideration.

Dealing with different parenting styles

Some (but by no means all) students who are bullied experience overprotective parenting. This may make it harder for them to be assertive and cause them to feel more anxious and insecure in their peer group (Sharp, 1993). They are more prone to seeing themselves as victims (Perry, Hodges & Egan, 2001). Research indicates that students with special educational needs are more likely to be bullied (Llewellyn, 1995; O'Moore & Hillery, 1989; Whitney, Nabuzoka & Smith, 1992). Their parents may overcompensate and overprotect. Overprotective parenting appears to be more common in the families of boys who are bullied, whereas some research shows that more commonly girls who are bullied have mothers who cope with conflict in an aggressive style (Finnegan, Hodges & Perry, 1998; Ladd & Ladd, 1998; Smith & Myron-Wilson, 1998).

Some students who are bullied come from families who are low on selflessly caring for others – something that some researchers believe they share in equally low measure with those who bully (Rican, 1995). This low-level genuine concern for others may partially explain why some children who are victimised are often lonely.

Finally, some students who are bullied are raised in families in which there is little practice in dealing with bantering or bullying. In this case it may be helpful for schools to provide books for parents to borrow that teach appropriate social survival skills (e.g. Field, 1999; Petersen, 2002) and to present parenting skills workshops that stress the need for parents to encourage age-appropriate independence and risk-taking and pro-social friendly behaviours in their children. Schools can reinforce the idea that, although all students have the right to be safe at school, there are ways they can behave that can make it more or less likely that they will be victimised. Students can be taught how to protect themselves by using social survival skills.

Ultimately, however, schools are limited in the degree to which they can change family factors. They are responsible for determining their limitations and need to know when to refer the student and their family to an external psychologist or similar appropriate professional. Counselling can assist parents to support their children (especially if the child has special needs or has been overprotected in some ways) and to parent in ways that increase resilience and decrease 'pick me' signals. It is important to assist parents in this way to ensure that they are giving their children messages that are consistent with the work being done by the school.

Working with parents whose child may be bullying another student

The way in which schools interact and work with the parents of a child who uses bullying behaviours can make a big difference to outcomes, both for the students involved and for the school as a whole. The most effective approach for the school is usually one that is sensitive and non-judgmental and focuses more on problem-solving than punishment. Separating the student from their behaviour when talking to parents – 'he/she is a fine person but his/her behaviour towards others is currently unacceptable and needs adjusting' – does this best. The parent requires empathy, support and a positive approach just as much as the parent of the student who has been victimised.

When parents of children who bully are informed about their children's behaviours they can have a variety of responses. Some react responsibly and work with the school to manage the problem in a helpful way that stops the bullying and enables their child to continue to be accepted and developed at school. Some become very angry with their children. Sadly, there is also a risk of some students being on the receiving end of harsh punishment from parents who themselves behave as aggressive role models. Others deny their child's involvement and become very defensive, refusing to accept any version of events from the victim and/or witnesses as true. Yet other parents directly approach the victim or their family and become abusive or try to get other parents to socially exclude them.

There is evidence that, in some cases, parenting styles and family processes may contribute to a higher likelihood of bullying behaviour in students who act as ringleaders in bullying situations. Exactly how much the behaviours and attitudes of a specific culture or peer group contribute to parenting styles that promote bullying is not clear, and has long been a topic of discussion by researchers into bullying (Higson, 2005; Smith & Myron Wilson, 1998). However, what is clear from research is that some aspects of parenting and family interaction are in many cases associated with whether a child bullies others

Influence of parenting styles and family factors on bullying behaviour

Students who consistently bully suffer from more family problems than students who don't (Roland, 2000). They are more likely to be raised in families in which parents show them and others less love and affection, use inconsistent and/or harsh discipline, and/or demonstrate lower levels of parental monitoring of their children's behaviour (Berdondini & Smith, 1996; Bowers, Smith & Binney, 1994; Rican, 1995; Rigby, 1997; Smith & Myron-Wilson, 1998). They are more likely to be on the receiving end of either abusive parental responses or harsh punishment (National Crime Prevention Council, 1997). They are more likely to have authoritarian father models (Knafo, 2003). Children's interactions with their siblings can also be a factor (Patterson, 1986). Aggression between siblings, especially when the power balance is uneven, is the most common form of family violence (Straus, Gelles & Steinmetz, 1981) and, if not checked, can contribute to bullying attitudes and patterns of behaviour.

Indifferent parents

There is some evidence that, in general, parents of students who bully do not speak very much to their children about their bullying behaviour at school (O'Moore, 1998). Some may be unaware that their child is bullying others. Some may not care. Some find it difficult to acknowledge and deal with their child's bullying behaviour. They may tend to ignore it or play it down. Parents being unaware of what their child is doing, is strongly linked with their teenager engaging in high-risk behaviour. This was the case with the behaviour of Eric Harris and Dylan Klebold, the two boys who were initially victims of school bullying but became perpetrators of the Columbine school massacre (Greenfield & Juvonen, 1999). Other parents are unaware of how their parenting style and/or their own 'modelled' behaviour may be contributing to their child's bullying behaviour. Some believe that their child's bullying behaviours are appropriate and acceptable and, indeed, desirable. In some instances one parent is unable to stop the other parent acting as a negative role model, because they find confrontation with an aggressive partner difficult.

One useful approach with less concerned parents is to highlight the difficulties that students who bully will encounter in the future. Then schools can re-label intervention as a productive preventative process for the child's work and relationships future. Students who often bully others are more likely to continue to use this style in dealing with their adult interpersonal lives (Rigby, Whish & Black, 1994) and are more likely to not finish high school, use drugs and alcohol, and engage in delinquent and criminal behaviour (Gottfredson, Gottfredson & Hybl, 1993; Olweus, 1994). They have a one in four likelihood of having a criminal record by the age of 30 (Huesmann, Eron, Lefkowitz, & Walder, 1984) and some will become workplace bullies.

Many studies, but not all, demonstrate that students who bully have high scores on depressive symptoms and suicidal thoughts and these may, in part, reflect family situations (Olweus, 1993; Roland, 2000). It is difficult for schools to have much direct impact on these family factors beyond the provision of information sessions on effective parenting. Effective parenting has many facets, but one core component is the use of an authoritative (NOT authoritarian) parenting style that is characterised by the attempts to develop age-appropriate autonomy for one's child while providing clear boundaries as to what is acceptable and unacceptable behaviour. Children who perceive that this is their parents' style are less likely to bully others (Rican, Klicperova, & Koucka, 1993).

Working with parents whose child may be a bully/victim

One category of child that schools find very difficult to understand and respond to is the child who alternates between bullying and being victimised. These children have been termed 'bully/victims'. One Australian study found that 8 per cent of students were in this category (Ahmed, Harris, Braithwaite & Braithwaite, 2001). 'Bully/victims' experience higher levels of anxiety and depression than do either students who just bully or are bullied. Parents of these students may find it difficult to see their child as both a victim and a perpetrator, despite evidence of their child bullying siblings at home (Crawford, 2002).

Once again, it is important that schools recognise the limitations of their role in some bullying situations and know when and where to refer parents for additional assistance. Parents of children who bully, or who are bully/victims, may require family counselling to assist them to change the home environment and encourage their children to become more empathic and learn appropriate respectful behaviours towards others. In cases where the school suspects that there is real violence at home that is perpetuating the child's use of bullying behaviours at school, mandatory reporting procedures should be followed. In some of these cases schools should also encourage parents to obtain help without the school being directly involved.

Guidelines for schools on working with parents

Schools need to collaborate regularly with parents and students in the formulation of general policies and procedures to deal with bullying. They need to inform all parents and students about possible crisis intervention procedures – a plan with a time frame – that may be implemented to stop specific bullying situations, including the time frame and intervention plan. Parents need to be informed of the appropriate protocol for reporting bullying and which staff member to talk to. They also need to be informed about the various types of bullying, the damage it causes and how to identify signs that it may be happening to their child (see appendix below). There needs to be a formal arrangement by which this consultative process is regularly reviewed and re-implemented.

Schools also need to advise parents of the schools' limitations in the type of help they can provide and of the possibility of being referred for assistance to a trained specialist external to the school. Schools need to be aware that if a parent considers taking legal action against a school over a bullying issue the lawyers engaged will ask whether the student who was bullied and the student(s) who bullied were referred for professional help. If the school counsellor was unable to provide the appropriate assistance, lawyers will ask why the child was not referred externally to an appropriate specialist.

These are more general guidelines for working with parents:

- Common parental complaints are that they were not informed about their child being bullied at an early stage or that nothing effective was done to stop the bullying. When bullying situations develop, communicate supportively with parents from the time the bullying is first reported until it is resolved – and even after that if needed. Monitor the situation over time and keep parents informed if things change. This can be done through phone calls or e-mails or in face-to-face interviews.
- As well as providing information as to how to make a complaint and discuss a bullying situation with a teacher, consider providing guidelines about bullying for parents (see next page and appendix at the end of the chapter) and communicate explanations, expectations and facts about bullying through information sheets, seminars, newsletters, drama and books they can borrow.
- Provide opportunities for parents to learn about effective and resilient parenting skills, as well as access to books and materials on parenting.
- Assist parents to develop resilience and good social skills in their children such as assertiveness, making friends, conflict resolution, non-aggressive anger management and empathy.
- Provide training to all school staff in effective and sensitive ways to talk with and reassure angry and worried parents. Staff may need to be reminded to remain non-judgmental and respect students' and families' confidentiality when the school is responding to a bullying situation. It can be very easy to forget what is being told to whom.
- If a student is not responding within four to six weeks to attempts by teachers, year level coordinators or welfare coordinators to help them cope emotionally and develop

positive relationships after being bullied, refer them and their parents to the school counsellor or an external psychologist, psychiatrist or child guidance clinic.
- If it is suspected that some of the factors contributing to a student's difficulties are beyond the school's role or expertise (e.g. marital problems, post-natal depression, drug and alcohol problems, sexual abuse, unemployment) then refer parents to an appropriate specialist.

General guidelines for parents about bullying

Bullying situations can be handled most effectively and with least damage to the child being bullied and the child who is bullying when parents work with the school to find appropriate solutions. Collaboration also increases the children's opportunities for future social success. A parent taking independent action always makes things worse for the children involved.

These guidelines for parents will help ensure that your child does not become a bully or a victim:

- Let your children regularly and firmly know how much you disapprove of bullying and why. Tell them you don't want them to take part in mistreating another student at any level, however small. Students who come from families that oppose bullying come to accept that bullying is wrong and are less likely to bully others because they know their parents would disapprove (Rigby, 1997).
- Avoid any type of bullying at home and deal firmly with any attempts by siblings to bully one another or engage in 'conflict' where there is a clear imbalance of power.
- Encourage your child to see the positive side of other students rather than express contempt and superiority.
- Model and encourage respect for others and pro-social behaviours and values, such as compassion, cooperation, friendliness, acceptance of difference and respect. Emphasise seeing things from another's point of view and the rights of others not to be mistreated.
- Stress to your children that bullying is everyone's problem and encourage them to act courageously and support any other student who is being bullied. Doing nothing usually means that the bullying continues or that bullying students become more arrogant and target more victims.
- Encourage all children in your family to become involved in a supportive way if a bullying situation develops at school and your child is involved. Students often know that someone is being bullied long before teachers and parents do. They can report

the bullying or encourage the victim to report it (Scottish Council for Research in Education, 1997).

- Report all incidents of bullying that you are aware of, not just incidents that happen to your child. Don't continue any young person's silent nightmare by saying nothing.
- Monitor your child's activities. Set limits and consequences.
- Your children will copy what you do, so it is important that you offer them a positive model for being empathic, resilient, compassionate and respectful of the rights of others.
- Most students cannot solve a bullying problem by themselves once it has gone past the initial one or two 'testing' incidents. They need support to stop it. Keep an eye out for signs that they may be being bullied (see appendix below) or bullying others. Cross-check with others (e.g. the school, friends) to find out what is happening in a non-obtrusive and non-confronting way.
- If you have been bullied in the past, you might wish to consider consulting a counsellor to ensure that your own memories don't adversely affect how you work with the school in resolving your child's bullying problem.
- Develop protective behaviours and resilient social skills in your child, such as speaking assertively, negotiating, expressing their own opinion, and using a confident voice and firm eye contact. Re-label this as a social skills learning exercise. Practise regularly using dinner conversations and social encounters with acquaintances and new people.
- Some students are bullied by peers they regard as friends. Although they can learn how to separate friendly banter from bullying, they need also to distinguish between peers who care about their feelings and those who don't. They should be encouraged to avoid peers who hurt their feelings and show no empathy when confronted.
- Students require the confidence and skills to avoid people who don't treat them with respect. They may need to know, later in life, how to make a complaint to someone in a position of authority if they are mistreated in a workplace context.
- Talk to your child about the qualities associated with developing true, caring friendships and assist them to build and maintain these friendships. This may mean taking an active role in encouraging social activities (e.g. after-school visits, sleepovers).
- Encourage emotional resilience and age-appropriate independence in your child. Give them responsibilities and a reasonable degree of choice in their lives.
- Assist them to develop effective ways of dealing with fear and anger instead of internalising their feelings, taking them out on others or losing face in front of the peer group by allowing them to spill over.

- If there are family issues that may be contributing to your child's bullying problems at school, such as marital difficulties, post-natal depression, drug and alcohol problems or unemployment, consider getting professional assistance for yourself and your child.
- If you grew up in a family where your own parental role models were authoritarian, physically or verbally aggressive and abusive, or lacked empathy and sensitivity, consider having some family therapy sessions with a psychologist to ensure that the parenting style you endured is not passed on down the generations.
- If you decide to move your child to another school, you need to take responsibility for ensuring, before the move, that your child has developed the necessary resilience and social survival skills. In particular, they need to be able to stand tall, make good eye contact and express their own opinions in an assertive manner. They should be encouraged to hide their fear that the bullying might happen again by presenting a calm body language and utilising an assertive interpersonal communication style.
- Although schools have an ethical and legal responsibility to manage incidents of bullying at school, they may be unable to completely eliminate bullying. You have the major responsibility to protect your child from injury and to help them learn how to deal with bullying, wherever they are. Bullying can occur outside school or once they leave school. If the school has not successfully resolved the bullying within six weeks, ask the school to refer you and your child to an external psychologist/psychiatrist or child guidance clinic for assistance. Professional assistance is generally short term – about four to six sessions – and usually includes a history-taking session, awareness of any trauma and painful emotions, skills to deal with bullying, and building self-esteem and effective and age-appropriate social skills. Most young people find such assistance empowering and they learn skills that they can use for a lifetime. You are involved at each stage of the process and are usually provided with appropriate information about bullying processes and shown how to review your parenting styles and responses to your child's situation. Assistance with payment may be available through private health fund rebates, victim's compensation schemes (in some cases) and Medicare rebates (if referred through a specific limited-sessions health plan by a GP). Sometimes the costs may be equivalent to those of expensive electronic toys or orthodontic treatment for your child and therefore initially seem prohibitive. However, this assistance may be a vital investment in a successful future for your child.
- Work closely with the school in preventing bullying, whether or not your child has been bullied. You can assist the school in providing resources and positive ways to encourage respectful behaviours at school. Consider becoming an assertive advocate

for school-wide bullying prevention programs and policies or volunteer time to help supervise on field trips, in the playground or in the lunchroom.

Conclusion

Although, in the past, research on effective ways to develop school-parent partnerships that could help to prevent and manage school bullying has been limited, emerging research is starting to identify the components of whole-school approaches that make a difference (e.g. Cross et al., 2005; Griffiths, 2001). This trend will hopefully continue.

REFERENCES

Ahmed, E. & Braithwaite, V. (2004). Bullying and victimization: Cause for concern for both families and schools. *Social Psychology of Education*, 7(1), 35–54.

Ahmed, E., Harris, N., Braithwaite, J. & Braithwaite, V. (2001). Shame management through reintegration (Vol. 1). Cambridge: Cambridge University Press.

Bastiani, J. & Wolfendale, S. (1996). Quoted by M. O'Moore, *Critical issues for teacher training to counter bullying and victimisation*. European Conference on Initiatives to Combat School Bullying: Keynote Addresses, London, May 1998.

Berdondini, L. & Smith, P. K. (1996). Cohesion and power in the families of children involved in bully/victim problems at school: An Italian replication. *Journal of Family Therapy*, *18*, 99–102.

Bowers, L., Smith, P. K. & Binney, V. (1994). Perceived family relationships of bullies, victims and bully/victims in middle childhood. *Journal of Social and Personal Relationships*, *11*, 215–232.

Choi, J. N. (2003). How does context influence individual behavior? Multilevel assessment of the implementation of social innovations: Commentary on Kallestad and Olweus. *Prevention & Treatment*, 6, Article 23. Retrieved January 2, 2005, from <http://journals.apa.org/prevention/volume6/pre0060023c.html>

Crawford, N. (2002, October). New ways to stop bullying. *APA Online: Monitor on Psychology*, *33*(9), 64. Retrieved April 23, 2005, from <http://www.apa.org/monitor/oct02/bullying.html>

Cross, D. (2004, November). *Helping to make schools even safer: Where policy meets the playground.* Paper presented at the National Coalition Against Bullying Seminar, Melbourne.

Cross, D., Hall, M., Erceg, E., Pintabona, Y., Hamilton, G. & Roberts, C. (2003). The Friendly Schools' Project: An empirically grounded school bullying prevention program. *Australian Journal of Guidance and Counsellors, 13(1)*, 36–46.

Cross, D., Hall, M., Hamilton, G., Pintabona, Y. & Erceg, E. (2004). Australia: The friendly schools project. In P. K Smith, D. Pepler & K. Rigby (Eds.), *Bullying in schools: How successful can interventions be?* (pp. 187–210). Cambridge: Cambridge University Press.

Field, E. M. (1999). *Bullybusting: How to help students deal with teasing and bullying*. Lane Cove, NSW: Finch.

Finnegan, R. A., Hodges, E. V. & Perry, D. G. (1998). Victimization by peers: Associations with children's reports of mother-child interaction. *Journal of Personality & Social Psychology*, *75*(4), 1076–1086.

Forgatch, M. S. (2003). Implementation as a second stage in prevention research: Commentary on Kallestad and Olweus. *Prevention & Treatment*, 6, Article 24. Retrieved January 2, 2005, from <http://journals.apa.org/prevention/volume6/pre0060024c.html>

Greenfield, P. M. & Juvonen, J. (1999). A developmental look at Columbine. *APA Online: Monitor on Psychology*, *30*(7). Retrieved April 23, 2005, from <http://www.apa.org/monitor/julaug99/vp.html>

Griffiths, C. (Ed.) (2001). *Countering bullying in schools: Training package*. Perth, WA: Department of Education.

Griffiths, C. & Weatherilt, T. (2004). *Ways that school support staff can help parents deal with bullying*. Perth, WA: Department of Education and Training.

Gottfredson, D., Gottfredson, G. & Hybl, L. (1993, Spring). Managing adolescent behaviour: A multiyear, multischool study. *American Educational Research Journal*, *30*(1), 179–215.

Higson, R. (2005, January 29–30). The devil's playground: School of hard knocks. *The Weekend Australian Magazine*, pp. 12–16.

House of Representatives Standing Committee on Employment, Education and Training (1994). *Sticks and stones: Report on violence in Australian schools*. Canberra: AGPS.

Huesmann, L. R., Eron, L. D., Lefkowitz, M. M. & Walder, L. O. (1984). Stability of aggression over time and generations. *Developmental Psychology*, *20*, 1120–1134.

Knafo, A. (2003). Authoritarians, the next generation: Values and bullying among adolescent students of authoritarian fathers. *Analyses of Social Issues & Public Policy (ASAP)*, 3(1), 199–204.

Ladd, G. W. & Ladd, B. K. (1998). Parenting behaviors and parent-child relationships: Correlates of peer victimization in kindergarten? *Developmental Psychology*, *34*(6), 1450–1458.

Llewellyn, A. (1995). The abuse of students with physical disabilities in mainstream schooling. *Developmental Medicine & Child Neurology*, *37*(8), 740–743.

National Crime Prevention Council (1997, June). *Bullying and victimisation: The problems and solutions for school-aged students*. Canberra: Virtual Library.

Olweus, D. (1993). *Bullying in school: What we know and what we can do*. Oxford: Blackwell.

Olweus, D. (1994). Bullying at school. In R. Huesmann (Ed.), *Aggressive behaviour: Current perspectives* (pp. 97–130). New York: Plenum Press.

O'Moore, A. M. & Hillery, B. (1989). Bullying in Dublin schools. *Irish Journal of Psychology*, *10*(3), 426–441.

O'Moore, M. (1998, May). *Critical issues for teacher training to counter bullying and victimisation*. European Conference on Initiatives to Combat School Bullying: Keynote Addresses, London.

Ortega, R. & Lera, M. J. (2000). The Seville Anti-Bullying in School Project. *Aggressive Behaviour, 26*, 113–123.

Patterson, G. R. (1986). The contribution of siblings to training for fights: A microsocial analysis. In D. Olweus, J. Broke & M. Randke Yarrow (Eds.), *Development of antisocial and prosocial behaviour: Research, theories and issues* (pp. 2335–2361). New York: Academic Press.

Perry, D. G., Hodges, E. V. & Egan, S. K. (2001). Determinants of chronic victimization by peers: A review and new model of family influence. In J. Juvonen & S. Graham (Eds.), *Peer harassment in school: The plight of the vulnerable and victimized* (pp. 73–104). New York: Guilford Press.

Petersen, L. (2002). *Social savvy: Helping your child fit in*. Melbourne: ACER.

Rapee, R. M. & Szollos, A. A. (2002). Developmental antecedents of clinical anxiety in childhood. *Behaviour Change, 19*(3), 146–157.

Rican, P. (1995). Family values may be responsible for bullying. *Studia Psychologica, 37*(1), 31–36.

Rican, P., Klicperova, M. & Koucka, T. (1993). Families of bullies and their victims: A children's view. *Studia Psychologica, 35*(3), 261–266.

Rigby, K. (1997). What children tell us about bullying in schools. *Children Australia, 22*(2), 28–34.

Rigby, K. & Barnes, A. (2002). To tell or not to tell: The victimised student's dilemma. *Youth Studies Australia, 21*(3), 33–36.

Rigby, K., Whish, A. & Black, G. (1994, August). Implications of school children's peer relations for wife abuse in Australia. *Criminology Australia*, 8–12.

Roland, E. (2000). Bullying, depressive symptoms and suicidal thoughts. *Educational Research, 44*(1), 55–67.

Scottish Council for Research in Education (1997). *Bullying at school: Advice for families*. Retrieved April 22, 2005, from <http://www.scre.ac.uk/bully/whatisbul.html>

Sharp, D. (1993, October). Bullies: A new look at an old problem. *Today's Parent*, 18–21.

Sharp, S. & Smith, P. K. (1991). Bullying in UK schools: The DES Sheffield Project. *Early Child Development and Care, 77*(1), 47–55.

Smith, P. K. & Myron-Wilson, R. (1998). Parenting and bullying. *Journal of Clinical Child Psychology and Psychiatry, 3*(3), 405–417.

Smith, P. K. & Sharp, S. (Eds.) (1994). *School bullying: Insights and perspectives*. London: Routledge.

Stevens, V., De Bourdeaudhuij, I. & Van Oost, P. (2001). Anti-bullying interventions at school: Aspects of programme adaptation and critical issues for further programme development. *Health Promotion International, 16*(2), 155–167.

Stevens, V., Van Oost, P. & De Bourdeaudhuij, I. (2000). The effects of an anti-bullying intervention programme on peers' attitudes and behaviour. *Journal of Adolescence, 23*, 21–34.

Straus, M. A., Gelles, R. J. & Steinmetz, S. K. (1981). *Behind closed doors: Violence in the American family*. New York: Anchor Books.

Whitney, I., Nabuzoka, D. & Smith, P. K. (1992). Bullying in schools: Mainstream and special needs. *Support for Learning, 7*(1), 3–7.

APPENDIX 13A: POSSIBLE SIGNS THAT YOUR CHILD MAY BE BEING BULLIED OR IS BULLYING (based on Field, 1999)

Being bullied

Physical signs

- They are being pushed, shoved, punched, hit, kicked.
- They are involved in fights in which they are unable to defend themselves.
- Their books, money, lunch or belongings have been taken, damaged, scattered around.
- They have bruises, cuts, scratches or torn clothing that cannot be given a natural explanation.
- They complain of minor aches and pains, other health difficulties, or they don't look well much of the time.
- They sleep poorly, begin (or resume) bedwetting and have bad dreams.
- They make frequent and unusual requests for money.
- They want to be taken to school even though it is close by.
- They try to stay close to a teacher or other adults during breaks.
- They lose their appetite.
- They are ravenous when they come home after school (their lunch or lunch money may have been taken).
- They start to bully younger siblings at home.

Academic signs

- They show sudden difficulty asking or answering questions in class.
- They participate less in class activities.
- There is deterioration in their class work and/or homework.
- They say they can't concentrate in class.

Emotional signs

- They appear anxious, distressed, sad, depressed, teary, withdrawn, or secretive.
- They show sudden changes in behaviour, e.g. they become moody, or use the 'bottle it up and burst' method.
- They become angry over nothing.
- When asked why they seem to be angry or sad, they deny it and say 'I'm OK'.
- They repeatedly say that they don't want to go to school anymore and/or that they want to leave the school.

- They seem unhappier at the end of weekends or holidays just before they have to go back to school.
- They start to talk about themselves in derogatory ways (e.g. 'I'm stupid'; 'No-one likes me').

Social signs

- They are teased a lot.
- They often tell you stories of how they felt embarrassed, ridiculed and/or humiliated at school.
- They are often alone and excluded from their peer group at recess and lunchtime.
- They no longer have the same friendship success and seem isolated.
- They no longer have contact with classmates after school hours.
- They are not chosen (e.g. for sharing cabins at camp).

Bullying others

- They often express a strong desire to dominate, win and/or be socially influential over others.
- They show very little empathy for people they consider to be inferior to them and express contempt for them.
- They have a very high self-opinion.
- They are not always compliant and cooperative with adults, including parents and teachers.
- They resist accepting responsibility for their behaviour, and tend to blame others.
- They show limited remorse or guilt.
- They bully siblings and show little empathy towards them.
- They are sometimes cruel to animals (usually boys rather than girls).
- They have additional spending money or come home with gifts without adequate explanation.

SECTION FOUR

PUTTING IT ALL TOGETHER: DEVELOPING POLICIES AND PROCEDURES

CHAPTER 14

A safe school (anti-bullying) template for schools

Helen McGrath and Maree Stanley

Acknowledgements

We would like to acknowledge the helpful feedback and comments received on the evolution of this template from members of the National Coalition Against Bullying.

Introduction

The process of establishing effective anti-bullying polices, programs and procedures usually takes between 12 and 18 months to be completed to the satisfaction of the overall school community (Eslea & Smith, 1998). The following template provides suggestions for directions in this process that are based on research evidence and constitute 'informed' practice.

Section A: The Eight Phases

The flow chart in Figure 14.1 provides a summary of the eight phases in the development of effective policy, procedures, programs and structures for the creation of a safe school. The section below provides more detail about each of the phases.

Figure 14.1 Bullying Phases Flow Template

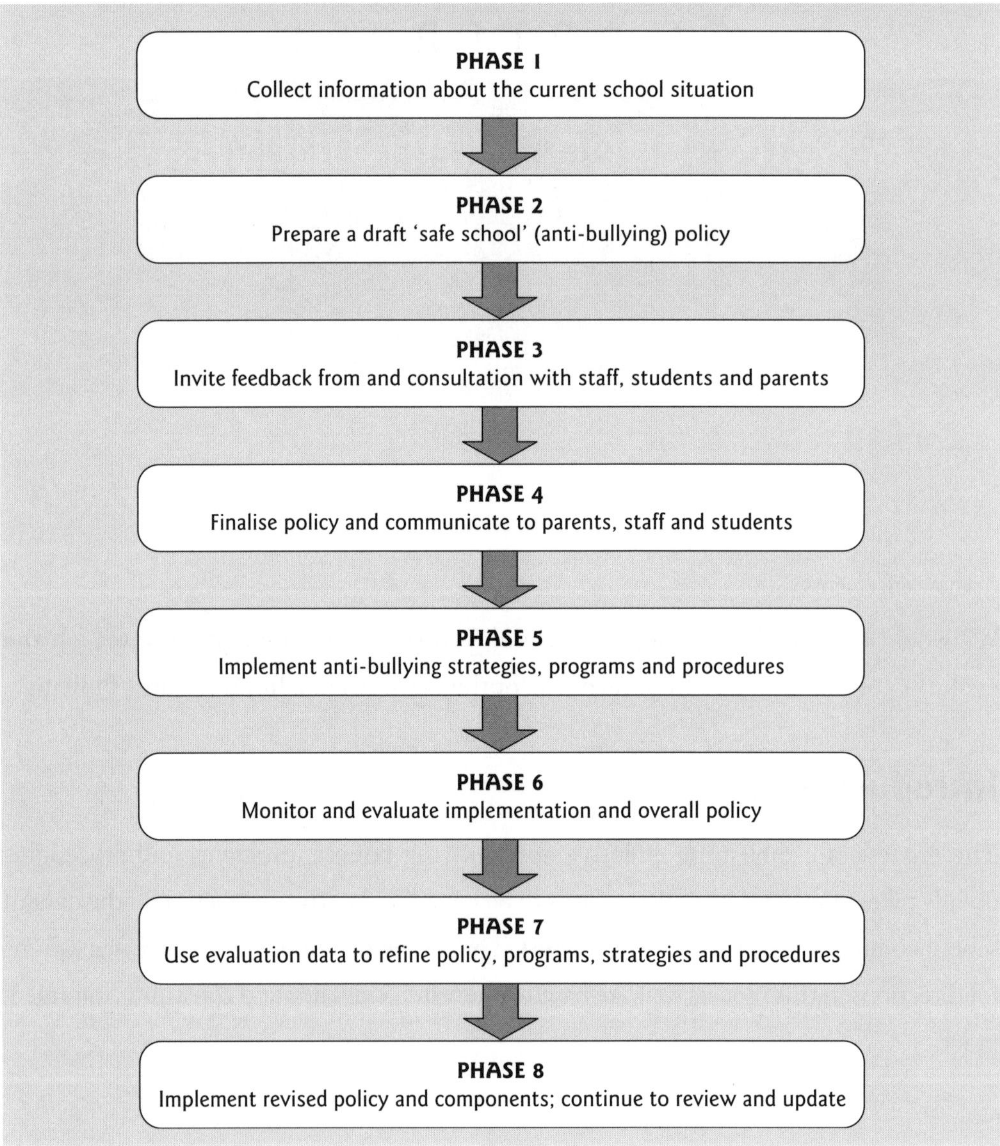

Phase 1: Collect information about the current school situation

It is a good idea to start by conducting an audit of your current policy, programs and procedures that relate to the prevention and management of bullying. A checklist accompanies this template for this purpose (see Appendix 14A). An audit of current practice highlights what progress has already been made as well as gaps that can help to identify where planning is needed for future goals.

Collecting information on the prevalence of bullying and attitudes about bullying held by students, staff and parents can help you to identify patterns in your school. In particular, surveying all stakeholders in the school community can help you to obtain information about how much bullying is happening, what types of bullying are happening and where they occur, and what students, teachers and parents know about current policy and bullying in general. Surveys can also help you to identify common but unhelpful attitudes that need to be addressed. It is a good idea to conduct surveys before and after changes that have been implemented to assess effectiveness and impact. Appendix 14B contains more information about a range of survey tools that can be used or adapted for this purpose.

Phase 2: Prepare a draft 'safe school' policy

A safe school (anti-bullying) policy is most commonly a separate and specific policy rather than part of the school's overall welfare and discipline policy. However, some schools prefer to make it a separate section of the welfare and discipline policy. The policy is best developed in consultation with staff, students and the parent community but some schools prefer the *initial* policy preparation to be undertaken by senior staff. The following components have been shown in a variety of research studies to contribute to an effective draft policy.

1. **A statement which emphasises the rights and responsibilities of everyone in the school community**
   - the rights of all to be safe at school
   - the responsibility of all not to take part in bullying in any way
   - the responsibility of all to let teachers or senior staff know about bullying situations of which they are aware.
2. **A statement that bullying at school is everyone's problem not a personal predicament**

   The approach should be that a person who is bullied does not have the problem alone because bullying damages everyone in the school community in one way or another, for example:
   - The student who is bullied and their family suffer emotional and physical distress.

- Students who are aware of bullying but do nothing about it often feel guilty and ashamed.
- Students who take part in bullying can become desensitised to cruelty and injustice, fail to develop social responsibility and, in some cases, become involved at a later stage in domestic abuse, workplace bullying and/or other forms of anti-social behaviour.
- No-one is safe whilst bullying is happening, because it creates a climate of intimidation and fear in which effective learning cannot take place.
- The school's reputation can be damaged.

3. **A statement of the school's commitment to prevent and minimise bullying**
   It is a good idea to include a strong commitment from the school and its staff to the prevention of bullying and put-downs. It is also helpful to include a clear statement that there is no one simple strategy to achieve this, and that the answer lies in the use of a combination of many approaches. Here is a sample statement that can get you started:

   > This school does not tolerate bullying in any form. All members of the school community are committed to ensuring a safe and caring environment which promotes personal growth, achievement and positive relationships for all students.

   A clear commitment to the non-acceptance of verbal and non-verbal putdowns can be included at this point as well.
4. **A clear definition of what bullying is (and is not) plus examples and agreed terminology**
   Some suggestions about definitions and examples of bullying can be found in Appendix 14C. Once there is agreement, acceptable common terminology can be stated. Currently, many schools agree with this approach:
   - The terms 'recipient' or 'target' are preferable to the term 'victim' as they do not imply powerlessness or weakness.
   - The term 'the student involved in bullying' or 'bullying student' is preferable to 'the bully', which may demonise individual students.
   - The term 'in a less powerful (or more vulnerable) position' is preferable to 'weaker' when talking about a student who has been bullied.

   O'Moore (2000) has cautioned schools and teachers to take great care in how they talk and write about victimised students. She notes that many schools perceive a victimised student as 'weak' rather than as someone who has the misfortune to be in the wrong place at the wrong time and, in most cases, the sensitivity and self-restraint to avoid a violent counter-attack. An approach which 'blames the victim' and asserts that some students bring bullying upon themselves because they are less socially skilful or 'weaker' and act in non-powerful ways which signal vulnerability is both insulting and misses the point: every student, no matter how their behaviour appears to others, has the right to be safe from harassment and violence. Even if a student acts in an annoying and provocative manner, other students are expected to handle their annoyance in an assertive, not an aggressive, way or just accept that different people do things differently. Care must be taken to avoid stereotypes that serve only to promote a negative and often inaccurate image of victims.

5. **Guidelines for students, teachers and parents on what to do in bullying situations**
   This section provides a step-by-step outline of what students should do if they are being bullied or are aware that another student is being bullied. It also informs parents as to what they should do (and not do) if they become aware that their own child is being bullied. Encourage parents to let the school know of any bullying situations involving students other than their child and explain to them how they can do this confidentially. This part of the policy should also state what actions teachers will take if a bullying incident or situation is reported to them (either by the bullied student or other students) or if they become aware of such a situation through observation. Stress that there will be some discretion at this point, based on the complexities of each individual situation. Consider including a diagram or flow chart to explain the options for action in both the short term and the long term.
6. **A summary of the school's preventative strategies and anti-bullying programs**
   See Section B of this chapter for more details.
7. **Provision for ongoing review of policy, procedures, programs and structures**
   It is useful to include in the policy a summary of the procedures that are in place to ensure that the school's safe school (anti-bullying) policy, procedures, programs and structures will be regularly reviewed and amended. Policies and programs that evolve and strengthen over time are more likely to continue to be effective.

Phase 3: Invite feedback from and consultation with staff, students and parents

Circulate the draft policy to students, staff and families. Invite feedback and discussion which can then be used to direct modifications. Consider holding parent meetings, using student, staff and parent focus groups (see Appendix 14D for some guidelines for conducting focus groups for this purpose) or inviting online feedback or written responses. Research has identified that wide consultation on the policy leads to a more effective policy which all members of the school community more readily support and adhere to (Eslea & Smith, 1998).

Phase 4: Finalise policy and communicate to parents, staff and students

Communicate the final policy to the school community in as many ways as possible, for example:

- send a copy home to every family and consider placing it on the school's website
- print it in student diaries
- give monthly reminders of its contents at school assemblies.

Phase 5: Implement anti-bullying strategies, programs and procedures

Implement evidence-based procedures, programs and strategies to address bullying (see Section B of this chapter for more detail).

Phase 6: Monitor and evaluate implementation and overall policy

It is important to regularly collect information and feedback on how effectively the school is preventing, minimising and managing bullying and creating a safe and positive school environment. This information can be used to refine the school's policy, procedures and programs. Some strategies for doing this are:

- continuing to collect information about the prevalence of bullying incidents/situations in the school over time to demonstrate decreases (see Appendix 14B for assessment tools)
- using focus groups of staff, parents and students (see Appendix 14D for information on conducting focus groups).

The ultimate aim is to create a positive feedback loop, which empowers and encourages all members of the school community to continue their struggle to counter bullying and promote positive relationships.

Phase 7: Use evaluation data to refine policy, programs, strategies and procedures

Make the changes you consider necessary based on your evaluation data.

Phase 8: Implement revised policy and components; continue to review and update

Implement the revised anti-bullying programs and procedures again and conduct regular reviews and evaluations.

Section B: Components of prevention and management

This section provides more detail about the big-picture diagram in Figure 14.2.

Figure 14.2 An Overview of Bullying Prevention and Management

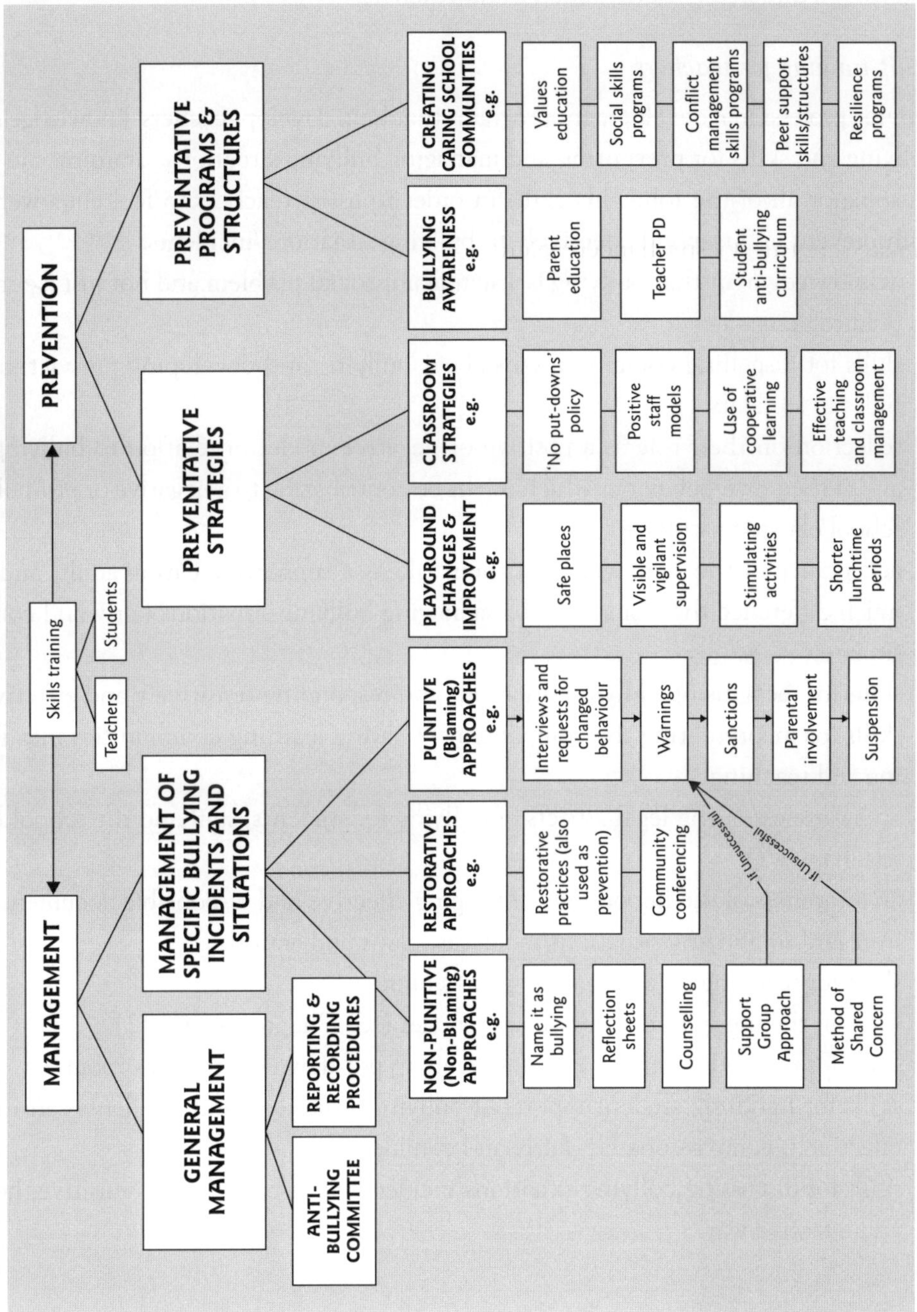

Skills training

Providing training in relevant skills is an aspect of both management and prevention and can be directed to both students and teachers.

Skills training for teachers

Provide professional development programs that help develop teachers' knowledge about bullying and skills for preventing and managing bullying situations. Training can focus on some or all of the following skills in order to assist teachers to feel empowered to both prevent and respond effectively to bullying situations/incidents:

- acknowledgment that bullying is a significant social problem and not just a personal predicament
- skills for dispelling common myths about bullying and developing pro-victim attitudes in students
- reflection on their role as a positive or negative model in relation to bullying and any of their own behaviour which might be contributing to a negative or pro-bullying school/classroom culture
- acceptance of the significance of their role as a supportive caring adult, and how much difference they can make by managing bullying situations fairly and compassionately
- skills for recognising bullying situations and responding sensitively and effectively
- skills for incorporating the components of caring learning communities into learning and teaching
- an awareness of the legal aspects of bullying for students, staff and the school (refer to Chapter 2)
- an awareness of the importance of keeping effective and responsible documentation in regard to bullying situations/incidents, plans and actions
- skills for teaching an anti-bullying curriculum
- skills in the use of non-punitive approaches (see Chapters 4 and 12)
- skills for responding firmly and effectively to put-downs in the classroom
- skills for handling student reports of bullying situations and incidents sensitively, effectively, compassionately, fairly and confidentially
- skills for discussing bullying situations/incidents with parents in a sensitive, helpful and effective way.

Skills training for students

Students need opportunities to learn and practise understanding and skills such as:

- the difference between asking for support, acting responsibly and dobbing (e.g. McGrath & Francey, 1991; McGrath & Noble, 2003)
- acting confidently and assertively (this should *not* lead students to believe that if they are bullied it is their fault)
- assisting students to respond adaptively to being bullied or put down, for example:
  - skills for 'saving face' under circumstances of harassment
  - skills in asking for support/help
  - skills of verbal and non-verbal assertiveness (only effective under conditions of initial, isolated and mild harassment)
  - skills for discouraging bullying and offering bystander support (see Chapters 6 and 8; McGrath & Noble, 2003)
  - social skills (McGrath, 1997; McGrath & Francey, 1991; McGrath & Noble, 2003), especially skills for effective and non-aggressive management of disagreement. Conflict is not the same as bullying – see definitions in Appendix 14C. However, teaching students skills for managing conflict well can contribute to a more positive and harmonious school culture in which it is more difficult for bullying to get a foothold.

General management

Many schools have found establishing an anti-bullying staff committee of teachers to be an effective general management strategy. Also important is the establishment of effective and confidential reporting and record-keeping systems.

Anti-bullying committee

The use of an anti-bullying committee is more effective if the members of the committee have the time needed to undertake the agreed responsibilities and intensive training in both prevention and management. Such a committee can be responsible for some or all of the following:

- identifying and disseminating information to staff about:
  - appropriate curriculum material for students about bullying
  - programs for teaching pro-social skills and values and developing a positive, caring and pro-social culture
  - strategies for promoting positive teacher/student relationships
- school-wide monitoring of the prevalence and patterns of bullying through the coordination of data collection (e.g. through surveys, incident reports, etc.)

- being available to students for the reporting of bullying
- consulting and collaborating with individual teachers on appropriate actions in bullying situations as required or requested
- collecting and disseminating relevant research information about bullying to staff
- coordinating and undertaking relevant professional development for themselves and other teachers
- working with staff to develop a code of conduct in regard to their own behaviour towards students and each other
- keeping senior staff informed about the bigger picture of bullying in the school
- monitoring staff responses to bullying situations/incidents across time to try to ensure that responses are reasonably consistent across teachers and contexts.

Reporting and recording procedures

These procedures help to protect students, parents and the school. The following features can contribute to effective reporting and record keeping:

- It is helpful for teachers on yard duty to have a clipboard containing a blank incident report form with them at all times so that they can report any behaviour or incidents that could be a cause for concern. This sheet can include sections such as:
  - What happened?
  - Where and when?
  - Who was involved?
  - Who was a witness?
  - What action was taken?
  - Is follow-up needed?
  - Teacher's signature or initials.

  These forms are then followed up and kept in a restricted access file to enable the appropriate person to identify patterns over time. If appropriate, teachers can use the incident report to alert other teachers at 'yard duty hand-over' about potential situations that need to be monitored or defused.
- Consider making at least one method of anonymous reporting available for students. This can be manual (e.g. a reporting box in the library) or electronic (e.g. e-mail).
- All reported incidents or complaints should be taken seriously and investigated.
- All records of possible or suspected incidents of bullying can be kept in a restricted file until confirmed.
- Each record of confirmed incidents of bullying plus action plans can be kept in the student's file. Schools need to consider how long such files will be kept and balance

the possibility of later retrospective legal action against the need to prevent labelling and stigmatisation.

- Depending on their age, students should be able to ask for teacher commitment to treat reports of bullying confidentially. Teachers should know methods of responding to a report in a way that does not break this commitment. For example:
  - A teacher or year level coordinator may only take action after conducting their own follow-up observations in the playground or elsewhere so that it seems that their response is based on their own information at a later point in time. Then they can say, 'The other day when I was near the canteen I noticed . . .'.
  - A teacher might say: 'Several staff members have reported to me over the last few weeks that . . .'.

  Note: If the Support Group Approach or the Method of Shared Concern is used, some incidents will not be routinely followed up and 'fact-checked' in this way in the early stages.
- Clear messages can be given to students as to what they should do if they are being bullied, and which staff members are available to support them. However, students also need to know that they can approach any teacher or staff member of their own choice to talk about a bullying situation if they wish.
- Students also need to be informed about what they should do if they witness others being bullied, or are aware of it in other ways.
- Clear guidelines can be provided for parents as to what they should do if they believe that their child (or another child) is being bullied.
- Clear guidelines can be provided for staff as to what they can do if a student reports to them that they are being bullied and what they can do if they are being bullied themselves.

Management of specific bullying incidents and situations

In collaboration with staff, establish step-by-step guidelines on actions to take when they become aware of bullying situations or incidents through observation, witness report or student/parent complaint. In particular, teachers need to agree with and be aware of:

- the differences between early and mild situations and more serious or persistent situations
- actions to take (and in what order) in newly reported/identified bullying situations
- actions to take (and in what order) in established situations where bullying persists despite the earlier adoption of a non-punitive support group or problem-solving approach

- the need to identify conditions under which teachers have the discretion to manage the situation in a different way
- how to document incidents and action plans
- which senior staff need to be informed or involved about bullying situations
- under what circumstances and at what point parents are involved
- from whom they can obtain advice or collaboration on the best way to respond to a bullying incident/situation
- how to involve the student who has been bullied in decisions about the most effective short-term approach to the situation. It is helpful for the student to have some say as to how the situation will be dealt with. Some choose to experiment with skills such as ignoring, being assertive and walking away if it happens again. Some, having already tried this unsuccessfully, prefer the option of the teacher discussing the issue with the offending students (refer to Chapter 12 on non-punitive approaches). Whatever the outcome, there need to be follow-up procedures. Follow-up ensures that the bullying has really stopped and that there has been no retaliation. This usually requires observations and informal chats but may also involve the use of a mentor-advocate teacher, i.e. a teacher who is not the student's regular teacher but who meets with the student on a regular basis for a chat or as requested.

Following are a number of strategies for responding to and managing bullying situations, all of which have been discussed in detail in previous chapters. Smith (2001) and Rigby and Thomas (2002) believe that the available evidence suggests that both punitive and non-punitive approaches can be effective.

Non-punitive (non-blaming) approaches (refer to Chapter 12)

Non-punitive approaches are those that neither openly blame the student nor involve the application of consequences and sanctions. The approaches described below involve teachers responding to bullying in a supportive way, without applying punishments. If these approaches are not successful within a short space of time, more punitive approaches are usually adopted.

Name the behaviour as bullying

One very important early step is to name the behaviour as bullying so that students are very clear about what they are doing. Some students may not fully see the connection between their behaviour and bullying behaviour.

Reflection sheets

Students who have been involved in bullying can be asked to complete a reflection sheet (or 'Time to Think' sheet) which asks them to write answers to questions such as:

- What happened?
- Who do you think has been affected by your behaviour and how?
- How did they feel?
- How can what happened be seen as bullying?
- Where was there a lack of respect?
- What can you do to make things better and/or make things right?
- What can you do to make sure this doesn't happen again?

Counselling

Identify school support staff or community support agencies that may be able to contribute additional counselling or support to the targeted student, the student/s doing the bullying and the parents. Individual and ongoing case management may be required where the bullying has persisted. Student support services and external counselling and support services may also be required.

Establish guidelines for effective and sensitive handling of reported bullying situations and incidents which emphasise:

- treating the student's report sensitively, seriously and fairly, through the use of genuine concern, respect, empathy and effective listening
- reassurance that actions will be taken to resolve the situation
- a degree of student choice as to how the situation will be handled.

Discuss bullying incidents in a helpful and sensitive way with parents and acknowledge their distress over the situation. Keep them informed of how the situation is being handled and what progress is being made. Stress that the problem is one on which the school and parents need to work together (see Chapter 13 for more details on working with parents).

The Support Group Approach and the Method of Shared Concern (refer to Chapter 12)

There is some evidence to suggest that many students who are bullied are hesitant to report it as they fear the possibility of retaliation or more damage to their social reputation if the students involved in bullying them 'get into trouble'. The adoption of a non-punitive group support/problem-solving approach to an initial bullying situation can be useful. Options include the Support Group Approach and the Method of Shared Concern (see Chapter 12). Some schools merge elements of both to create their own approach but the active ingredients are:

- not openly blaming or lecturing
- not applying punishments
- working with the students involved to solve the problem.

Restorative approaches

Restorative approaches can be difficult to classify as they are not really punitive or non-punitive. They certainly focus directly on students taking responsibility for their actions and so cannot be considered a 'non-blaming' approach. On the other hand, they don't apply authority-based consequences but rather ask the students involved to negotiate and determine a way to make amends for the harm that has been done. Therefore, they are not punitive approaches. It appears that they may be best treated as a separate approach, with some features of both punitive and non-punitive approaches.

Restorative approaches ask students who have harmed another to accept responsibility for that behaviour and, in that sense, students are 'blamed' for their action. However, a restorative approach also stresses the importance of fairness, empathy, remorse, making amends and restoring relationships that have been damaged as a result of their actions. The assumption is that students who harm another are also harming themselves and their school/classroom community and that punishment breeds defensiveness and retaliation, whereas a restorative approach focusing on taking responsibility and making amends develops thoughtfulness and repairs relationships.

Restorative practices involve the systematic use of this 'restorative' approach to manage anti-social behaviours ranging from not putting your own rubbish in the bin up to bullying. Restorative practices involve the use of Circle Time and Classroom Meetings to handle issues that directly or indirectly affect the class group (see McGrath & Noble, 2003a, for details of how to use Circle Time).

The more serious process of *community conferencing* involves a meeting which aims to help the students involved in bullying (or any other harm-doing, such as vandalism or theft) feel remorse and empathy and make amends. Such meetings can include the students who have offended, the student who has been harmed, their families and/or supporters/advocates, and the appropriate senior or support staff from the school. Some conferences are more informal. The following basic guidelines (Wachtel & McCold, 2000) are used:

- Help the student develop some awareness of how others have been affected by what they have done. This process can be fostered by hearing others saying how they feel about what happened to them and what impact it made on them.
- Don't tell the student off or lecture them. This leads them to react defensively and

become alienated and they tend to see *themselves* as the person who has been mistreated. Don't focus on the impact of their behaviour on others.
- Ensure that students take an active role in the process. Ask them to speak about the impact of their actions and help them decide how to repair any harm that has been done. Encourage them to make a commitment to that action.
- Accept that some situations are ambiguous and that it can be difficult to ascertain who has caused the harm. Students can still be encouraged to take responsibility for their part.
- Separate the student from what they have done. Let them know that you assume that they did not *mean* to cause harm and that their behaviour has surprised you. If appropriate, mention some of their strengths and accomplishments. It is important to recognise their worth as well as disapprove of what they have done.
- See every instance of harmful or thoughtless behaviour as a constructive opportunity to teach and build in students empathy and a sense of responsibility and community.

For more detail on these approaches, refer to Chapter 11.

Punitive approaches

Some schools opt for a punitive approach in some or all situations. Generally, there is additional discussion with those involved and reference made to documented graduated consequences. A typical sequence may be, for example:
- a verbal warning
- a written warning
- interview with a teacher, which may include a written commitment to change the behaviour
- interview with a senior staff member
- further small group learning opportunities in relation to pro-social values and social skills
- sanctions such as detention, the suspension of playground privileges for a number of days, or some form of time out or social exclusion
- parental involvement (but this may occur at an earlier stage)
- more serious consequences such as in-house or external suspension
- very serious consequences such as expulsion.

Preventative strategies

Successful preventative practices can minimise bullying. There is a wide range of options to choose from.

Playground improvement

Most bullying in primary schools occurs in the playground whereas in secondary schools, although there is still a considerable amount of bullying that occurs in the playground, more occurs in the corridors and classrooms (Ahmad & Smith, 1990; Craig, Pepler & Atlas, 2000; Rivers & Smith, 1994; Whitney & Smith, 1993). This makes it essential that schools identify changes and improvements that can reduce the likelihood of bullying in the school yard. Some of these are discussed below.

Safe places

'Safe places' provide a refuge for students who are being victimised. Examples are:

- special games rooms containing a variety of board games and organised activities, which can be supervised and facilitated by a teacher, parent volunteer or older students
- club activities
- organised activities in the gym or library.

Visible and vigilant supervision

High-risk situations often include crowded areas (e.g. the canteen; excursion buses; footy games), areas with lower levels of teacher supervision (e.g. toilets and locker rooms, classrooms when the teacher is late) or places where teachers are less visible (e.g. bus queues). It is a good idea to identify high-risk areas by observation or through student report. Students can be asked to answer the question as part of a survey or they can be asked to draw red dots on a school map to show either where they have been bullied or have witnessed bullying or where they have not felt safe. These areas can then be more vigilantly supervised or reorganised. This has been shown to be a highly effective strategy for reducing bullying (Eslea & Smith, 1998).

In general, teachers can be asked to ensure that they supervise in the playground more effectively. Effective supervision is characterised by a highly visible teacher presence, teachers actively looking for potential bullying situations, and thorough and wide-reaching monitoring of all areas of the school. Yard duty teachers can be supplied with a clipboard and forms for recording observations and reports of behaviour which suggests the possibility of bullying.

Stimulating activities

Creating safe, stimulating and structured activities for break times can help to reduce bullying at lunchtime and recess (Cross, 2004; Cross, Hall, Hamilton, Pintabona &

Erceg, 2004; Eslea & Smith, 1998). A range of options can be developed that offer students safe and engaging activities when they feel isolated and vulnerable, for example:

- provision of a variety of outdoor games equipment
- an 'all welcome' play area where students can go to find a temporary playmate
- special cooperative outdoor games and sporting activities which are facilitated and supervised by a teacher, parent volunteer or older students.

It can be helpful to have a playground committee composed of teachers, students and perhaps parents. The task of the committee is to plan and monitor activities and equipment and to evaluate how effectively they increase student safety.

Shorter lunchtime periods

Some schools have found that more bullying occurs in the last 10 minutes of lunchtime than at any other time (Cross, 2004). If, after structured observation and data collection, your school finds this to be so, consider shortening the break time and making adjustments elsewhere in the daily schedule (Cross, 2004).

Classroom strategies

Research has shown that even in some schools where bullying is a significant problem there are often specific classrooms or class sessions where very little bullying occurs and that this can be attributed to the actions and teaching competence of the individual teacher(s) (Roland & Galloway, 2002). Clearly, what happens in the classroom makes a significant difference to whether or not students bully others. Teachers can make a large contribution to the reduction of bullying in a school by using the following approaches.

'No put-downs' policy

Establish a 'no put-downs' policy and culture and make sure that all teachers have the skills to act firmly when put-downs are used (see McGrath, 1997; McGrath & Noble, 2003a). Once established, this expectation can be firmly endorsed in all classrooms. A culture of disrespectful put-downs is a starting point for the evolution of a bullying culture. Students need to be made aware of the strongly non-verbal nature of put-downs. The differences between put-downs and stirring need to be highlighted so that stirring/bagging doesn't become a smokescreen for what is often the early stage of bullying.

Positive staff models

Gain commitment from all staff to model appropriate behaviour towards both students and colleagues. Appropriate teacher behaviour has the following characteristics:

- It reflects mutual respect, negotiation and fairness towards students and colleagues and the avoidance of put-downs or 'words that wound'.
- It is optimistic, cooperative, friendly and inclusive.
- It avoids the use of bullying or put-down behaviour.
- It is non-coercive and does not involve demonstrations of power or dominance.

Staff can be asked to make plans for enhancing their own positive and respectful behaviour in these ways and to consider developing a published staff code of conduct.

Cooperative learning

There are many studies which support the effectiveness of cooperative learning as a strategy for effective student learning and classroom management and also for reducing bullying, creating connectedness, and developing respect, acceptance of difference and a sense of community (Cowie & Sharp, 1998; Cowie, Smith, Boulton & Laver, 1994; Johnson & Johnson & Stanne, 2000).

Effective teaching and classroom management

Effective teaching and classroom management minimises bullying and stops it quickly if it starts. Students who are fully engaged are less likely to be bored and looking for entertainment through annoying or harassing classmates. Roland and Galloway (2002) found that teachers who were perceived by their students as demonstrating the following characteristics and competencies had less bullying in their classrooms:

- They were caring and supportive towards students and helped them with problems when needed.
- They were competent and able to engage students.
- They constantly monitored what was happening in the classroom and quickly intervened when there was any type of conflict or problem between students.
- They developed clearly stated class rules and expectations in conjunction with their students.

Preventative programs and structures

There are many types of preventative programs and structures available that can be used to minimise the likelihood of bullying. In general, schools that implement more options get better results (Eslea & Smith, 1998).

Bullying awareness for parents, teachers and students

All members of the school community need opportunities to be informed about the seriousness of bullying and to become aware that bullying is everybody's problem.

Parent education

Cross et al. (2004) have noted that a lack of appreciation by parents about the benefits for all students from anti-bullying initiatives, especially those that are preventative, can be an obstacle to success. Therefore, it is important to stress to parents what their family can gain from awareness programs, even if their child is not *currently* being bullied or involved in bullying.

Effective awareness programs for parents can focus on:

- how the development of connectedness and relationships and a sense of community is of benefit to all students
- the concept that bullying is everyone's problem, not just a personal predicament
- what bullying and put-downs are, examples of both, and why they are unacceptable
- how pro-social values, programs and strategies can create a pro-social connected culture and prevent bullying
- indicators that their child may be being bullied or be bullying others
- the peer dynamics that are often involved in bullying
- the importance of working with the school to deal with bullying situations rather than trying to solve the problem themselves.

Consider introducing parent information sheets or holding parent forums or evening sessions. More information can be obtained in Chapter 13.

Teacher professional development

Information and suggestions for appropriate professional development can be found in most chapters of this book. It is also important to address the loss of staff who have been trained in anti-bullying skills (Cross et al., 2004) and identify opportunities for professional development for new staff, as well as procedures and strategies for program maintenance (see McGrath & Noble, 2003a, pp. 79–81).

Anti-bullying curriculum

Consider teaching children an anti-bullying curriculum at every year level (e.g. McGrath & Noble, 2003b). In the Sheffield study in the UK, one of the most effective strategies, and the most popular choice of teachers, for bullying prevention was the use of an anti-bullying and pro-social curriculum (Eslea & Smith, 1998). Ideas for what to include can be found in Chapters 3 and 4. Effective anti-bulllying curriculm programs for students focus on:

- the unacceptability of bullying and put-downs
- the school's commitment to preventing and minimising bullying and put-downs
- a clear definition of bullying (examples, expectations, rights, responsibilities and consequences)
- that bullying is everyone's problem
- the importance of positive peer relationships, social inclusion, pro-social values (especially acceptance of differences)
- the legal side of bullying (it can be helpful to involve a legal expert or police officer)
- the links between bullying and global and historical examples of religious, sexual or racial oppression (for older students)
- issues related to workplace bullying (for senior students).

Curriculum activities can be incorporated across many different key learning areas, for example English (e.g. writing and poetry), Arts (e.g. drawings and posters) and Drama. They can also be undertaken in pastoral care, Personal Development or RE lessons. Students can also undertake group projects and create group products (e.g. a DVD or drama production) related to bullying. There are a variety of resources that can be used such as videos, DVDs and children's literature (fiction and non-fiction) that carry anti-bullying messages, as well as performances by professional theatre groups that communicate anti-bullying messages (see resources in Appendix 14E).

Creating caring learning communities

Research supports the effectiveness of implementing programs and structures that contribute to a positive, pro-social, connected and caring school community in which all members experience a sense of safety and belonging (Cross, 2004). More details are outlined in Chapters 3 and 4. This culture is also consistent with a non-violent approach to conflict and differences. Some of the direct options are:

- values education programs which focus on pro-social values such as cooperation, acceptance of differences, friendliness and respect (e.g. McGrath & Noble, 2003b)
- social skills programs which teach students skills such as including others and playing fairly
- conflict management skills programs which teach skills such as negotiation and being assertive
- peer support systems such as buddy programs (see Chapter 6), peer counselling, peer mediation, and student anti-bullying committees and campaigns (peer support skills

that bystanders can use to defuse or intervene in bullying situations can also be taught – see McGrath & Noble, 2003b)

- resilience programs (which usually include social skills, conflict management skills and anger-management skills)
- community service programs, such as those that focus on caring about others in the community (e.g. the elderly, homeless youth, etc.).

The appendixes which follow provide more detail to support aspects of this template.

REFERENCES

Ahmad, Y. & Smith, P. K. (1990). Behavioural measures: Bullying in schools. *Newsletter of Association for Child Psychology and Psychiatry*, *12*, 26–27.

Cowie, H. & Sharp, S. (1998). Tackling bullying through the curriculum. In P. K. Smith & S. Sharp (Eds.), *School bullying: Insights and perspectives*. London: Routledge, pp. 84–107.

Cowie H., Smith, P. K., Boulton, M. & Laver, R. (1994). *Co-operation in the multi-ethnic classroom*. London: David Fulton.

Craig, W. M., Pepler, D. J. & Atlas, R. (2000). Observations of bullying on the playground and in the classroom. *International Journal of School Psychology*, *21*, 22–36.

Cross, D. (2004, November). *Helping to make schools even safer: Where policy meets the playground*. Paper presented at the National Coalition Against Bullying Seminar, Melbourne.

Cross, D., Hall, M., Hamilton, G., Pintabona, Y. & Erceg, E. (2004). Australia: The friendly schools project. In P. K Smith, D. Pepler & K. Rigby (Eds.), *Bullying in schools: How successful can interventions be?* (pp. 187–210). Cambridge: Cambridge University Press.

Eslea, M. & Smith, P. K. (1998). The long-term effectiveness of anti-bullying work in primary schools. *Educational Research*, *40*, 203–218.

Johnson, J. & Johnson, R. & Stanne, M. B. (2000). Cooperative learning methods: A meta-analysis. Retrieved March 30, 2005, from <http://www.co-operation.org/pages/cl-methods.html>

Limper, R. (2000). Cooperation between parents, teachers and school boards to prevent bullying in education: An overview of work done in the Netherlands. *Aggressive Behavior*, *26*, 125–134.

McGrath, H. (1997). *Dirty tricks: Classroom games which teach students social skills*. Melbourne: Addison Wesley Longman.

McGrath, H. & Francey, S. (1991). *Friendly Kids, Friendly Classrooms*. Melbourne: Longman.

McGrath, H. & Noble, T. (2003a). *BOUNCE BACK! A Classroom Resiliency Program: Teacher's Handbook*. Frenchs Forest, NSW: Pearson Education. <http://www.bounceback.com.au>

McGrath, H. & Noble, T. (2003b) *BOUNCE BACK! A Classroom Resiliency Program*. Frenchs Forest, NSW: Pearson Education (Bullying units in all three Teacher Resource Books) <http://www.bounceback.com.au>

O'Moore, A. M. (2000). Critical issues for teacher training to counter bullying and victimisation in Ireland. *Aggressive Behaviour*, *26*, 99–111.

Rigby, K. & Thomas, E. (2002). *How Australian schools are responding to the problem of peer victimisation in schools*. Canberra: Criminology Research Council. Retrieved February 16, 2005, from <http://www.aic.gov.au/crc/reports/200001-10.html>

Rivers, I. & Smith, P. K. (1994). Types of bullying behavior and their correlates. *Aggressive Behavior*, *20*, 259–368.

Roland, E. & Galloway, D. (2002). Classroom influences on bullying. *Educational Research*, *44*, 299–312.

Smith, P. K. (2001). 'Should we blame the bullies?'. *The Psychologist*, *14*(2), Retrieved May 15, 2005, from <www.luckyduck.co.uk>

Wachtel, T. & McCold, P. (2000). Restorative justice in everyday life. In J. Braithwaite & H. Strang (Eds.), *Restorative justice in civil society* (pp. 117–125). New York: Cambridge University Press.

Whitney, I. & Smith, P. K. (1993). A survey of the nature and extent of bully/victim problems in junior/middle and secondary schools. *Educational Research*, *35*, 3–25.

APPENDIX 14A: THE ANTI-BULLYING TEMPLATE FOR SCHOOLS

Phase 1 Collect information about current school situation	Audit of the school's current policy	Yes	Needs Work	Not Started
	Audit of the school's current programs	Yes	Needs Work	Not started
	Audit of the school's current procedures	Yes	Needs Work	Not Started
	Initial staff survey about bullying	Yes	Needs Work	Not Started
	Initial student survey about bullying	Yes	Needs Work	Not Started
	Initial parent survey about bullying	Yes	Needs Work	Not Started
Phase 2 Prepare a draft anti-bullying/'safe school' policy	Statement of rights and responsibilities	Yes	Needs Work	Not Started
	Statement that bullying at school is everyone's problem	Yes	Needs Work	Not Started
	Statement of the school's commitment to prevent and minimise bullying	Yes	Needs Work	Not Started
	Definition of what bullying is (and is not) and a range of examples and agreed terminology	Yes	Needs Work	Not Started
	Guidelines for students to follow if they are bullied	Yes	Needs Work	Not Started
	Guidelines for students to follow if they witness or are aware of bullying	Yes	Needs Work	Not Started
	Guidelines for parents to follow if they believe their child has been bullied	Yes	Needs Work	Not Started
	A statement of the schools processes which will occur after a bullying incident	Yes	Needs Work	Not Started
	Guidelines for teachers to follow if they are bullied	Yes	Needs Work	Not Started
	A statement about the school's actions if the bullying persists	Yes	Needs Work	Not Started
	A statement about how the school will investigate to clarify what has actually happened	Yes	Needs Work	Not Started
	A statement about the recording procedures used for bullying incidents	Yes	Needs Work	Not Started
	A statement of the school's prevention strategies and other anti-bullying programs	Yes	Needs Work	Not Started
	An indication of the point at which parents will be involved	Yes	Needs Work	Not Started
	A statement of the procedures that are in place to ensure policy revision every two years	Yes	Needs Work	Not Started
Phase 3 Invite feedback from and consultation with staff, parents and students	Circulation of a draft policy to elicit feedback from the school community	Yes	Needs Work	Not Started
	Invite feedback and discussion via meetings, focus groups, online feedback or written responses	Yes	Needs Work	Not Started
	Revision of the policy after analysis of feedback	Yes	Needs Work	Not Started

(continued)

Phase 4 Finalise policy and communicate to parents, staff and students	A copy of the policy sent home to every family	Yes	Needs Work	Not Started
	A copy of the policy is printed in student diaries	Yes	Needs Work	Not Started
	Reminders of policy are given at assemblies	Yes	Needs Work	Not Started
	A copy of the policy is printed in the school's newsletter	Yes	Needs Work	Not Started
Phase 5 Implement anti-bullying strategies, programs and procedures	Establishment of a school anti-bullying committee	Yes	Needs Work	Not Started
	Bullying awareness programs for students at all year levels	Yes	Needs Work	Not Started
	Bullying awareness programs for parents	Yes	Needs Work	Not Started
	Bullying awareness programs for teachers	Yes	Needs Work	Not Started
	Collaboratively developed teacher guidelines for responding to and managing bullying situations	Yes	Needs Work	Not Started
	Establishment of effective confidential reporting and record-keeping procedures and systems	Yes	Needs Work	Not Started
	Collection of data about bullying in the school and analysis of patterns	Yes	Needs Work	Not Started
	Establishment of a 'no put-downs' culture	Yes	Needs Work	Not Started
	Implementation of a range of anti-bullying prevention program options at all year levels	Yes	Needs Work	Not Started
	Implementation of a range of program and strategy options that contribute to a caring pro-social school, e.g. buddy buddy structures, community service	Yes	Needs Work	Not Started
	Provision of a variety of anti-bullying resources for both teachers and students	Yes	Needs Work	Not Started
	Creation of safe and structured indoor and outdoor activities/places for break times	Yes	Needs Work	Not Started
	Ensuring effective yard duty supervision	Yes	Needs Work	Not Started
	Identification of high-risk areas and situations and responsive planning to address them	Yes	Needs Work	Not Started
	Staff commitment to model appropriate positive behaviour and provide positive role models	Yes	Needs Work	Not Started
	Ongoing collection of data at the school to direct changes and provide a positive feedback loop	Yes	Needs Work	Not Started
	Ongoing professional development in areas such as Support Group Approach, Method of Shared Concern, restorative practices, social skills programs, resilience programs	Yes	Needs Work	Not Started
	Establishment of guidelines for effective and sensitive handling of bullying reports and complaints	Yes	Needs Work	Not Started
	Establishment of guidelines for effective and sensitive handling of parent discussions about bullying	Yes	Needs Work	Not Started

(continued)

	Counselling available for all students involved in bullying situations	Yes	Needs Work	Not Started
	Follow-up procedures in place for students who have been bullied	Yes	Needs Work	Not Started
Phase 6 Monitor and evaluate implementation and overall policy	Ongoing collection of data about bullying to direct changes and provide a positive feedback loop	Yes	Needs Work	Not Started
	Information collected about the prevalence of bullying incidents and situations to demonstrate any decrease	Yes	Needs Work	Not Started
	Focus groups held with staff, parents and students	Yes	Needs Work	Not Started
Phase 7 Use evaluation data to refine policy, programs, strategies, and procedures	Changes made to policy based on data	Yes	Needs Work	Not Started
	Changes made to strategies used based on data	Yes	Needs Work	Not Started
	Changes made to programs used based on data	Yes	Needs Work	Not Started
	Changes made to procedures used based on data	Yes	Needs Work	Not Started
Phase 8 Implement revised policy and components; continue to review and update	Revised anti-bullying programs implemented	Yes	Needs Work	Not Started
	Revised anti-bullying procedures implemented	Yes	Needs Work	Not Started
	Changes communicated to staff, students and parents	Yes	Needs Work	Not Started
	Regular reviews and evaluations are carried out	Yes	Needs Work	Not Started

APPENDIX 14B: ASSESSMENT TOOLS

This section describes a range of measures for assessing perceptions of students, teachers and parents about bullying in their school. These are:

- The MindMatters Bullying and Harassment Survey
- Life in School Checklist
- Rigby and Slee's PRQ (Peer Relations Questionnaire)
- Olweus's Revised Bully/Victim Questionnaire
- Andrew Fuller's SSS-R (School Safety Survey – revised) for secondary schools
- NCAB's DIY (Do-It-Yourself) Bullying Surveys.

The MindMatters Bullying and Harassment Survey

You will find a summary of the types of questions used in its survey in its publication entitled *A Whole School Approach to Dealing with Bullying and Harassment: Facing Facts* at <http://cms.curriculum.edu.au/mindmatters/resources/download.htm>.

Many of the questions do not focus specifically on bullying as there is no mention of repeated behaviours. Types of questions used include:

- Name the places where you notice name-calling and put-downs happening at school.
- Name the places where you notice pushing and shoving.
- Name the places in the school where you feel least comfortable or safe because of the way people behave.
- Name the places where you notice hitting and fighting.
- Have these things happened to you at this school? (9 specific behaviours are listed)
- Name the people (if any) in the school who have bullied or harassed you.
- Name the people (if any) in the school you have seen bullying other people.
- Name any class in which you don't feel safe.

Life in School Checklist

You will find a copy of this British survey, which was developed by Tiny Arora, at <eduwight.iow.gov.uk/the_lea/behaviour_policies/images/PreventingBullyingApp1.pdf> More details about this instrument can be followed up in:

Arora, T. (1994). Measuring bullying with the Life in School checklist. *Pastoral Care in Education*, *12*(3).

Arora, C. M. J. (1999). Levels of bullying measured by British schools using the 'Life in School' checklist: A case for benchmarking? *Pastoral Care in Education*, *17*(1).

Types of questions used include:

- How often this week did another child do these things to you? (40 specific behaviours listed, some positive, most negative)
- How often have these bullying behaviours happened to you and where?
- What would you do if you saw someone being bullied? (9 specific behaviours specified)
- Where did the unpleasant behaviour that upset you most happen and who did it?
- What did you do and who did you tell when they did it?
- Should the school be doing more to stop this?
- How do you feel at school?
- Where at school do you feel unhappy?
- Does the school take bullying seriously and what could it do to stop bullying?

Peer Relations Questionnaire (PRQ)

Dr Phillip Slee and Dr Ken Rigby developed this first Australian questionnaire (Rigby & Slee, 1993). It has 20 items and is designed for students aged 8–18 years. It takes about 30 minutes to complete. However, because of its length and complexity, computer-based analyses are needed to obtain results. There are 6 items focusing on the tendency to bully others, 6 focusing on the tendency to be bullied, 4 measuring social behaviour and 4 'fillers'. There is reasonable evidence to support the conclusion that the PRQ is a reliable and valid measure of bullying (Duncan, 1999; Perry, Kusel & Perry, 1988; Rigby, 1997; Rigby & Slee, 1995).

Peer Relations Assessment Questionnaires (PRAQs)

There are three versions of this shorter questionnaire developed by Dr Ken Rigby. The areas covered are very similar to those in the original PRQ but there are fewer questions and less work involved in analysing and summarising the results.

1. **Questionnaire for students**. There is one version for older students (over 8 years), which uses written questions. There is a second version for younger students (8 years and younger), which includes visual images and simpler questions.
2. **Questionnaire for teachers**. This allows staff to provide information anonymously about their perceptions and judgments regarding bullying at their school and their preferred ways of dealing with it.
3. **Questionnaire for parents**. This provides the opportunity for parents of students to report on their children's experiences of school bullying and express their views on how they think bullying should be prevented and managed.

The Professional Reading Guide is the publisher and sole distributor of the Peer Relations Questionnaire and the Peer Relations Assessment Questionnaire. Schools buying the questionnaires will have the right to photocopy the questionnaires for survey use in their own school, subject to certain conditions. To obtain further information contact:
Dr Barrington Thomas
Editor and Publisher
The Professional Reading Guide
PO Box 104
Point Lonsdale
Victoria, Australia, 3225
Telephone (03) 5258 2340
Fax (03) 5258 3878
E-mail: profread@pipeline.com.au

References

Duncan, R. (1999). Maltreatment by parents and peers: The relationship between child abuse, bully victimization, and psychological distress. *Child Maltreatment, 19*, 45–56.

Perry, D. G., Kusel, S. J. & Perry, L. C. (1988). Victims of peer aggression. *Developmental Psychology, 24*(6), 807–814.

Rigby, K. (1997). What children tell us about bullying in schools. *Children Australia, 22*(2), 28–34.

Rigby, K. & Slee, P. (1995). *Manual for the Peer Relations Questionnaire (PRQ)*. Adelaide: University of South Australia.

Rigby, K. & Slee, P. T. (1993). *The Peer Relations Questionnaire (PRQ)*. Adelaide: University of South Australia.

Revised Olweus Bully/Victim Questionnaire

Olweus's Revised Bully/Victim Questionnaire (Olweus, 1994) consists of 40 questions for students aged 8–16 years to respond to anonymously. There are two versions of the questionnaire. One is amended slightly for younger students in Years 3–5. A modified version of this instrument has been developed by Whitney and Smith (1993).

The questionnaire measures perceived bullying of various kinds, where the bullying occurs, pro-bully and pro-victim attitudes, and the extent to which teachers, peers and parents are aware of and respond to the bullying. There is a small amount of published research support for the reliability and validity of the instrument (Bendixen & Olweus, 1999; Olweus, 1993, 1994; Pellegrini, Bartini & Brooks, 1999; Tobin & Irvin, 1996), although Eslea and Smith (2004) and others, for example, <http://vinst.umdnj.edu/VAID/TestReport.asp?Code=ROBVQ> have expressed some concern about the lack of published data on validity and reliability.

Crothers and Levinson (2004), however, agree with the conclusion of Austin and Joseph (1996) that this is one of the best methods available for establishing the incidence of bullying with middle school students and older.

Types of questions used include:

- How often have you been bullied at school in the past couple of months? (frequency options are specified for each category and a range of types of bullying is provided)
- In which class(es) is the student or students who bully you?
- Have you been bullied by boys or girls?
- By how many students have you usually been bullied?
- How long has the bullying lasted?
- Where have you been bullied?
- How often do the teachers or other adults at school try to put a stop to it when a student is being bullied at school?
- How often do other students try to put a stop to it when a student is being bullied at school?
- How do you usually react if you see or understand that a student your age is being bullied by other students?
- What do you think and feel when you see someone else being bullied?
- How often have you taken part in bullying another student(s) at school in the past couple of months? (frequency options are specified for each category and a range of types of bullying is provided)
- Do you think you could join in bullying a student you didn't much like?
- How often are you afraid of being bullied by other students in the school?
- How well do you like school?

This is not an easy instrument to quickly get hold of. You can contact Professor Dan Olweus directly at the University of Bergen at:

E-mail: dan.olweus@psych.uib.no
Phone: +47 55 58 28 08; Direct Phone: +.+47 55 58 23 27
Fax: +47 55 58 98 87
Websites: <www.colorado.edu/cspv/ blueprints/model/BPP_OrderForm.pdf>
<http://www.uib.no/psyfa/hemil/ansatte/olweus.html>

References

Austin, S. & Joseph, S. (1996). Assessment of bully/victim problems in 8 to 11 year-olds. *British Journal of Educational Psychology*, 66, 447–456.

Bendixen, M. & Olweus, D. (1999). The measurement of antisocial behaviour in early adolescence and adolescence: Psychometric properties and substantive findings. *Criminal Behaviour and Mental Health*, 9, 323–354.

Crothers, L. M. & Levinson, E. M. (2004). Assessment of bullying: A review of methods and instruments. *Journal of Counseling and Development*, 82, 496–503.

Eslea, M. & Smith, P. (2004, June). Developmental trends in attitudes to bullying. Poster presented to the Thirteenth Biennial Meeting of the International Society for the Study of Behavioural Development, Free University, Amsterdam.

Olweus, D. (1993). *Bullying at school: What we know and what we can do*. New York: Blackwell.

Olweus, D. (1994). Annotation: Bullying at school: Basic facts and effects of a school based intervention program. *Journal of Child Psychology and Psychiatry*, 35, 1171–1190.

Pellegrini, A. D., Bartini, M. & Brooks, F. (1999). School bullies, victims and aggressive victims: Factors relating to group affiliation and victimization in early adolescence. *Journal of Educational Psychology*, 91, 216–224.

Tobin, T. & Irvin, L. K. (1996). The Olweus Bully/Victim Questionnaire: Evidence and consequences regarding use in the United States: Reclaiming children and youth. *Journal of Emotional and Behavioural Problems*, 5(1), 29–33.

Whitney, I. & Smith, P. K. (1993). A survey of the nature and extent of bullying in junior/middle and secondary schools. *Educational Research*, 35, 3–25.

School Safety Survey – Revised (SSS-R) for secondary schools

See more details in:

Fuller, A. (1998). *From surviving to thriving: Promoting mental health in young people*. Melbourne: Australian Council for Educational Research Press.

Types of questions used include:

- Which of these behaviours have ever happened to you at your current school and how often? (10 behaviours specified)
- If you have been bullied how long has it been happening?
- What are the worst times of day for bullying? (options specified)
- How much of a problem is bullying and harassment at this school?
- Who does the bullying? (e.g. gender/year level)
- If you were being bullied who would you talk to about it? (options specified)

- Can teachers stop bullying?
- What would you tell a friend to do if they were being bullied? (options specified)
- Would you be interested in helping to stop bullying and/or harassment in your school?

The NCAB Do-It-Yourself Student Bullying Surveys

A CD version of these surveys, which can be modified and 'cut and pasted', can be obtained from NCAB. See <http://www.ncab.org.au> for details of how to order the CD. There is a parent survey plus a survey for each of the following year levels:

- Years K–1 (ages 5–6)
- Years 2–4 (ages 7–10)
- Years 5–6 (ages 11–12)
- Years 7–9 (ages 12–14)
- Years 10–12 (ages 15–18).

The school can select and include the types of questions they want to know the answers to. Surveys can offer insights into how students and parents currently perceive bullying at the school. They can also be completed before an anti-bullying program or procedure is implemented and again after the program. This can give you some encouraging feedback on how attitudes, feelings and behaviours related to bullying have changed and/or information to direct changes and refinements. They can also be used initially to direct program planning.

Sample questions that can be put together into a survey include:

- What is bullying?
- How do you feel about being at this school? (options specified)
- Do you agree with these statements about bullying? (a selection of statements and three response options are provided, e.g. 'If someone is being picked on, it's best to mind your own business')
- How much bullying happens at this school? (options specified)
- What kinds of bullying have you seen at this school? (options specified)
- If you saw a classmate bullying another student, what would you probably do? (options specified)
- How often do you see other students try to put a stop to bullying? (options specified)
- What is the best advice to give to someone your age who is being bullied? (options specified)
- What does the school expect you to do if you are being bullied? (options specified)
- What does the school expect you to do if you are aware that someone else is being bullied? (options specified)

- Where do you feel unsafe and worried about being bullied? (options specified)
- Could you personally use some help because you are being bullied at school? (options specified)
- What kind of bullying is it and do you need some help with it? (options specified).

Note: You need to carefully consider the ethical implications of the following questions:

- Who is bullying you?
- Are you aware of someone in your year level who you think is being bullied?
- Who do you think is bullying them?

The NCAB DIY Parent Bullying Survey

This survey is featured on the NCAB DIY Bullying Surveys CD along with the Student Survey. Types of questions used include:

- What is bullying?
- Do you agree with these statements about bullying? (a selection of statements related to myths about bullying are provided plus three response options)
- How much bullying do you think happens in this school? (options specified)
- Are you aware of the school's bullying policy? (options specified)
- How seriously does the school take bullying? (options specified)
- What advice would you give to your child if they were being verbally bullied? (options specified)
- When do you think parents should be contacted about bullying situations that involve their child? (options specified).

APPENDIX 14C: TEMPLATE – DEFINITIONS AND EXAMPLES

Defining bullying

To prevent and reduce bullying it is necessary to begin with a clear definition of it so that everyone in the school community has a shared understanding. The tendency to 'over-include' is a major obstacle in preventing and managing bullying. If every single act of meanness or social rejection is categorised as bullying, then schools find it difficult to respond firmly to the complex situations of repeated and deliberate harassment that most researchers agree constitutes bullying.

Is bullying the same as harassment or aggression?

Harassment can be defined as unwanted and one-sided words or actions towards another that demean, annoy, alarm or abuse. Harassment may involve a single incident or an ongoing pattern of behaviour. It may be deliberate or unintentional.

Aggression can be defined as words or actions that are intended to harm another.

Bullying can be viewed as both a subset of harassment and a subset of aggression. It is a specific form of harassment that is *repeated and deliberate*. It is a specific kind of aggression that is *repeated*.

Below is a more detailed definition which can help to clarify bullying behaviour for teachers.

Bullying behaviour has the following key features:

- It is *deliberate*. It is neither incidental nor accidental. There is either an intention to distress the recipient or a willingness to use the recipient for their own outcomes (e.g. have fun at their expense, be accepted by the group, demonstrate social power over another, etc.).
- The behaviour *does cause distress* for the recipient. They feel oppressed and apprehensive about the possibility of future attacks. The distress may be physical, psychological or social, or involve damage to reputation or property.
- It is directed towards a *specific* person or group.
- There is a *repeated pattern* of attacks.
- There is an *imbalance of power* between those bullying and the recipient.
- The behaviour is *unreasonable and unjustifiable*.
- The recipient usually *finds it difficult to leave or avoid* the bullying situation(s) without personal cost (but feels rightly that he/she shouldn't have to).

The power advantage of those who are bullying makes it very difficult for the recipient to single-handedly stop the attacks. A power advantage can be gained by students in many ways such as:

- having enough social power to get other students to back them up or act as their agents
- damaging the reputation of the targeted student(s) so that others fail to support them
- being bigger, older, stronger, more aggressive or more articulate
- misusing official power (e.g. as a prefect, chairperson, captain).

There may be the occasional exception to the key features listed above. For example, one single but prolonged episode (e.g. over three hours of a sporting match or on an excursion) in which an individual student is verbally abused and humiliated in several different ways may be an example of bullying even though it is not a repeated pattern *across time*.

The issue of 'deliberateness' can be complex too. 'Deliberate' means that the behaviour is chosen, and is not just accidental or incidental. Most students who take part in bullying (especially the ringleaders) are aware that what they are doing is distressing for the recipient and unacceptable, especially if they are in a school which has focused on communicating an awareness of what bullying is. However, some may believe (incorrectly) that what they are doing is justified (e.g. because they 'blame the victim' or believe rumours about them) and so they deny to themselves and others that they are taking part in bullying. Some students who take part in bullying, although aware that the recipient does not like the behaviour that is being directed towards them, are genuinely unaware of the *severity* of the distress for the recipient.

Simple definitions of bullying

Here are some examples to select from for different ages, audiences and purposes:

- Bullying is a repetitive attack which causes distress not only at the time of the attack, but also by the threat of future attacks. It is characterised by an imbalance of power and can be defined by the negative impact on the vulnerable person who is targeted. It can be verbal, physical, social or psychological. It can be done in person, by manipulating others to take part, or by electronic means such as e-mail, text messages or chat rooms.
- Bullying is when someone repeatedly misuses their power to try to hurt, scare or exclude another person. It can be done by one person or a group. It can be physical, social, verbal or electronic.
- Bullying is when a student or group keeps picking on another student. They try to hurt their body, feelings, property, reputation or social acceptance. This behaviour is

repeated and directed towards the same person. A fight or disagreement between equal students isn't bullying.

- Bullying is when a student is repeatedly harassed or ganged up on by a group. The people doing it act in ways that upset or harm the student's body, peace of mind, property, reputation or social life. A disagreement between students where both have the same power isn't bullying.
- Bullying is when one child (or a group of children) picks on another child. They keep trying to hurt them or they keep saying and doing mean things to make them feel bad.
- Sometimes children pick on someone. Sometimes they try to hurt them or their things. Sometimes they say and do mean things to hurt their feelings. Sometimes they try to make others not like them and leave them out. If a child keeps on doing this to another child, we call this bullying.

Bullying behaviours

There is a wide range of bullying behaviours, including:

- direct physical attacks such as hitting, tripping, pushing, throwing things towards others, etc.
- name calling, mocking, setting up, belittling and insulting someone
- making insulting racist or sexual comments or comments about (perceived) sexual orientation
- trying to damage someone's reputation amongst other students by spreading rumours, exposing private information, telling lies, etc.
- using verbal and non-verbal put-downs in a public context such as a discussion or meeting
- playing nasty practical jokes on others
- damaging or hiding other people's personal property
- using covert forms of physical intimidation such as blocking the way and making the other person walk around them or bumping them and claiming it was an accident
- encouraging others to socially exclude the recipient
- 'cyberbullying' (e.g. making malicious comments or playing nasty practical jokes on someone via e-mail, chat rooms, text messages, etc.)
- accusing someone of things they haven't done.

Some students are very skilled at making plans for bullying selected recipients and then getting others to actually perform the bullying behaviours.

What bullying is NOT

There are many distressing behaviours that are NOT examples of bullying even though they may require teacher intervention and management. It is essential that incidents of bullying be clearly differentiated from incidents of mutual conflict or single-episode/random aggression as the strategies for effectively responding vary for each situation (McGrath & Noble, 2003a and b). Inappropriate school responses may result in matters becoming worse for those involved.

There are three typical negative social situations which are often confused with bullying, namely:

- mutual conflict
- social rejection or exclusive friendships
- single-episode or random acts of aggression or intimidation.

Mutual conflict

Bullying is not the same as mutual conflict. In mutual conflict situations there is an initial argument or disagreement between the parties at the core of the exchange of negative feelings and behaviours. However, these situations are not characterised by an imbalance of power. Both parties are upset and usually both want a resolution to the problem. Mutual conflict is usually best dealt with through mediation procedures.

Social rejection and exclusive friendships

Students often decide not to be friends with someone anymore or they don't want to play with or associate with that person. Only when social rejection involves deliberate and repeated attempts to cause a specific student distress is it categorised as bullying. When social rejection/exclusion *is* used as a form of bullying it often has one or more of the following features:

- There are repeated comments which draw attention to the deliberateness of the exclusion (e.g. 'We don't want you in our game') and/or nasty comments about the perceived unacceptability of the recipient (e.g. 'No-one here likes you').
- The targeted student is deliberately and repeatedly excluded in a broad range of contexts, not just in a specific social context (e.g. students refuse to work with them on a group task, sit near them in class, etc.).
- There are repeated non-verbal gestures of exclusion and unacceptability (e.g. the use of the 'germ lock' symbol to imply that the recipient is dirty or unhygienic OR the use of the 'L for Loser' gesture).

- A series of nasty tricks or practical jokes are played on the recipient to highlight their social exclusion (e.g. students do not turn up to a prearranged meeting point).
- Other students are also urged to exclude the recipient whenever possible.

Single-episode or random acts of meanness, intimidation or violence

Bullying is a sub-set of aggressive behaviour and is often characterised by meanness, intimidation and physical violence. However, these aggressive behaviours are *not* categorised as bullying if they occur only once or are random in nature (i.e. directed towards several different people) and not repetitive. These types of incidents are usually best dealt with through the school's discipline and counselling procedures.

REFERENCES

McGrath, H. & Noble, T. (2003a). *BOUNCE BACK! A Classroom Resiliency Program: Teacher's Handbook*. Frenchs Forest, NSW: Pearson Education. <http://www.bounceback.com.au>

McGrath, H. & Noble, T. (2003b) *BOUNCE BACK! A Classroom Resiliency Program*. Frenchs Forest, NSW: Pearson Education (Bullying units in all three Teacher Resource Books) <http://www.bounceback.com.au>

Smith, P. (2004). Bullying: Recent developments. *Child and Adolescent Mental Health*, 9(3), 98–103.

APPENDIX 14D: USING FOCUS GROUPS WITH STUDENTS, STAFF AND PARENTS

Focus groups are a qualitative method of collecting information through one or more organised small group discussions. They are 'focused' in two ways:

- The persons being interviewed in a focus group have something significant and relevant in common, *e.g. they are all parents at the school; they are all students from Year 9 at the same school.*
- The purpose of the interview is to gather more detailed, in-depth information about one or more specific aspects of bullying by using a set of predetermined and sequenced discussion questions.

In focus groups, the emphasis is on perceptions, insights, responses and opinions about bullying rather than specific facts or statistical data. They enable the researcher to probe for perceptions and views that might otherwise remain unspoken (Elliott & Lambourn, 1999). The result often is a richer understanding of what is needed in an anti-bullying program or of which aspects of a new program are making a difference and how. Focus groups can help to provide understanding of issues such as:

- What perceptions students have of the extent of bullying in the school.
- Whether the new anti-bullying program is having any impact in the student community.
- How parents are reacting to the new or revised school policy.
- What students already know about bullying and school procedures in relation to reporting it.
- The level, knowledge or skill staff have about bullying and put-downs in the classroom.
- How aware staff are of the school's policy and procedures in relation to bullying.
- How students in the school perceive teachers' responses to put-downs and bullying.
- Whether parents really understand what staff are trying to do in the school with the anti-bullying policy, program and procedures.

Focus groups can also be used following the administration of a bullying survey to explore in more depth some of the themes that have been identified.

There are several advantages of using the focus group method for collecting data. For example:

- Using focus groups allows the interviewer(s) to probe responses and ask for elaboration and clarification in a way that is difficult to do with questionnaires (Krueger, 1994).
- The focus group method is relatively low in cost and time compared with other methods of data collection such as surveys.

There are also some disadvantages in using focus groups, such as:

- Focus groups do not represent random feedback from participants but rather feedback from selected individuals. The participants may be atypical. This can be countered to some degree by careful and varied selection or by having two or more focus groups from the same population (e.g. two groups of Year 6 students instead of just one).
- The researcher may have less control in a focus group interview than he/she does in an individual interview.
- Data from focus groups may be more difficult to analyse than data from a questionnaire (Krueger, 1994).

Focus groups are not always an appropriate choice. For example, focus groups would not be used if you wanted to gather specific, quantifiable, factual and statistical information such as rates of bullying or the extent of participation in a program (Krueger, 1994).

Participants

Each focus group needs to be small enough for all participants to have an opportunity to share insights but large enough to provide a diversity of perceptions (Krueger, 1994). In general a group size of 6–8 works best for students and 8–10 works best for groups of parents or teachers.

The selection strategies for obtaining participants need to be carefully planned to maximise diversity within the same population and minimise bias. It is better if the participants in any one group are not close friends or relatives (Krueger, 1994). It is also important to determine whether the topic being discussed might produce different responses from boys versus girls. When in doubt, use single-sex groups.

Archer (1993) believes that students under six aren't sufficiently articulate to be able to relate their feelings to an interviewer. Therefore, the youngest age at which students can actively and meaningfully participate in a focus group discussion is probably about eight years. In a study which investigated the focus group participation of students between 8 and 14 years of age, Heary and Hennessy (2002) found that students aged 8–10 years were just as able to contribute meaningfully as older students (11–14 years). In particular they found that:

- Both younger and older students genuinely engaged in the discussion, i.e. offered their own opinions, disagreed with some comments and agreed with others.
- Younger groups (8–10-year-olds) were much livelier and more time was spent keeping them focused on the activity.

- There were more irrelevant comments in the younger groups than in the older groups. Since the quality of the contributions by younger students was still good, it may be necessary to allow some of these irrelevant comments in order to stimulate the flow of ideas.
- The younger groups tended to apply all situations to themselves and to people whom they knew (e.g. family and friends). This was much less common among the 11–14-year-olds.

Both younger and older students said they enjoyed taking part in the focus groups, they believed that they had had a chance to say everything they wanted and that the focus group was a good way to talk to their age group.

Number of focus groups

Consider having a range of focus groups to cover age levels, parent groups and staff groups. For example, you could have one focus group for each year level in the school, or you could join two levels together. You could have a focus group for parents of younger students and one for parents of older students. You could have a focus group of staff from the younger levels of the school, one from the middle school, one from the upper school and one of year level coordinators or senior staff.

Setting up a focus group

Reserve a time and place well before the interviews and let participants know the time and location promptly. The total time for a group interview should be 30–60 minutes for students and 60–90 minutes for parents and teachers. Determine what equipment will be needed (e.g. audiotape, microphone, note-taking kit, etc.).

Decide on your pool of participants and then select the appropriate number. For student focus groups, consider selecting a large potential pool of every third student on the relevant class lists. Then balance the final selection from the pool by using criteria such as ethnic background, gender, etc. For teacher focus groups, firstly decide on the categories that you want to use (e.g. junior staff, specialist staff, senior staff, coordinators, etc.), list the potential pool for each category and then balance the final selection using criteria such as gender, teaching experience and discipline specialty. For parent focus groups, it can be helpful to send a letter to all parents asking them to fill out a sheet like the one below:

> We will be conducting small group discussions on the topic of (…………..). These will be held on (………………) at (……….).
>
> We will need about (……) people and it will take approximately (…..).

If you are interested in taking part, please provide the following information. We will probably not be able to use everyone who offers but we thank you for your interest.

Name .... Phone Number ....

I would be able to attend on the following days and at the following times (provide options to select from).

From your potential pool, decide on a varied group of interested people (balanced for gender, number of children they have had at the school, etc.) for each focus group and contact them by phone. Assume that despite agreeing to be involved some people won't turn up and that you may need to ask one or two extra people to cover this possibility. Alternatively, use strategies that will make non-attendance less likely, e.g. ring and remind them three days beforehand, saying: 'We are just ringing to confirm that you are still available to . . .'.

If possible, provide simple refreshments (even for students) and make sure that everyone has a name tag.

The interviewer(s)

You only need one or two interviewers. However, there also needs to be someone who takes notes and, preferably, also records the discussion on audiotape. The interviewer(s) should not have had regular contact with the participants of the focus group. Preferably they are people who are outside the system.

Structure of the discussion

There are usually five stages in the discussion:

1. **The opening (2–5 minutes)** This includes the welcome and introduction, statements about the purpose of the interview, how the information will be used and the length of the session.
2. **The ground rules (2 minutes)** This includes rules such as:
   - Everyone's ideas matter and should be respected.
   - Everyone should have an opportunity to speak.
   - The adoption of a 'no names' rule, i.e. students are asked not to say the names of any other students if they talk about incidents or situations.
   - Confidentiality will be maintained in that no-one's names will be mentioned in the report. Ask participants to 'keep whatever is said in this room private' but remind them that you cannot guarantee that all participants will do this.

3. **The interview questions** See below for more details (30–40 minutes).
4. **Summary and closure (3 minutes)** This can include a brief 'go-round' activity, such as asking everyone in turn to say 'one thing you would like to emphasise about . . .', or 'one small way in which the school's approach to bullying can be improved'. It also includes an expression of thanks to the participants, and a restatement of how the information will be used.
5. **Follow-up** Send all participants a follow-up letter to thank them for their involvement.

The interview questions

Here are some guidelines for selecting discussion questions:

- Prepare a set of between five and eight questions about the issue you want to explore. Indicate the order in which the questions should be presented to participants (Krueger, 1994). Questions don't simply emerge as the discussion flows. Even though some unplanned directions may occur, the interviewer still needs to return each time to the prepared questions (in planned sequence).
- Allocate an approximate time for each question to make sure that all questions are covered.
- Questions should be relatively unstructured but still specific (e.g. it is better to ask 'What was your reaction to the policy?' than 'Did you like the policy?').
- Avoid questions which have only two choices of answer (e.g. those that require a YES or NO response).
- Avoid asking 'why?' questions. Use 'how' and 'what' questions instead.
- Ask only one question at a time even if other questions, or parts of a question, go together. Asking multiple questions makes it difficult for participants to know where to start.

The questions that you use will depend on what you want to investigate with a specific focus group, but some possible questions to consider are:

- What do you know about bullying at this school? (parents or students)
- What is your perception of how bullying is managed by teachers in the school? (parents)
- What is your opinion about what has changed in our school as a result of our anti-bullying policy and programs? (students or parents)
- What is your reaction to the new program/policy/procedures etc. that the school is planning to use/has implemented? (parents)
- What are some of the things you would like to see done in the school that might reduce bullying? (students or parents)

- Do you have a clear idea of what bullying is? What are some examples? (students, teachers or parents)
- What impression have you gained from your children about bullying in this school? (parents)
- How do you deal with put-downs in the classroom and what assistance do you need? (teachers)
- As teachers at the school, what would be the most helpful ways to assist you to prevent and manage bullying and put-downs more effectively? (teachers)

Here are some sound general guidelines for managing the overall discussion of the predetermined questions:

- The same sequence of pre-planned questions should be followed in all focus groups.
- The interviewer should communicate trust, respect, tolerance, humour, and a willingness to listen.
- It is important to convey to participants in focus groups that they are the experts and that the focus group facilitator and other staff have come to learn from them and get information from them.
- Be aware of your potential biases as a facilitator. Avoid 'leading' or 'directing' participants by making 'approving' or 'empathic' responses to their comments.
- Use information-seeking responses that help a participant to clarify and elaborate, e.g:
  - *Can you tell me some more about that?*
  - *Can you explain what you mean by . . .?*
  - *Can you give me an example of what you are saying?*
  - *What might that look like in practice?*
- Try to keep the discussion on the topic without stifling participant responses.
- Try to ensure that the discussion occurs between and among group members under your guidance rather than on a one-to-one level with you.
- Be comfortable with silence and don't jump in to fill space quickly. This avoids directing participants and gives them time to consider the question. Some participants may make a contribution that they wouldn't have otherwise made if they hadn't had time to consider the question before they spoke.
- Use active listening, i.e. give a brief summary of what you believe a participant has said so that they feel 'heard' and you can check the accuracy of your understanding (e.g. 'So what you're saying is that the written communication didn't match what was being said to the students?').
- If an answer given is vague or unclear, ask for more clarification from the respondent

(e.g. 'I think I have some idea of what you mean but it would be helpful for me if you could give some more details/examples and restate your key point').

- Find ways to include non-contributing participants and 'limit' overly talkative ones in a respectful way. Try to make sure everyone has a chance to answer every question. If one person does not speak up, ask them directly but do not 'spotlight' them (e.g. 'Jack, I'm interested in your views on this particular issue').

Documenting participants' responses

The simplest and most reliable way to document a focus group's ideas is to both audiotape each discussion and also use a note-taker. Two note-takers can be used to help increase accuracy and direct attention to the more subtle communications. It is okay to link individuals' names to comments and views in these notes but names should not be used in the report and notes should not be seen by anyone else.

Analysing the data

Analyse each question separately for each 'set' of focus groups (e.g. a set could be two focus groups of parents of older students). Use the sequence in which the questions were asked (e.g. Question 1, Question 2, etc.). Focus on common themes that emerged in each group and the strength of these themes (i.e. how many people referred to each theme).

Then put the data from each of the groups together to make a summary of how groups agreed and differed. What points were made in more than one type of group? Did older students have different views or examples compared with younger students? Did parents of younger students express more/less concern about an issue than parents of older students? Were any unexpected issues raised?

Writing up the report

Summarise the data in a brief report. Reports usually follow this format:

- Description of the purpose, site, and the participant details for each group. Give each group a letter (e.g. Group B and each participant that letter plus a number (e.g. B5 made the point that . . .). If several participants in one group agree on a point, it is not necessary to refer to them all specifically (e.g. all of the group except one agreed that . . .).
- Summaries of themes and common responses (question by question and in sequence) for each focus group.
- Summary of how groups agreed and differed across the bigger picture.

- Comments that might have been expressed only by one person but seem relevant or worthy of consideration.
- An overall summary of what was learned from the groups.

REFERENCES

Archer, T. M. (1993). Focus groups for kids. *Journal of Extensions*, *31*(1). Retrieved April 23, 2005, from <http://www.joe.org/joe/1993spring/tt2.html>

Elliott, K. & Lambourn, A. (1999). Sex, drugs and alcohol: Two peer-led approaches in Tamaki Makaurau/Auckland, Aotearoa/New Zealand. *Journal of Adolescence*, *22*, 503–513.

Heary, C. & Hennessy, E. (2002). The use of focus groups in pediatric health care research. *Journal of Pediatric Psychology*, *27*, 47–57.

Krueger, R. A. (1994). *Focus groups: A practical guide for applied research*. Thousand Oaks, CA: Sage.

APPENDIX 14E: USEFUL RESOURCES

This section lists some further resources that you may find useful for specific bullying-related purposes.

Template resources

Internet sites

There are many websites dealing with bullying but these are some of the best of those currently available. Most have sections for both teachers and students.

Australia

<http://www.bullyingnoway.com.au>
<http://www.kidshelp.com.au/INFO7/contents.htm>
<http://www.ncab.org.au>
<http://www.rch.org.au/cah/research/index.cfm?doc_id=1012>

New Zealand

<http://www.police.govt.nz/service/yes/nobully/>

Scotland

<http://www.antibullying.net/database.htm>

Canada

<http://www.bced.gov.bc.ca/sco/resources.htm>

ERIC/EECE resource list: Bullying in schools

<http://www.ericdigests.org/2002-3/bullying.htm>
<http://www.ericdigests.org/2003-1/bullying.htm> (prevention)

General resources on bullying

Fuller, A. & King, V. (1995). *Stop bullying!* Melbourne: VicHealth.

Juvenon, J. & Graham, S. (Eds.) (2000). *Peer harassment in schools: The plight of the vulnerable and the victimised*. New York: Guilford.

McGrath, H. & Noble, T. (2003). *BOUNCE BACK! A Classroom Resiliency Program: Teacher's Handbook*. Frenchs Forest, NSW: Pearson Education. <http://www.bounceback.com.au>.

Morita, J., Smith, P. K., Junger-Tas, J., Olweus, D., Catalano, R. F. & Slee, P. T. (1999).

School bullying around the world: Challenges and interventions. Tokyo: Kaneko Shobo Co.

Rigby, K. (2002). Bullying in childhood. In Peter K. Smith & Craig H. Hart (Eds.) *Handbook of childhood social development* (pp. 549–569). Oxford: Blackwell.

Rigby, K. (2002). *A meta-evaluation of methods and approaches to reducing bullying in pre-schools and in early primary school in Australia*. Canberra: Commonwealth Attorney-General's Department. Phone 1800 703 777 for free copies.
Access on line through one of these three websites:
<http://www.ncp.gov.au/agd/WWW/ncpHome.nsf/Page/Publications> OR
<http://www.education.unisa.edu.au/bullying/meta.pdf > OR
<http://www.ag.gov.au/agd/WWW/ncpHome.nsf/Page/Publications_All_Publications_Early_Intervention_A_META-EVALUATION_OF_METHODS_AND_APPROACHES_TO_REDUCING_BULLYING_IN_PRE-SCHOOLS_AND_EARLY_PRIMARY_SCHOOL_IN_AUSTRALIA_>.

Rigby, K. (2002). *New perspectives on bullying*. London: Jessica Kingsley. Obtainable in Australia from Footprints Distributors (Phone 02 9997 3973; Fax 02 9997 3185; E-mail: <sales@footprint.com.au>; Website: <http://www.footprint.com.au>).

Rigby, K. (2003). *Stop the bullying: A handbook for schools* (2nd ed.). Melbourne: ACER. (Phone 03 9835 7447; Fax: +61 3 9835 7499; Email: <sales@acer.edu.au>).

Rigby, K. & Slee, P. (1997). *Bullying in schools* (video and manual). ACER, Melbourne.

Sharp, S. & Smith, P. K. (Eds.) (1994). *Tackling bullying in your school: A practical handbook for teachers*. London: Routledge.

Smith, P., Pepler, D. & Rigby, K. R. (2004). *Bullying in schools: How successful can interventions be?* Cambridge: Cambridge University Press.

Smith, P. K., Morita, J., Junger-Tas, J., Olweus, D., Catalano, R. & Slee, P. T. (Eds.) (1999). *The nature of school bullying: A cross-national perspective*. London: Routledge.

Smith, P. K. & Sharp, S. (1994). *School bullying: Insights and perspectives*. New York: Routledge.

Suckling, A. & Temple, C. (2001). *Bullying: A whole-school approach*. Melbourne: Australian Council for Educational Research.

Sullivan, K. (2000). *The anti-bullying handbook*. Oxford and Melbourne: Oxford University Press.

Anti-bullying curriculum programs

Clements, D. & Godinho, S. (2003). *Read and reflect: Literature discussion in small groups.* South Melbourne: Curriculum Corporation.

Linning, L., Phillips, M. & Turton, R. (1997). *A literature based approach to bullying: For upper primary and lower secondary students.* Hamilton, Qld: The Literature Base.

McGrath, H. & Noble, T. (2003). *BOUNCE BACK! A Classroom Resiliency Program* (bullying units in all three Teacher Resource Books). Frenchs Forest, NSW: Pearson Education. <http://www.bounceback.com.au>

Anti-bullying programs

Cross, D. (2004, November). *Helping to make schools even safer: Where policy meets the playground.* Paper presented at the National Coalition Against Bullying Seminar, Melbourne.

Friendly Schools Friendly Families Program Materials:

- The Friendly Schools team handbook: *Making it work*
- Six whole-school component handbooks
- CD ROM: *Bringing the program alive*
- Family booklet: *How to make friends and stop bullying*
- Five Classroom Pack

The Friendly Schools Friendly Families Program can be ordered by contacting (08) 9273 8268 or e-mailing <chpru@ecu.edu.au>

Slee, P. T. (1997). *The P.E.A.C.E. Pack: A programme for reducing bullying in our schools.* Adelaide: Flinders University.

Smith, P., Pepler, D. & Rigby, K. R. (2004). *Bullying in schools: How successful can interventions be?* Cambridge: Cambridge University Press.

Reducing put-downs in the classroom

McGrath, H. (1997). *Dirty tricks: Classroom games which teach students social skills.* Melbourne: Addison Wesley Longman.

McGrath, H. & Noble, T. (2003). *BOUNCE BACK! A Classroom Resiliency Program.* (bullying units in all three Teacher Resource Books). Frenchs Forest, NSW: Pearson Education. <http://www.bounceback.com.au>

Videos/DVDs about bullying

Bullying (1994). Jane Balfour Films video. Melbourne: ACER.

Bullying: No way (Available from Open Access Unit, Education Services Directorate,

Education Queensland, PO Box 220, Ashgrove Qld 4006; Phone: 07 3377 1000; Fax: 07 3366 3849).

Bullying: The inside story. Video Education Australia. <http://www.vea.com.au/Home.asp>

Hurting on the inside: Girls and bullying. Video Education Australia, 111A Mitchell Street, Bendigo, Vic 3550. (Aus) freecall 1800 034 282. <http://www.vea.com.au/Home.asp>

Theatre groups performing shows on bullying for students

Brainstorm Productions
Freecall: 1800 676 224
Website: <http://www.brainstormproductions.com.au/>
E-mail: <info@brainstormproductions.com.au>

Fair Play and Shades of Grey
<http://education.qld.gov.au/publication/reporting/parents/2_03bull.html>
<http://www.qac.org.au/htm/inschools.asp>

Books and resources on bullying for parents

Australian Department of Education, Science and Training (DEST). Bullying: Information for parents. <http://www.dest.gov.au/schools/publications/2000/bullying/index.htm>

Berne, S. (1996). *Bully-proof your child*. Melbourne: Lothian.

Elliot, M. (1991). *101 ways to deal with bullying: A guide for parents*. Stoke-on-Trent: Trentham.

Field, E. (1999). *Bullybusting: How to help children deal with teasing and bullying*. Lane Cove, NSW: Finch.

Horton-Jones, L. (2004) *Raising bullywise kids: Everything you need to know to protect your kids from bullying*. Newport, Vic.: The Soaring Phoenix. <http://www.thesoaringphoenix.com.au/Raising-Bullywise-Kids-review.pdf>

Resources on conflict management

Cohen, R. (1995). *Students resolving conflict: Peer mediation in schools*. Glenview, Illinois: Good Year Books.

Girard, K. & Koch, S. J. (1996). *Conflict resolution in the schools: A manual for educators*. San Francisco: Jossey-Bass.

Johnson, D. W. & Johnson, R. T. (1991). *Teaching students to be peacemakers*. Edina, Minnesota: Interactions Book Co.

Johnson, D. W. & Johnson, R. T. (1995). *Reducing school violence through conflict resolution*. Virginia: ASCD.

McGrath, H. & Noble, T. (2003). *BOUNCE BACK! A Classroom Resiliency Program*. Frenchs Forest, NSW: Pearson Education. (Activities for teaching conflict-management skills can be found in the relationships units in all three Teacher Resource Books.)

McMahon, C. (1996). *Implementing conflict resolution and peer mediation skills into the school community*. Noosa Heads, Qld: Conflict Resolution Network Schools Development.

Teaching social skills

McGrath, H. (1997). *Dirty tricks: Classroom games which teach students social skills*. Melbourne: Addison Wesley Longman.

McGrath, H. (2000). *Behaviour management*. Ready to Go Series. Sydney: Blake Ed.

McGrath, H. & Francey, S. (1991). *Friendly Kids, Friendly Classrooms*. Melbourne: Longman.

McGrath, H. & Noble, T. (1993). *Different kids, same classroom*. Melbourne: Longman.

McGrath, H. & Noble, T. (2003). *BOUNCE BACK! A Classroom Resiliency Program* (relationships units in all three Teacher Resource Books). Frenchs Forest, NSW: Pearson Education. <http://www.bounceback.com.au>

MindMatters
<http://cms.curriculum.edu.au/mindmatters/>

Petersen, L. & Gannoni, A. (1992). *Stop, Think, Do*. Melbourne: ACER.

You Can Do It!
<http://www.youcandoit.com.au/>
Refer to the *Getting along* unit

Developing resilience

Fuller, A., Bellhouse, B. & Johnston, G. (2001). *The heart masters: A program for the promotion of emotional intelligence and resilience in the junior to middle years of secondary school*. Dandenong, Vic.: G. N. & E. J. Ridgway, © 2001.

McGrath, H. & Noble, T. (2003). *BOUNCE BACK! A Classroom Resiliency Program* (see relationships units in all three Teacher Resource Books). Frenchs Forest, NSW: Pearson Education. <http://www.bounceback.com.au>

MindMatters
<http://cms.curriculum.edu.au/mindmatters/>

INDEX